A Pictorial Record of

GREAT WESTERN COACHES (1903 – 1948)

including the Brown vehicles

A Pictorial Record of

GREAT WESTERN
COACHES (1903 – 1948)

including the Brown vehicles

J. H. Russell

Oxford Publishing Co.

A FOULIS-OPC Railway Book

British Library Cataloguing in Publication data
Russell, J.H. (James Harry), 1915–
  A pictorial record of Great Western Coaches (1903–1948).
  1. England, Railway services: Great Western Railway.
  Rolling stock: Coaches, history
  I. Title
  625.230942
  ISBN 0-902888-04-8

Library of Congress catalog card number
90-81299

Published by:
Haynes Publishing Group
Sparkford, Near Yeovil, Somerset BA22 7JJ

Haynes Publications Inc.
861 Lawrence Drive, Newbury Park, California 91320,
USA.

Printed by: J.H. Haynes & Co. Ltd

This book is
dedicated to all my modelling friends
in general,
and to Jack Slinn and the Pendon boys
in particular.

Publisher's note: A number of the line illustrations are taken from
official drawings and due to the age of these some of the detail has
faded. These have been included because of their historical interest
and importance.

Preface

How odd it is, to realise that twenty-two years after the Great Western Railway ceased to exist as a private Company enthusiasts are still clamouring for more and yet more details of how this fine English railroad built, operated and maintained it's superb fleet of locomotives and rolling stock.

Books are being produced every month, it seems, on every facet of the Great Western scene. Senior devotees who can recall the fascinating sense of rightness and permanence-which a visit to any station on the line engendered, will always be interested in a new work which will help bring back nostalgic memories; but the strangest thing is that hundreds of young enthusiasts, many of whom have no knowledge of the old Great Western, buy books, drawings, and photographs, and can hold learned discussions on the relative merits of one locomotive against another, or quote sizes, lot numbers and code names of rolling stock. Boys of all ages still spend hours and pounds, laboriously constructing exquisite models of not only engines, track and lineside buildings, but also near-perfect miniatures of wagons, vans, and coaches.

So it is to the latter that I devote this work, I have tried hard to see that as much material as space will allow has been crammed within its pages, but if the particular vehicle our reader is searching for is missing from these books, please accept my apologies and appreciate the dilemma which faced me, namely . . . which, out of so many? At least the omission does leave the door open for a supplement at a later date!

However, to sum up, what better than to use a quote of John Binney, "Let reader and writer never forget that from the word 'go', memory weakens and imagination strengthens, but any record is better than no record at all."

PART II — GREAT WESTERN CARRIAGE STOCK
1903 – 1948

Introduction

This collection of photographs and drawings is the third in a series of five which attempts to portray, albeit briefly, some of the many and varied vehicles which were made at Swindon and operated by the Great Western Railway during the 113 years of the Company's existence, before finally becoming nationalised in 1948. As there are many readers who will only be interested in one particular section, I have overlapped the two parts rather generously, and even duplicated some pictures in order to make each volume as complete as possible within itself.

I crave reader's indulgence, therefore, for any omissions from Part 1 which may appear in this section, and vice versa. My aim has been to show the change from Dean to Churchward briefly in Part 1, and to cover the development onwards more thoroughly in Part II . . . space of course always dictating what to include and what to omit.

The steam rail-cars are covered fully in this section, as I feel the development of these interesting vehicles influenced the main-line stock to a large degree. The progression of design through the large 'Dreadnoughts' and 'Concertinas' to the 'Toplight' vehicles, followed by the bow-ended stock of the 1920's, with some examples of the open 'Excursion' coaches of the mid-thirties, to the magnificent Super Saloons and Centenarys of the 1935 era, can be seen; followed finally by a few examples of the comparatively modern vehicles built under Mr. Hawkesworth in the last years before state ownership.

As well as coaches and the early Diesel cars, there are many of the interesting 'brown' vehicles, in picture and diagram form, (with number list where I have been fortunate enough to secure this information), as I have had many requests for more details of these wagons from modellers. These books do not set out to be technical or historical, but are rather albums of pictures, with drawings, to help the modeller and enthusiast alike. Nevertheless, in this volume, I have tried wherever possible, to follow the *Lot* numbers through consecutively, which, therefore, gives a good idea of the year by year building progress, and shows the gradual changes in design. Readers who are interested in the purely historical angle of Great Western coaches are recommended to the excellent work by Michael Harris, which deals specifically with the technical aspect and ties up nicely with this series. My publisher and I have tried wherever possible to reproduce the majority of the diagrams (most of which are the official Swindon originals) to a scale of 4mm to 1 foot, as this just allows the longest vehicles to fit within the pages. Even so, in some extreme cases the buffing gear has had to be omitted, as this was thought better than to have taken a slice out of the centre of the drawing. Where the drawing is to a different scale a note is made to this effect.

Modellers are warned, however, that even Swindon 'general arrangement' drawings are fallible, and greater accuracy is ensured by working from a photograph. This will be apparent from some of the Steam Rail Car drawings, where occasionally the coach builders have not followed the diagram, or where the drawing might show the vehicle at a different date to the original. So be warned, a drawn line does not prove anything!

As with my other two books, I have had unstinting help and assistance from many sources, Pendon Museum supplying many coach diagrams and photos; David Lee again coming to my aid with information about Rail cars and Browns; Jim Fraser lending drawings of the T.P.O.'s; Jim Whittaker helping with Siphons and Monsters, etc.; and above all, Mr. Sprinks of P.R.O. Paddington, together with Mr. Froud at Swindon, whose unfailing assistance has been invaluable in locating and printing official photographs.

Last but by no means least, I have to thank another good friend of mine, Mr. J. Slinn of the H.R.M.S., whose tireless efforts producing data and reading the manuscript has put so much detail into the work, which I hope will cause it to find favour with the majority of Great Western devotees.

Jim Russell 1973.

FIG 1

FIG 2

In order to get an overlap and to make this part as complete as possible for the reader who only has access to this section, I am starting this collection with some early vehicles, built originally before 1900, but afterwards converted and given longer life in another guise.

The two vehicles shown on *page 1* come under this category, and as can be seen, are of the low roof variety, originally built in 1898. The coach next to the engine is one of the composites of *diagram E58 series*, 50' in length and virtually as built, but the leading carriage is one of the brake 3rds, which was altered in early 1920's to work as an auto unit. Originally, these brake 3rds were ordered on *lot 872 to diagram D27*. When converted, the two coaches saw service on the Bristol — Clifton — Avonmouth branch; the system so became known as the *'Clifton Down'* arrangement. Drawing on page 3.

The conversion consisted of fitting three windows in the van end of the brake 3rd, constructing a driver's compartment and fitting the usual auto-car gear so that the unit could be driven from this end, thus obviating the need for turning or running round after each trip. My photograph (*Figure 1*) shows these coaches when on their last workings at Marlow in September 1947. It is interesting to note the sanding gear on the leading bogie and the guard irons extending down from the bogie frame. *Figure 2* shows the train standing in the old bay at Bourne End, where the connection was made with the Maidenhead—High Wycombe trains.

The drawing on this page is another from the pen of John Binney, and is of interest as it shows one of the 1896 series of dining cars which were built to *diagram H.2* and converted from 1st class to composites in 1903 or thereabouts. The seating was limited and the kitchen was situated at one end of the vehicle. Only three vehicles were so converted, but two others of 1900 were altered to be of composite accommodation also. At the outbreak of the First World War this carriage and its sister were used as refreshment cars in the home ambulance trains, and eventually finished life in 1936, after a long and varied career. Original numbers in 1896 were 250-252, later altered to 9503, 9517 and 9504 eventually, the two cafe cars being numbers 9516 and 9502 (see G.W.R. Coaches by Harris page 56 and below).

DIA H.2
LOT 801

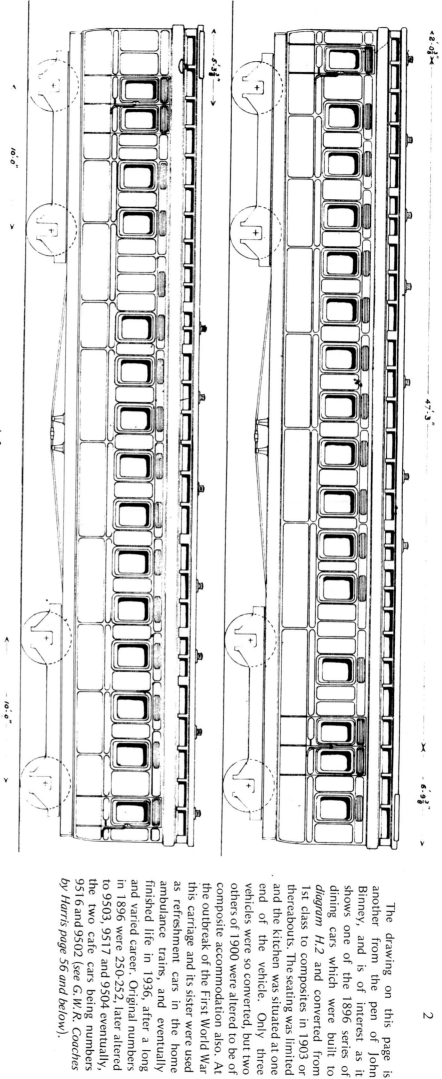

FIG 2A

Lot 929
No. 236 to H.3 dia.
renumbered 9502 cafe car

Lot 929
No. 237 to H.3 dia.
renumbered 9516 cafe car

This official drawing shows the arrangement of the 'Clifton Down' trailer car conversion.

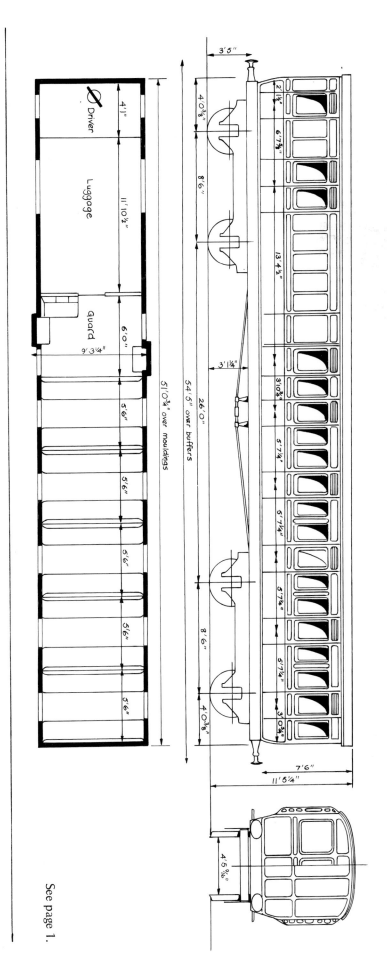

See page 1.

The history of the Steam Rail Motors on the Great Western really merits a work of its own, and no doubt one day someone who has made a particular study of the subject will do just that, but as these interesting vehicles formed such a vital part of the carriage programme I have presumed to include a few in this series, if only to preserve continuity. Although already mentioned in *Part I*, I have gone into rather more detail in this part, as the evolution of the large 70' carriage can be seen clearly in these examples of the steam rail car and trailers. For the drawings and some of the photographs I am indebted to David Lee again, who has collected a complete folio of the S.R.M.'s official drawings, and Mr. Slinn who with Mr. Binney has compiled copious notes about these interesting vehicles.

It would appear that the first self-propelled coach was one which appeared on the Fratton and East Southsea branch in 1901 and which was noted by the Great Western authorities, who then decided to run similar carriages on some of the Company's shorter branch lines.

A proposal was made to construct a clerestory coach with a petrol engine in one end and compartments to seat 1st and 3rd class passengers in the other. The diagram is said to have shown guards' lookouts at both ends, the whole vehicle being 58' long and 8'6" wide. However, there is no evidence that this vehicle was proceeded with and Steam Rail Car No.1 shown on *page 4*, (*figure 3*) was the first of its kind, but totally different from the clerestory described above. Built in October 1903 under *Lot 1037 diagram A*, this steam car was 57' long and

3

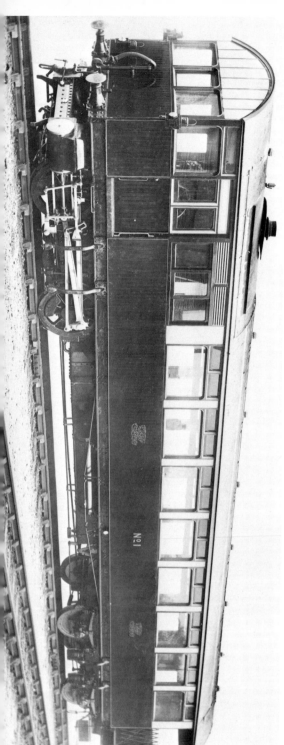

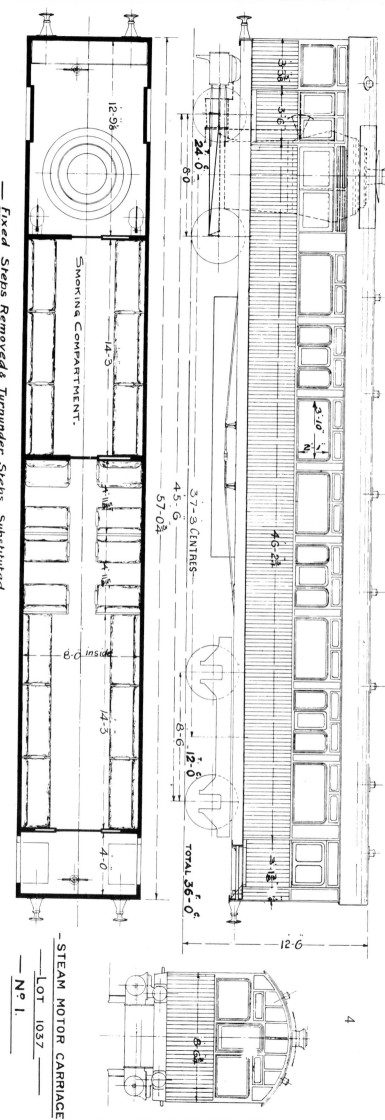

SMOKING COMPARTMENT.

STEAM MOTOR CARRIAGE
LOT 1037
No. 1.

— Fixed Steps Removed & Turnunder Steps Substituted. —

FIG 3

LOT.1037

DIA.A

8'6" wide, with a large high roofed full body and vertical boarded sides. There was only one saloon, served by lazy-tong gates at one end only. Each end was flat and had three windows therein. A large water tank was slung underneath and the coach was lit by gas lighting. Both this car and its sister No.2 started service on the Stonehouse-Chalford branch in Gloucestershire. The drawing shows doors at the passenger end but, as with all drawings, licence should be allowed and photographs are much more accurate in revealing what actually was fitted to the vehicles. Doors came later as an alteration. So the reader is always cautioned about the falli-bility of drawings, official and otherwise. Notice that the buffers are of the round head loco type.

The next steam rail car to be made was No.3, illustrated here in *figure 4* and in the accompanying drawing. Made to *diagram B* in May 1904, together with 4 to 14, they were rostered to work on the Westbourne Park to Southall, via Greenford branch, the Brentford branch, and the Plymouth, Millbay, Plympton route. As can be seen they differed from Nos. 1 and 2 by having shaped ends, bigger end windows, and the eliptical roof in place of the single arc type. Also, the length was increased to 59'6". Under this same *lot number 1054* were vehicles 4 to 8, made similar to No.3. A further six, numbered 9 to 14, were made in the same year but with a slight change in the seating plan; having all the longitudinal seats at one end instead of being divided by series of seats set across the central gangway. These latter cars were given *diagrams C and D*.

Long buffered standard gangway fitted on No. 5 and 6. Driving apparatus fitted on No. 5.

As in later years, many of the steam rail cars were converted into trailer cars. *Figure 5* shows No.99 so treated, which originally was S.R.M. No.3 itself. The conversion was carried out in 1915. The photograph shows the vehicle in the lake livery with white roof.

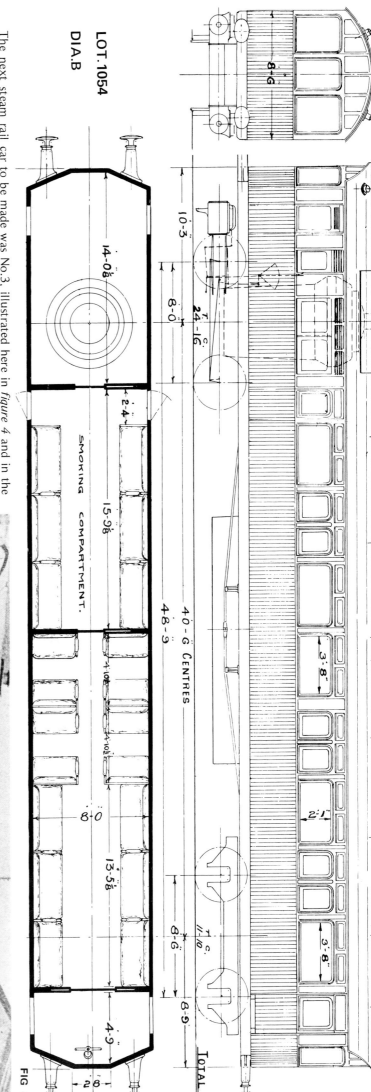

LOT.1054
DIA.B

FIG 4

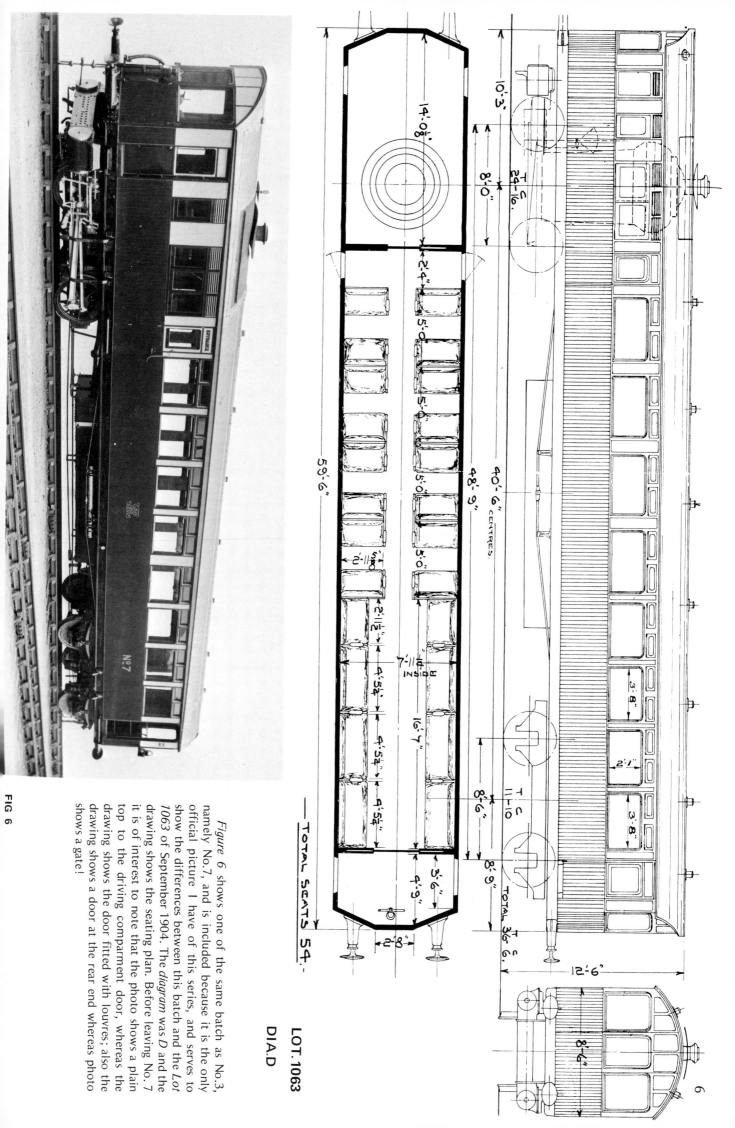

FIG 6

LOT. 1063

DIA.D

— TOTAL SEATS 54 —

Figure 6 shows one of the same batch as No.3, namely No.7, and is included because it is the only official picture I have of this series, and serves to show the differences between this batch and the *Lot 1063* of September 1904. The *diagram was D* and the drawing shows the seating plan. Before leaving No.7 it is of interest to note that the photo shows the top to the driving compartment door, whereas the drawing shows the door fitted with louvres; also the drawing shows a door at the rear end whereas photo shows a gate!

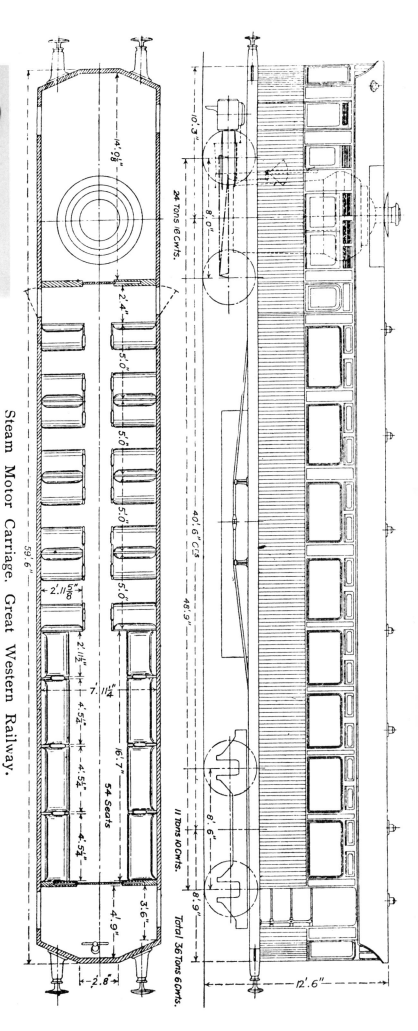

Steam Motor Carriage, Great Western Railway.

LOT.1054
DIA.D

DIA.P7

The drawing, taken from a 'Railway Engineer' of 1903, is of No.10 in the *Lot 1054* series, and does show the proper iron gate-way at the rear end, and is included solely for this reason. *Diagram is D.*

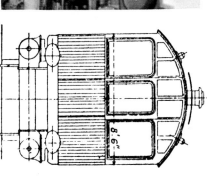

The two small photographs are of the very short 'Python' to DIA 'P.7'. Interesting as they show two styles of lettering. Nos. are 353 and 180 (Service No.) respectively. No. 180 running as a Loco Accumulator van.

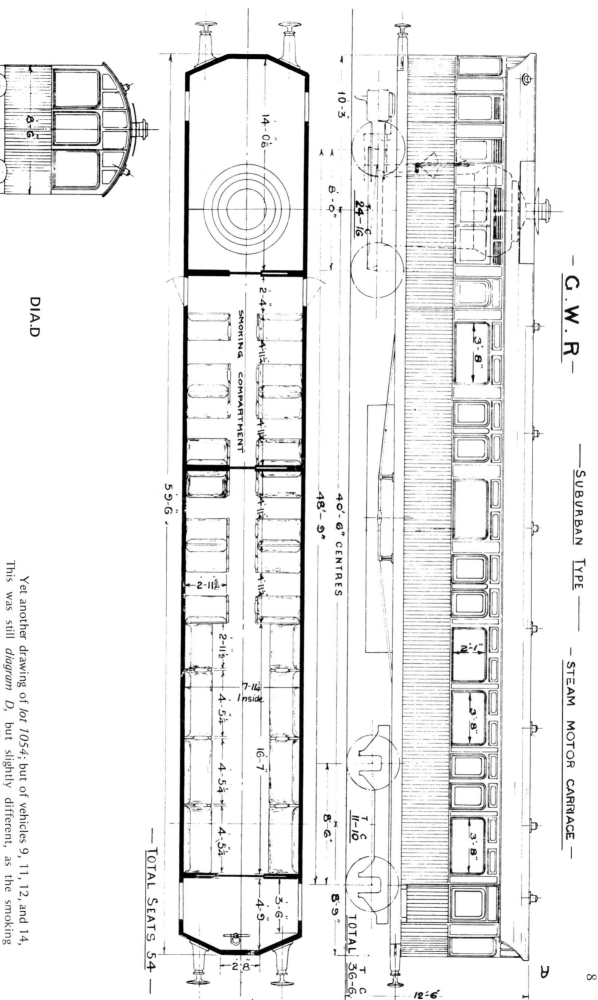

— G.W.R —

— SUBURBAN TYPE —

— STEAM MOTOR CARRIAGE —

DIA.D

— LOT 1054 —

— Nos 9,11,12,13 —

— SWINDON APRIL 1904 —

Yet another drawing of *lot 1054*; but of vehicles 9, 11, 12, and 14, This was still *diagram D*, but slightly different, as the smoking compartment has been closed off.

8

The steam rail-cars soon established themselves as money spinners, and extra accommodation was necessary. Therefore, special vehicles known as Trailers were constructed, which were akin to the steam rail cars, but without the motive unit. The driving gear was arranged through universal joints between the two vehicles, so that the unit could be driven from one end of the trailer. This official drawing shows No.1, the 59'6" prototype, and it can be seen how closely the design followed the rail-cars. Built under *lot 1055* there were only two, this one to *diagram A* and a longer version of 70' to *diagram B*.

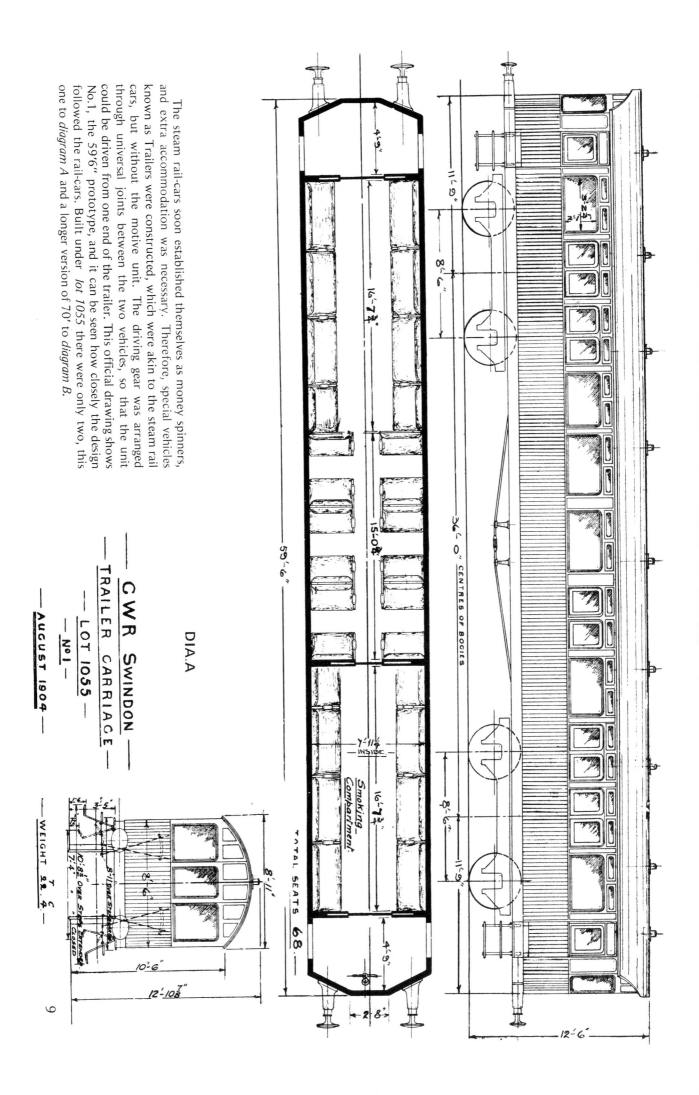

DIA.A

— GWR Swindon —
—— TRAILER CARRIAGE ——
— LOT 1055 —
— No.1 —
—— August 1904 ——

TOTAL SEATS 68.

Smoking Compartment.

9

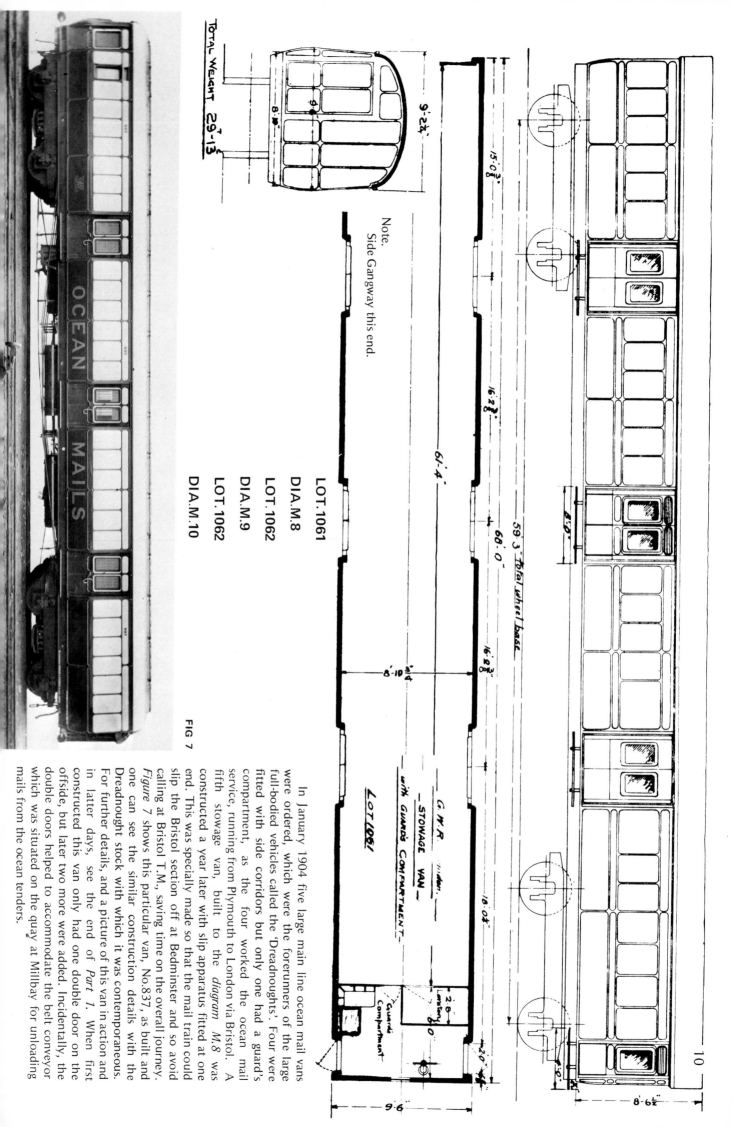

LOT.1061
DIA.M.8
LOT.1062
DIA.M.9
LOT.1062
DIA.M.10

FIG 7

Note.
Side Gangway this end.

LOT.1061

— G.W.R. —
— STOWAGE VAN —
with GUARD'S COMPARTMENT.

Guards Compartment

In January 1904 five large main line ocean mail vans were ordered, which were the forerunners of the large full-bodied vehicles called the 'Dreadnoughts'. Four were fitted with side corridors but only one had a guard's compartment, as the four worked the ocean mail service, running from Plymouth to London via Bristol. A fifth stowage van, built to the *diagram M.8* was constructed a year later with slip apparatus fitted at one end. This was specially made so that the mail train could slip the Bristol section off at Bedminster and so avoid calling at Bristol T.M., saving time on the overall journey. *Figure 7* shows this particular van, No.837, as built and one can see the similar construction details with the Dreadnought stock with which it was contemporaneous. For further details, see the end of *Part 1*. When first constructed this van only had one double door on the offside, but later two more were added. Incidentally, the double doors helped to accommodate the belt conveyor which was situated on the quay at Millbay for unloading mails from the ocean tenders.

FIG 8

FIG 10

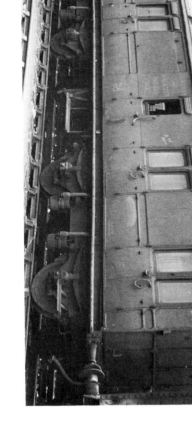

LOTS.1017.1048.1116.1121

Four examples of the 40' Passenger Brake Van are shown on this page, all of them photographed at the end of their lives between 1948 and 1958. *Figure 8* is of No.1121 which was built in January 1904 to *diagram K15* under *lot 1048*. This van is electrically lit and although some of the panelling still shows, most of the side has disappeared under the repair sheeting. Bogies are of the Dean 8'6" pattern, and the van carries gangways.

Figure 9 is of a similar, but non gangway, vehicle, shown when in departmental use with the Signal & Telegraph Department. Interesting

K.15

K.16

nevertheless, as this example still carries the guard's lookout with which they are all fitted when built. No.242 is fitted with gas lighting.

Another *K15* is shown in *figure 11* but this time running on Churchward American 8' bogies. Running number of this vehicle was 239 and its *lot No.* was *1116*.

No. 209 illustrated in *figure 10* is of the *K.16* variety and was built under *lot 1017* in 1903. The van at the time of photographing was rostered to work between Trowbridge and Worcester, mostly with parcel traffic of the sausage trade I would assume.

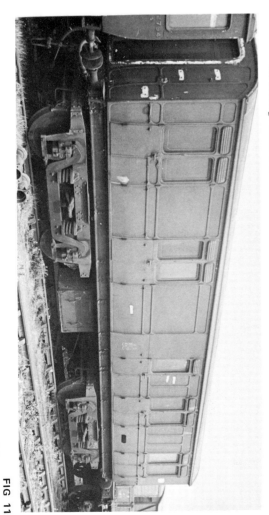

FIG 9

FIG 11

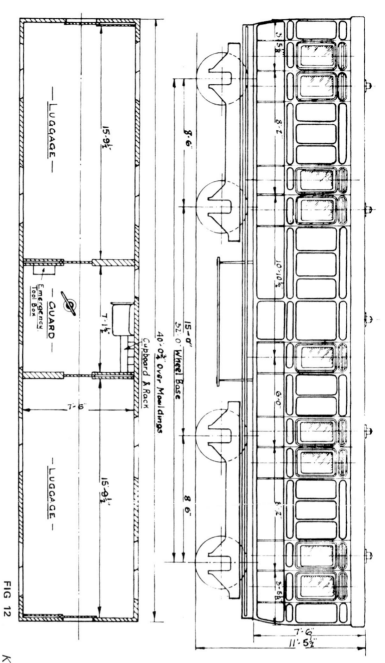

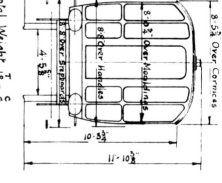

LUGGAGE

15-9½

Emergency Tool Box

GUARD

Cupboard & Rack

7-1½

7-6

LUGGAGE

15-9½

40-0¾ Over Mouldings

FIG 12

3-5⅝   8-2   8-6

10-10¼

15-0

52-0 Wheel Base

9-0   8-6   8-2   3-5⅝

7-6

11-5½

3-5   1-7

8-9¾ Over Mouldings

8-8 Over Handles

8-5¼ Over Cornices

8' 8" Over Stepboards

4-5½

10-3¾

11-10¾

Total Weight 18 - 6 T C

LOT. 1075
DIA. K.15

The photograph (*figure 13*) and drawing on page 13 are of the Steam Rail Car No.17. This was the first of a set of 12 ordered in February 1904 and completed in April of that year. It had a diagram classification of F and was 59'6" in length, 8'6" wide. Notice that a small double door luggage compartment has been added to the design. No.17 completed the greatest mileage of this series clocking up 330,146 miles by the end of 1917 and was converted into Trailer No.113 in April 1919 to *diagram A.9*.

Here are shown both drawing and photograph of No.231, another K.15 passenger brake van, built in November of 1904 to *lot No. 1075*. The picture, taken at Ebbw Vale in 1947, shows one end altered to accommodate three windows, the centre being a droplight. At one time the vehicle was used for sleet cutter working, which would necessitate this fitting. Note the American type 8' bogies and the large number of roof ventilators.

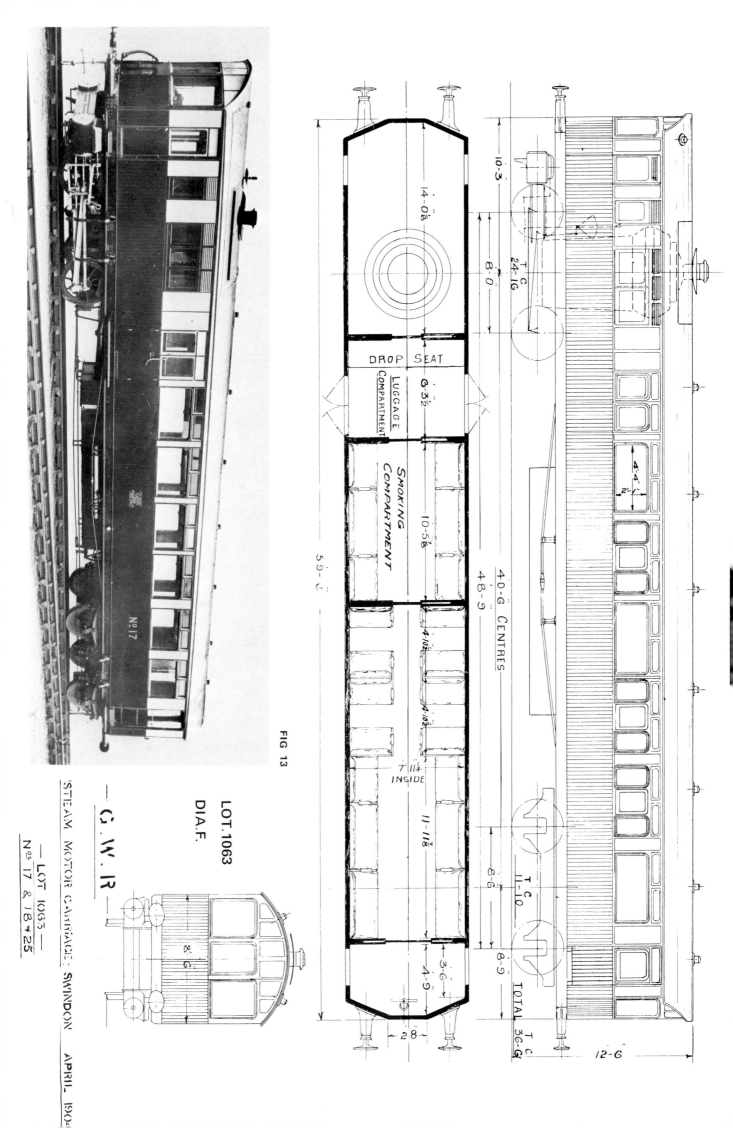

FIG 13

LOT.1063
DIA.F.

— G.W.R —

STEAM MOTOR CARRIAGE SWINDON APRIL 190?

— LOT 1063 —
N°s 17 & 18 +25

DROP SEAT

LUGGAGE COMPARTMENT

SMOKING COMPARTMENT

14-0⅝

6-3½

10-5⅜

59-?

48-9

40-6 CENTRES

4-10½

4-10½

7 11¼ INSIDE

11-11⅛

3-6

4-9

28

8-6

8-9

12-6

TOTAL 36-6

T C 24-16

10-3

8-0

4-4

2

T C 11-10

8-6

8 6

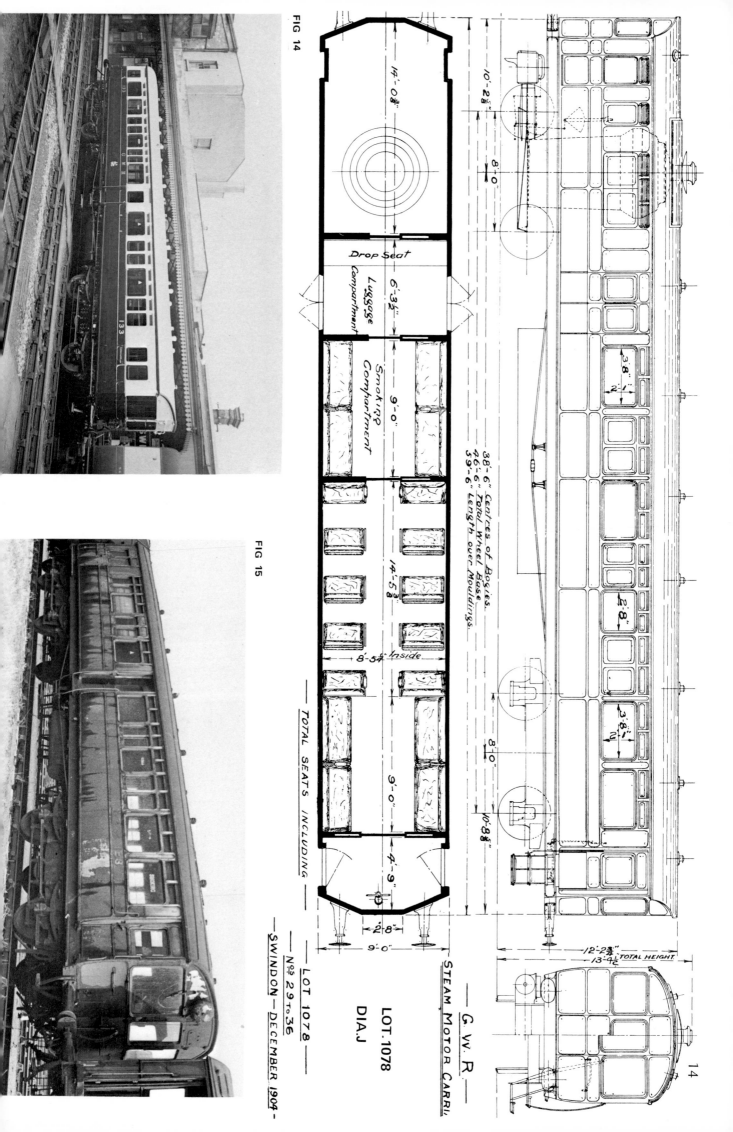

FIG 14

FIG 15

Drop Seat

Luggage Compartment

Smoking Compartment

6'-3½"   9'-0"   14'-5⅜"   9'-0"   4'-9"

8'-5¼" Inside

2'-8"

9'-0"

14'-0¾"

38'-6" Centres of Bogies.
26'-6" Total Wheel Base.
59'-6" Length over Mouldings.

10'-2⅜"   8'-0"

8'-0"   10'-8⅝"

— TOTAL SEATS INCLUDING —

— N⁰ 29 to 36 —

— SWINDON — DECEMBER 1904 —

— LOT 1078 —

LOT.1078
DIA.J

— G.W.R. —

STEAM MOTOR CARR.

3'-8"
2'-1"

2'-8"

3'-8"
2'-1"

12'-2¾"
13'-4½" TOTAL HEIGHT

14

was J. Notice that the body construction is of the full-boated panelled stock instead of the flat, slab-sided construction. The driving wheels on these S.R.Ms were of 3'6½" diameter, instead of the usual 4' diameter. The two photographs in *Figures 14 and 15* show the same vehicle, No.133, which was converted from Car No. 36, also of *lot 1078*, in 1923. *Figure 14* was taken by Roye England at Swindon in 1932 (notice the white roof) and *figure 15* was taken by myself at Reading in the early 1950s. One picture shows the driving end and and the other the trailing luggage section.

This page is filled by a large detailed picture, kindly loaned by David Lee, of steam Rail Car No.43. Reproduced as large as possible like this it enables many details to be seen. The overall length of these cars has now risen to 70', which has called for a large 9' bogie with volute springs at the trailing end. Two vacuum cylinders are now fitted, and there is also a partition to keep the smokers apart from the non-smokers.

There were twelve cars in this series, numbering from 41 to 52, to *lot 1079*, and *diagrams were L, M, and N*. Although not originally fitted with gangways (see photo.), these were fitted in December of 1910 to enable the Steam Car to be coupled to a trailer and so increase its payload. No.43 itself became trailer No.134 in 1923 to *diagram A.17* after running 346,888 miles.

LOT.1079
DIA.M.1

The drawing is the side elevation of *lot 1079* reduced from the official diagram. The interior furnishings of S.R.M. No.43 are clearly shown in *Figure 17*. One can see in the foreground the fixed side-benches and further down the seat with backs which could be swung over to face the seat the other way. Notice the gas lamps, leather straps for standing passengers, the usual Great Western wall photographs, and the slatted floor. Sliding doors were provided at compartment ends, and ventilators were fitted in the roof and over the windows.

On this page is the plan of the *L diagrams*, showing the seating layout, and on page 16 the end elevation for the benefit of modellers. *Figure 18* is a Swindon photograph of Trailer No.4 which shows a new line of thought in 1905. It was found that the Steam Rail Cars were a little on the weak side for hauling tail traffic, and trials had been taking place using a small 0—4—2T engine, sandwiched in between two trailers, instead of the S.R.M. and trailer method. No.4 shown here was one of the first built expressly for this job, and one can see the driving gear in the right hand end of the vehicle. Together with a similar trailer marshalled at the other end of the engine, and again reversed, this gave a driving compartment at each end, and this avoided the necessity of either turning or running round at a terminus. When formed in pairs like this, one unit would be for smokers and the other for non-smokers.

LOT.1081
DIA.B

FIG 18

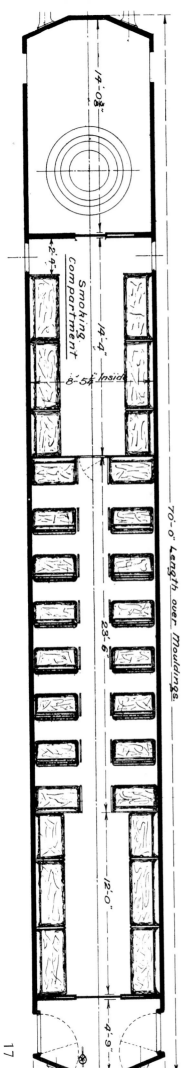

— TOTAL SEATS. 64 —

14'-0⅜"

2'-4"

14'-4"

8'-5¼" Inside

Smoking compartment

23'-6"

12'-0"

4'-9"

70'-0" Length over Mouldings.

9'-0" over mouldings

17

FIG 19

FIG 20

Two photographs and an official drawing illustrate Trailer No.119. In *figure 19* the luggage end is shown and in *figure 20* the driving compartment can be seen. This car was originally Steam Rail Car No.23, and was converted to a trailer in 1920. With engine the *diagram was F* and after conversion this became *diagram A.9.*

A B C A

59'-6" Over Mouldings.

63'-6" Over Buffers.

12'- 6"

DIA.A.9

18

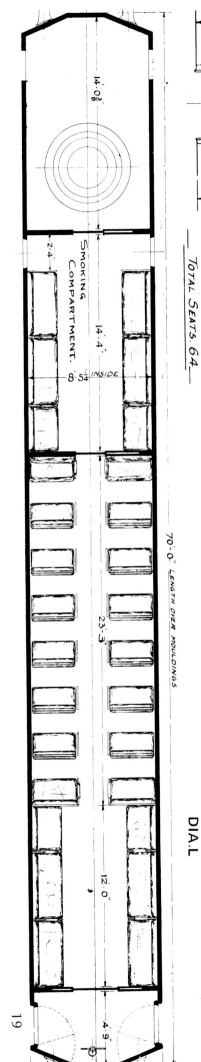

TOTAL SEATS. 64.

SMOKING COMPARTMENT.

14'-0⅜"

14'-4'

8'-5¼" INSIDE

2'-4"

23'-3"

12'-0"

70'-0" LENGTH OVER MOULDINGS

4'-9"

19

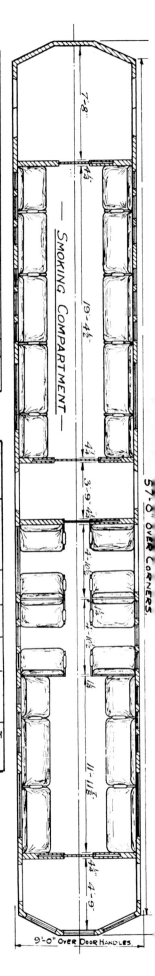

SMOKING COMPARTMENT

7'-8"

4¼"

19'-4½"

4¼"

3'-9¼"

11-10½"

1¼"

11-11⅝"

4¼"

4'-9"

57'-0" OVER CORNERS

9'-0" OVER DOOR HANDLES

DIA.A.9

10'-6"

9'-0"

8'-10"

8'-6"

9'-0" OVER STEP RAILS (SCORED)

13'-1¼"

— TOTAL SEATS. —

— G.W.R — TRAILER CAR — LOT 1063 —

TRAILER No.	LATE MOTOR No.	A	B	C	TARE	TOTAL SEATS
113	17	8'-6"	33'-6"	42'-0"	24-9	58
114	18	9'-0"	32'-3"	41'-3"	25-6	"
115	19	8'-6"	29'-0"	37'-6"	24-15	"
116	20	9'-0"	31'-8"	40'-8"	25-14	62
117	21	8'-6"	29'-0"	37'-6"	24-14	"
118	22	9'-0"	31'-8"	40'-8"	26-0	"

TRAILER No.	LATE MOTOR No.	A	B	C	TARE	TOTAL SEATS
119	23	8'-6"	29'-0"	37'-6"	25-8	62
120	24	9'-0"	31'-3"	40'-8"	25-12	"
121	25	8'-6"	32'-0"	40'-6"	24-16	"
122	26	9'-0"	31'-8"	40'-8"	25-19	"
123	27	8'-6"	29'-0"	37'-6"	25-17	"
124	28	9'-0"	31'-8"	40'-8"	25-19	"

On this page are two end elevations and two plans, which show quite well the difference in the seating arrangements, and, in the end profile, the slab-sided trailer which used to be a motor, and the 70' new-look steam rail cars of the lot 1079 series. Also for interest is a table which gives conversion numbers and variable dimensions of the A.9 series.

LOT.1079
DIA.L

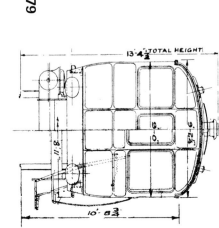

13'-4½" TOTAL HEIGHT

9'-0"

8'-11"

9'-2¼"

10'-8¾"

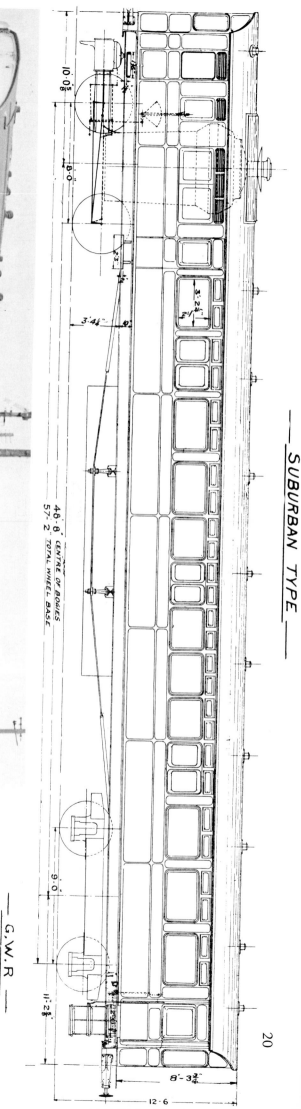

- G.W.R -
STEAM MOTOR-CARRIAGE
LOT 1079
Nos 50 TO 52
SWINDON — NOVEMBER 1904

DIA.A.19 DIA.N

FIG 21

At the risk of repetition, and to keep this *Part II* as self-contained as possible, I am showing on page 21 examples of the superb 'Dreadnought' coaches of 1905. *Figure 22* illustrates No.3277, a full third class corridor coach of 1905, to the classification of C.24. Note how the corridor changes sides near the halfway point; constructed like this it was said, to distribute the passenger weight evenly. Apart from sleepers and diners, these carriages were some of the longest ever to run on British railways. There were many unusual features about this stock, including the flat slab-doors at ends and middle and fitted with double hinges, the high eliptical roof which gave an inside measurement floor to ceiling of 8', and sliding doors which shut off the side corridors from the end vestibules. Upholstery was dark green for 1st class, and dark red rep for the 3rd class compartments.

The drawing at foot of the page is of the brake 3rd version of the same series. Incidentally, would-be modellers of these massive coaches with their complicated panelling can be saved much hard work, as Trevor Charlton has produced some photo-engraved sides of the vehicles in zinc for 4mm scale, which are really superb.

Trailer No.140 shown on this page, is recorded here as it does show clearly the surgery used at Swindon to convert the steam rail cars to trailers. This particular vehicle was originally Steam Car No.52, the outline of which is shown in the official drawing at the top of the page. As a steam rail car, the diagram was *N* and differed from the *M* series in that the internal door dividing the saloons was sliding instead of swinging. Looking again at the photograph which I took at Reading in 1948, one can see that the left hand end is the driving compartment, as it was with the S.R.M. and the right hand end is where the engine was originally situated. In other words, the drawing is reversed to the photograph.

10' 0⅝"
8' 0"
3' 44"
3' 2¼"
48' 8" CENTRE OF BOGIES
57' 2" TOTAL WHEEL BASE
9' 0"
11' 2⅝"
8' 3¾"
12' 6

20

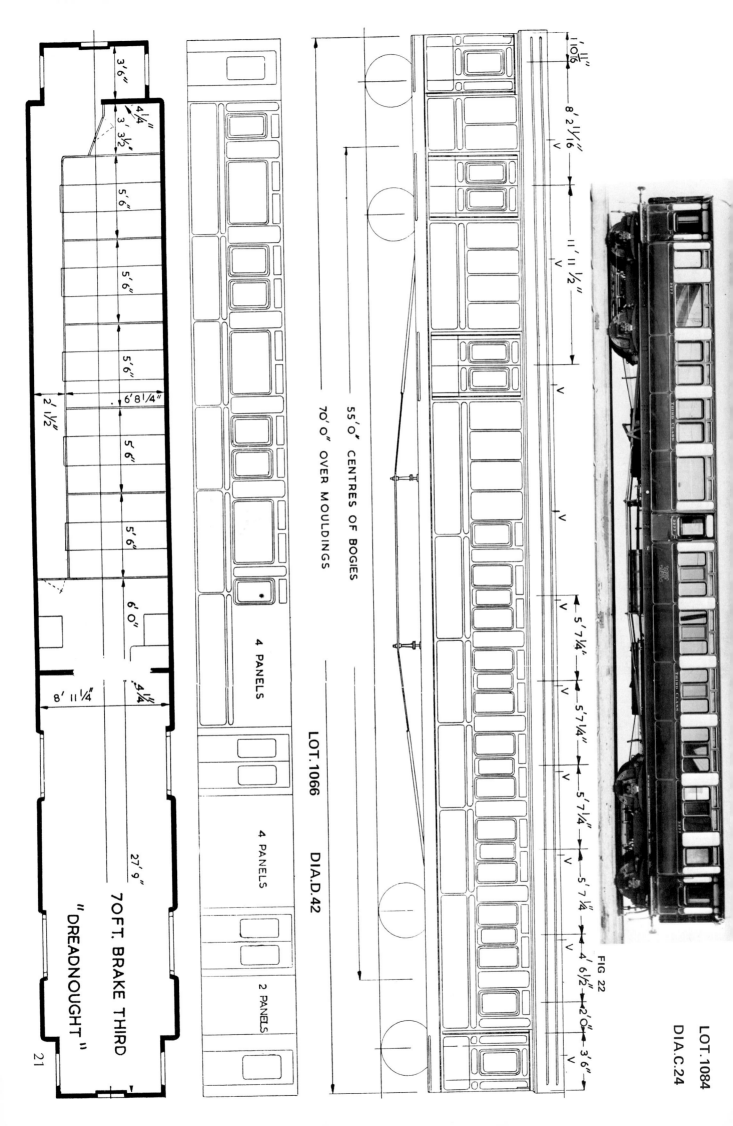

70FT. BRAKE THIRD
"DREADNOUGHT"

LOT.1066   DIA.D.42

LOT.1084
DIA.C.24

FIG 22

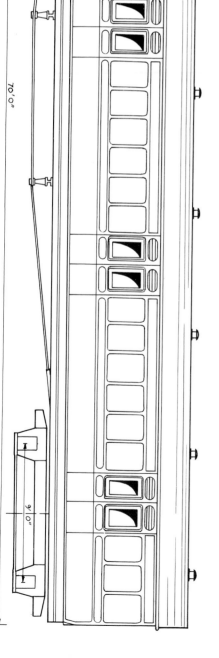

70'0"

9'0"

FIG 23

Also in 1905 five large 70' stowage vans were built under *lot 1091* to *diagram M.11*. They were constructed to implement the growing T.P.O. traffic which was in need of more up-to-date vehicles. As can be seen from the photograph and drawing, they were to the full extent of the loading gauge, namely 70' x 9' and were very large vehicles. I managed to photograph No.825 at Henley in 1947, when it was painted in the war-time all brown livery, (*figure 23*).

The drawing and inset show the slight difference in the placing of the guard's door.

Inset

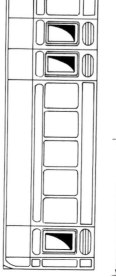

9'0"

LOT.1091

DIA.M.11

22

FIG 24

LOT.1092
DIA.E.78

Paddington received many complaints from the travelling public against the Dreadnoughts, because of the difficulty experienced with ingress and exit. In fact these vehicles were known at Swindon as 'Deathtraps'! The conservative British were used to a door to each compartment, so Churchward finally had to abandon the massive 3 doors-a-side Dreadnoughts. Another 70' type was the Tri-composite brake shown on this page. Built in 1905, also to *diagram E.78* under *lot 1092* it still retained full width and length, but had doors for each compartment. It was an unusual vehicle in having not only small lookouts for the guards (which can be seen in *Figure 26*) but also 3 lavatories. By virtue of this, my old friend the late Mike Longridge gave these carriages the soubriquet of 'Tri-Bog Brake Compo', and they proved to be a very useful coach in traffic, although little has been written about them! Originally they were designed to be clerestory roofed!

FIG 26

FIG 25

FIG 27

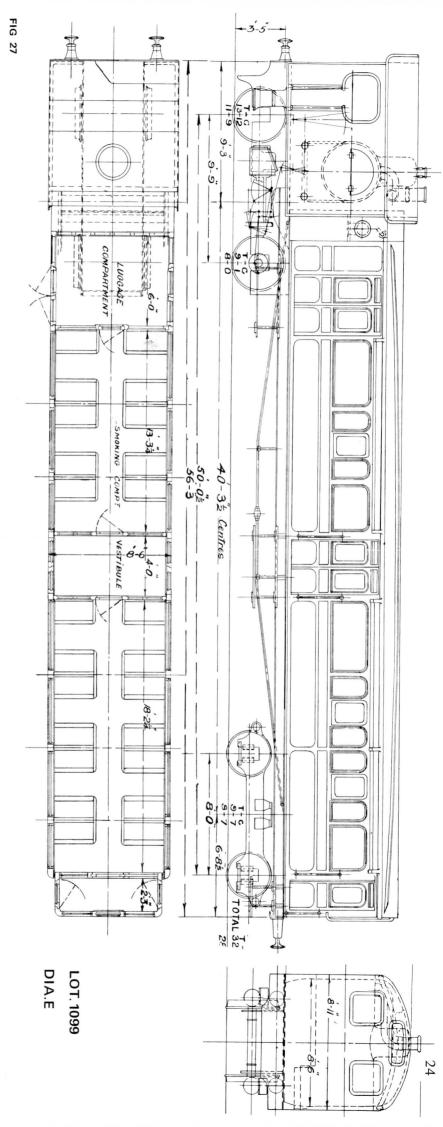

LUGGAGE COMPARTMENT

SMOKING COMPT

VESTIBULE

LOT. 1099
DIA. E

Although completely non-Swindon in both design and build, it is thought worth while to include both photo and drawing of No.15 if only for interest's sake, and to show how far superior were the Churchward rail cars to contemporary designs by other Companies. This particular version was one of two (Nos.15 and 16), designed and built by Kerr-Stuart & Company, ordered by the Great Western Railway in 1904, and completed in November 1905. It can be seen that the boiler was horizontal and mounted transversly. Drive was on to one axle only, making the engine unit a 2—2—0 in fact, which might have accounted for its weak performance. It is not known why these cars were ordered, as little of value seems to have resulted from their purchase, and indeed No.15 only ran 87,000 miles before being sold to the Nidd Valley Light Railway in 1920. No.16 ran even less than this, and, failing to find a buyer, was broken up in 1927.

More steam rail cars in picture form, and a natural follow-on from the previous page, because Nos.61 to 72 had their engines and bodies made by Kerr-Stuarts to Great Western design. No.61, shown at the top of the page in *figure 28* coupled to trailer No.34, was the first of the series and carries the unusual monogram, which was tried out in 1906 but quickly abandoned. Bogies fitted to this series were the 9' 'Motherwell' type as can be seen from the official photographs. The works plate of Kerr-Stuart can just be seen to the left of the central steps in *figure 29* of No.67. The official drawing accompanying the pictures is of the same series *diagram O of lot 1088 and 1100 of 1905.*

FIG 28

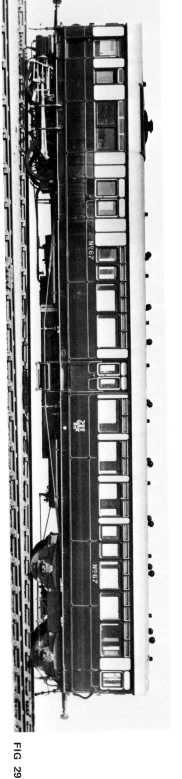

FIG 29

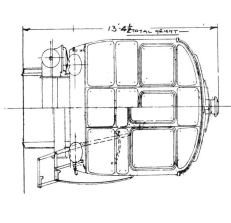

G.W.R SWINDON
STEAM MOTOR CARRIAGE.
SCALE ¼" = 1 FOOT
APRIL 1905
LOTS 1088, 1100,
N°S 53 to 58
„ 61 „ 72

DIA.O

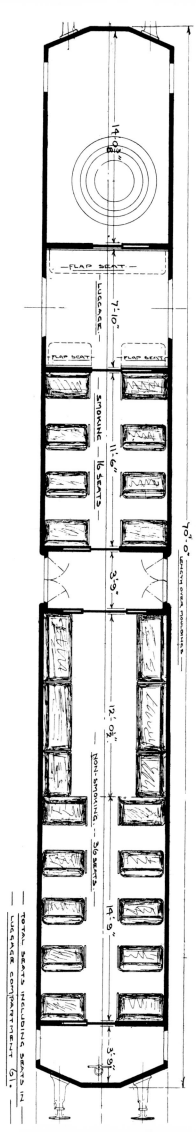

FLAP SEAT

LUGGAGE

FLAP SEAT · FLAP SEAT

SMOKING — 16 SEATS

NON-SMOKING — 36 SEATS

14'0" 7'10" 11'6" 3'9" 12'0½" 14'9" 3'9"

70'0" LENGTH OVER MOULDINGS

— TOTAL SEATS INCLUDING SEATS IN —
— LUGGAGE COMPARTMENT 61. —

LOT.1100

DIA.O

FIG 30

The interior of No.61 is illustrated on this page in *figure 30* and it is possible to see the departure from Great Western practice in the fitting of raffia-backed swing seats; everything else is standard.

Figure 31 shows No.63 of the same series, from the opposite, or off-side, in approximately 1910. Note that the double windows of the engine compartment have now been reduced in width, and the water-filler cover fitted in place, which was to become standard from here on. The diagram given to these cars was "Q" and the seating and general arrangement can be seen in the plan at the head of the page.

Another series of steam rail cars which were built outside Swindon was the *lot 1101* on which the engine and frames were of Great Western manufacture, but the bodywork was carried out by the Gloucester Carriage & Wagon Company. Numbers were from 73 to 80 and depicted on page 27 is No.75 in drawing and photograph. The diagram number was Q and they were put into stock in mid-1906. A further series of three were built at Swindon to virtually the same design twelve months later under *diagram Q1*. Length was 59'6", and width 9', running numbers 81 to 83.

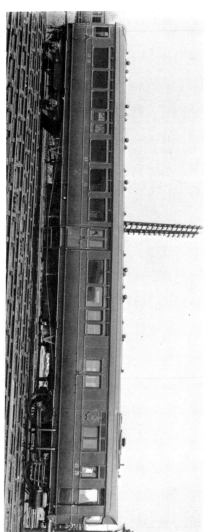

FIG 31

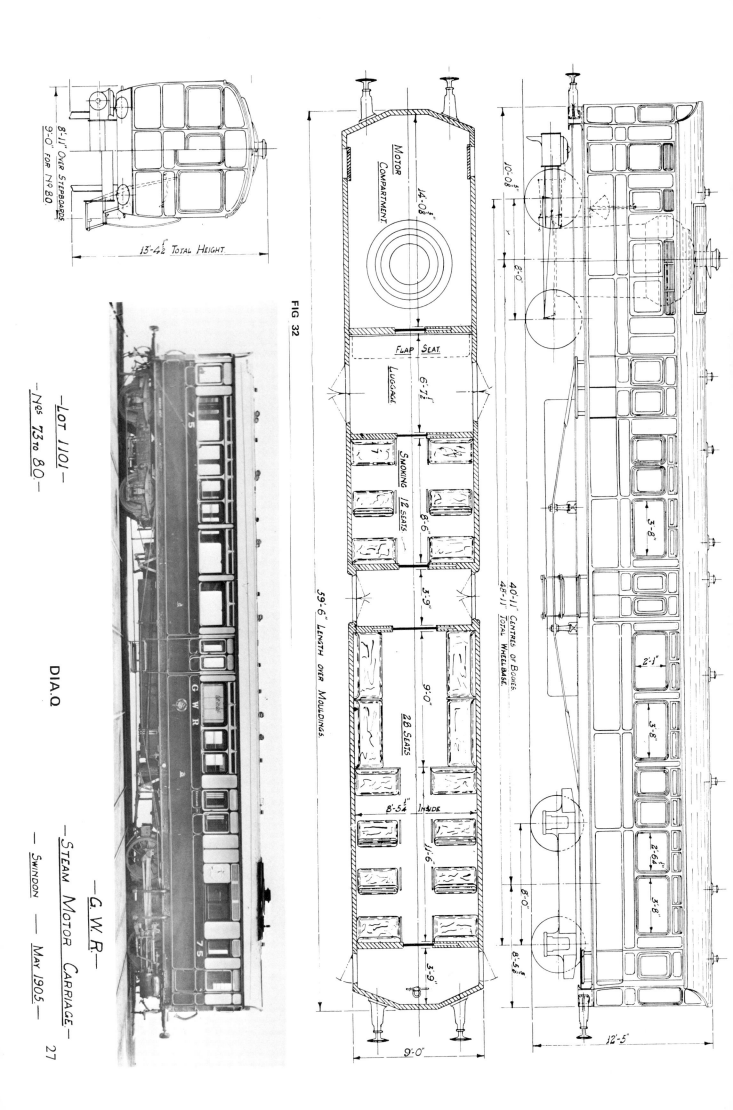

FIG 32

8'-11" OVER STEPBOARDS
9'-0" FOR Nº 80.

13'-4½" TOTAL HEIGHT.

MOTOR COMPARTMENT

14'-0⅜"

FLAP SEAT.

LUGGAGE

6'-7½"

SMOKING
12 SEATS

8'-6"

3'-9"

9'-0"

28 SEATS

8'-5¼" INSIDE

11'-6"

3'-9"

59'-6" LENGTH OVER MOULDINGS.

9'-0"

10'-0⅝"

8'-0"

40'-11" CENTRES OF BOGIES
48'-11" TOTAL WHEELBASE.

8'-0"

8'-5⅝"

3'-8"

2'-1"

3'-8"

2'-6¼"

3'-8"

12'-5"

— LOT 1101 —
— Nᵒˢ 73 ᴛᴏ 80. —

DIA.Q

— G.W.R. —
— STEAM MOTOR CARRIAGE. —
— SWINDON — MAY 1905 —

27

FIG 33A

FIG 33

LOT.1108   DIA.L

LOT.1097   DIA.E

FIG 34

Lot 1108 of January 1906 contained six 70'
trailers of the *L diagram* pattern, 29 to 34. In *figure
33* we see one of these cars, No.34, photographed in
1948 just leaving Hook Norton viaducts and passing
the home signal *en route* for Banbury. One can just
see the old-type vacuum cylinder with its joggled
hangers (the other sides were straight) and the driver
sitting down in the leading compartment.

Figure 34 illustrates No. 11 which was one of three
70' trailers built to *lot 1097* of 1905. The photograph was taken in the Up bay at Banbury and one
can just see the old Brunel all-over roof, over the top
of the trailer. Notice the car has been refitted with
short 7' bogies and has blank ends next to the engine.
The small inset picture is a full front shot of the
driving compartment of these vehicles, which might
prove of interest to model-makers (*figure 33a*).

It is not generally known that six clerestory coaches were altered to form trailer cars. In 1905 four clerestory 3rds were converted by fitting a driving compartment into one end, complete with large windows, using the single lavatory as a cubby hole with tip-up seats, and equipping them with through regulator gear. *Figure 35* shows No.14 which was to *diagram G of lot 1097* and the drawing is for Nos.16 and 17 which were *diagram H.* Two more were so dealt with under *lot 1108*, being *diagrams M and M1.*

LOT.1097   DIA.G

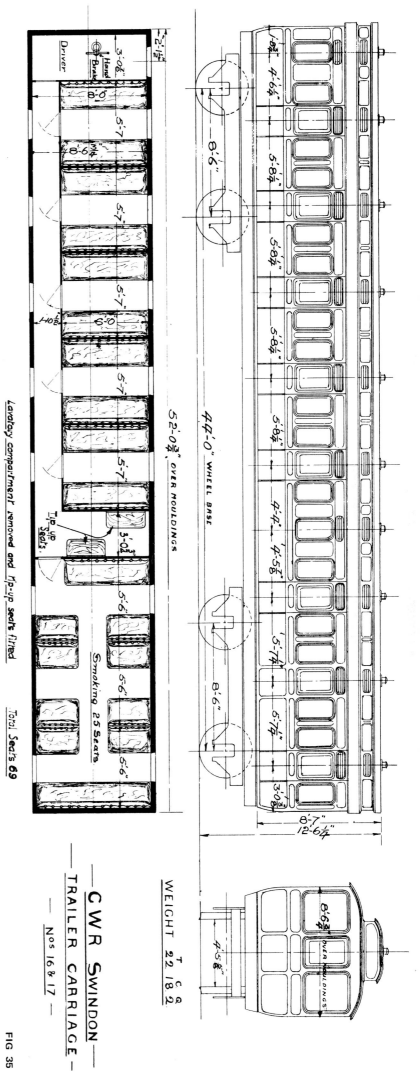

Through *Regulator Gear* fitted on Nos 16 & 17   Total Seats 69

Lavatory compartment removed and tip-up seats fitted

Driver

Hand Brake

Tip up Seats

Smoking 25 Seats

52'-0¾" OVER MOULDINGS

44'-0" WHEEL BASE

WEIGHT 22 18 2 T C Q

— G W R SWINDON —
— TRAILER CARRIAGE —
— Nos 16 & 17 —

FIG 35

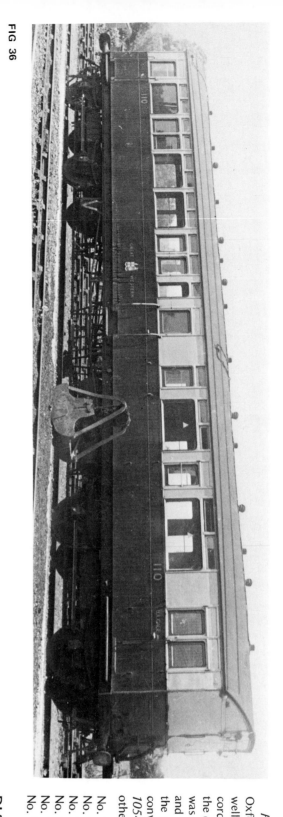

FIG 36

Figure 36 is a photograph of trailer No.110 standing at Oxford North in 1947 and shows the luggage end quite well. The wire hanging down from the roof is the whistle cord by which the driver could operate the whistle from the driving compartment. This car, which in this condition was to *diagram A 7*, started life as S.R.M. No.12 in 1904 and was converted in 1916 to a trailer. The diagram on the same page shows the outline and plan of the vehicle as converted to this *A 7* form. The original lot number was 1054 and half were converted to the A.7 drawing and the other six to *diagram Z* seen on the next page.

No. 107	Trailer late No. 9	Motor
No. 108	" " No. 10	"
No. 109	" " No. 11	"
No. 110	" " No. 12	"
No. 111	" " No. 13	"
No. 112	" " No. 14	"

DIA.A.7

— SMOKING COMPARTMENT —

7'-7½"   4¼"   17'-11½"   4½" 3'-9" 4½"   9'-11½"   13'-5½"   4½" 4'-9"

59'-6" Over Mouldings

A   A   B   C   C   A   A

A⁷

— G.W.R —
— TRAILER CAR —
— LOT 1054 —
Nos 107, 108, 109, 110, 111, 112
— SWINDON JULY 1917 —

Another picture of trailer No.110 is shown here and the front end details are revealed together with roof ventilators and lamp tops. This car was stationed at Oxford when I knew it and worked with engine No.1196 on the Woodstock branch. The bucket grab alongside the carriage was the means of coaling locomotives at Oxford when the coal stage was either too busy or out of commission.

Below *figure 37* is shown slab-sided conversion drawing, the same *lot No. 1054* but given *diagram Z*, being slightly different to the drawing on the previous page in several measurements and panelling.

DIA.Z

FIG 37

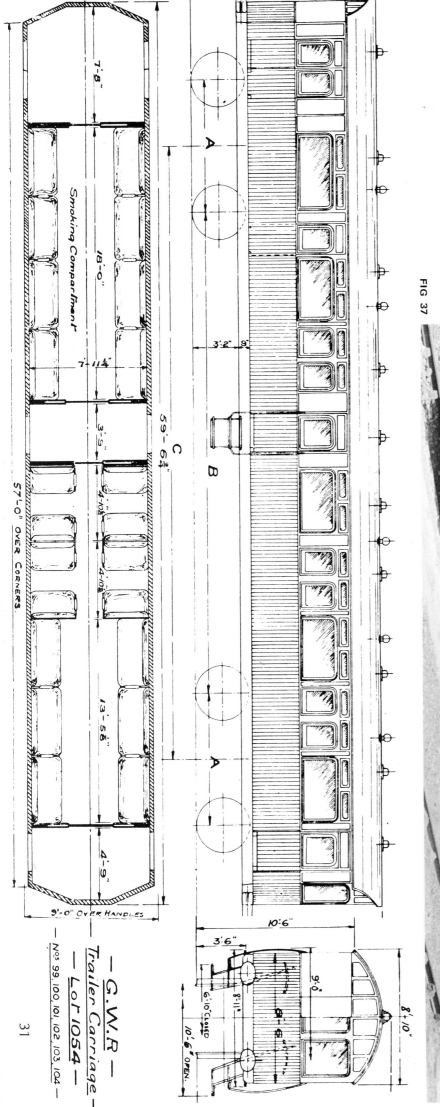

Smoking Compartment

7'-8"
18'-0"
7'-11¼"
3'-9"
4'-10½"
4'-10½"
13'-5⅝"
4'-9"
59'-6¼"
C
57'-0" OVER CORNERS
9'-0" OVER HANDLES

3'-2"   9"
A   A   B

10'-6"
3'-6"
9'-0"
8'-11"
6'-10" Closed
10'-6" Open
9'-6" Open
8'-10"

— G.W.R —
Trailer Carriage
— Lot 1054 —
Nos. 99,100,101,102,103,104

31

Whilst still dealing with the early steam rail cars it might be of interest to both enthusiasts and modellers to describe the steam unit itself, which was fitted into these carriages. The drawing shown is also from the 1904 issue of the R.E. and gives a lot of useful dimensions. It can be seen that the boiler was of the upright type, carried on the top of the bogie side frames by means of angle-iron brackets riveted to the boiler shell. They were fitted with 477 tubes of 1⅛" dia. which, together with the firebox area, gave a total heating surface of 672.33 sq.ft. The regulator, mounted in the main steam pipe from a turret in the top of the boiler, worked in a quadrant, transversely across the body, whilst the reversing lever moved in a fore and aft direction, operating the link of the Walschaerts gear which shifted the position of the D valves. The engine bogies were of the Dean pattern, 8.0' W.B. with scroll irons and transverse beams, and were fitted with sand boxes for working in both directions, and the driving wheels were coupled and driven by 12" × 16" two cylinders. Water was carried in a large 450 gallon tank slung underneath the car amidships, and filled through fillers located one on each side just behind the boiler. When first constructed, water hoses were directed into these fillers by lowering the drop-lights directly opposite, but later the glass windows were reduced in size and a special panel with a filler flap was fitted in their space. Coal was brought to the cars in sacks and dumped into bins in the front of the compartment, which held 15 cwts. There was a gas lamp in the cabin, and although quite light inside because of all the windows, my dim memory of a ride in the engine unit is one of heat combined with draughts and wet steam, mixed with coal dust. As a small boy I remember I was rather scared of all the noise and the smoke and flames which blew back from the firehole when going into tunnels. Old friends of mine who used to be firemen on these motors have told me that they were always shy of steam and much of the trouble was caused by ashes collecting on the top tube plate, so obstructing the draughting. Much of the firing had to be done at stations when the cars were stopped, rather than when running; in fact it was not an easy turn for firemen rostered to the motors, as when the driver was at the other end of the vehicle the fireman was responsible not only for firing, keeping the boiler full, but for re-creating the vacuum when required, and also notching up the reversing lever (setting the cut-off).

The smaller drawing is to 4mm scale for modellers.

Steam Motor Carriage, Great Western Railway.

A plan, end elevation, valve gear and picture appear in companion volume "G.W. Engines".

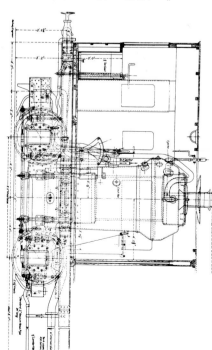

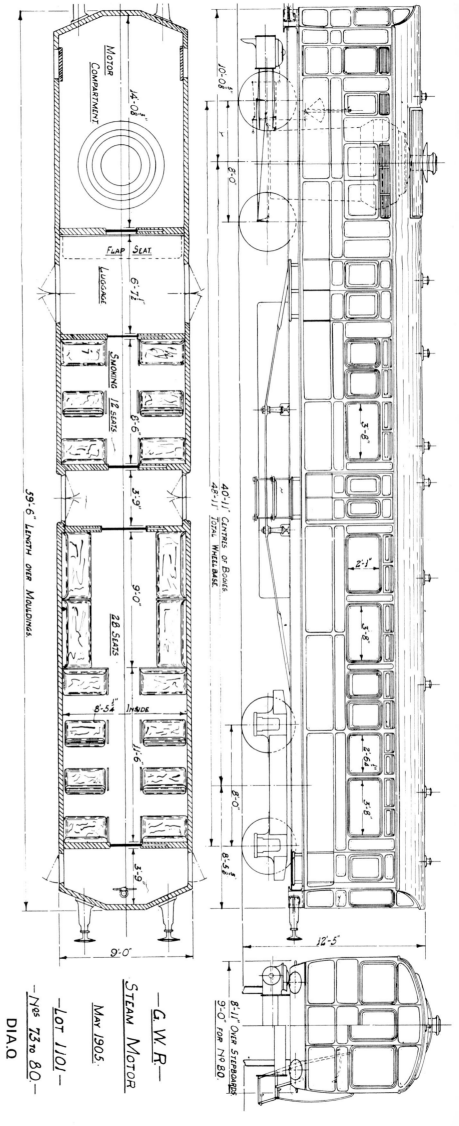

No.77 is one of eight steam rail cars which were built in April 1906 under *lot 1101* to *diagram Q*. These eight, Nos.73 to 80, had their bodies built by the Gloucester Carriage & Wagon Company and the frames and engines by the Great Western at Swindon. This particular car, shown in the picture *figure 38*, was never converted to a trailer car and was finally condemned in October 1935 after an active life of 28 years.

There are one or two points of interest in the picture: to the left of the driving cab can be seen No.86, one of the cars built to *diagram R*, described on the next page. Note also the loco-type sand boxes fitted to the front stretcher bar of the bogie, protection for the driver's face in the form of a series of bars at the front windows (several men were injured by broken glass, as large birds and other missiles often hit against the end windows). Also note the fitting of the hand-worked windscreen wiper, nearside only, and the double doors in the centre, which usually indicated that the body was not built at the Great Western factory, but by private companies.

FIG 38

33

MOTOR COMPARTMENT

14-0⅜"

FLAP SEAT

LUGGAGE

6-7½"

SMOKING 12 SEATS

8-6"

3-9"

28 SEATS

9-0"

8-5¼" INSIDE

11-6"

3-9"

9-0"

59-6" LENGTH OVER MOULDINGS.

DIA.Q

10-0⅝"

5-11"

9-0"

40-11" CENTRES OF BOGIES.
48-11" TOTAL WHEELBASE.

3-8"

2-1"

3-8"

2-6¼"

3-8"

8-0"

8-5⅛"

12-5"

8-11" OVER STEPBOARDS
9-0" FOR Nº 80

— G.W.R —
STEAM MOTOR

MAY 1905.

— LOT 1101 —

— Nºs 73 to 80 —

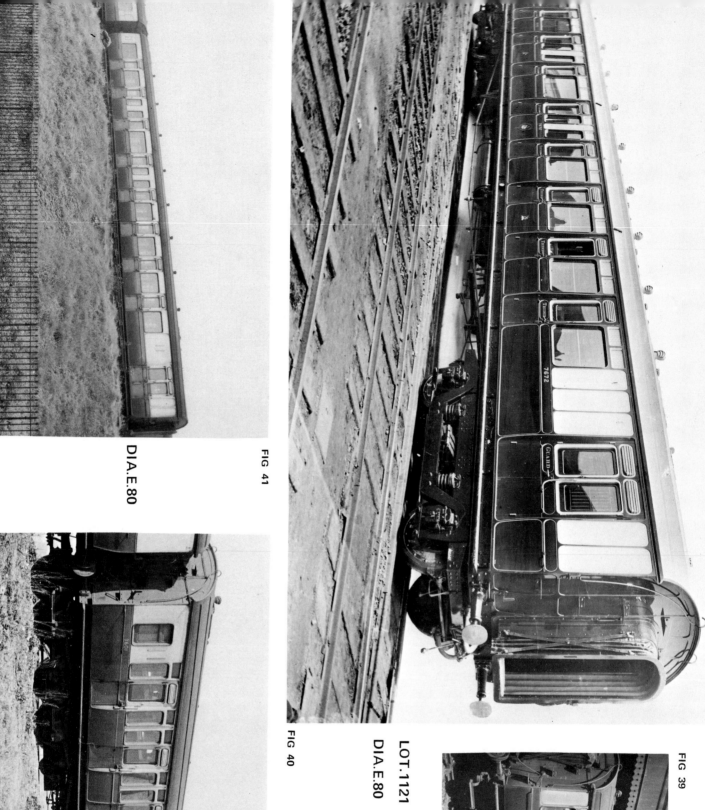

FIG 39

LOT.1121
DIA.E.80

34

DIA.E.80

FIG 41

FIG 40

LOT.1119
DIA.E.81

LOT.1110

DIA.C.27

FIG 42

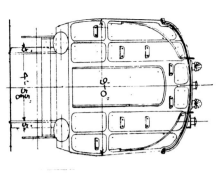

LOT.1112
DIA.D.43

The next development in the main line coach building programme was the large 70′ stock nicknamed 'Concertinas'. After the passenger resistance to the 'Dreadnoughts', due to their restricted number of doors, and the success of *lot 1092* the brake composites, Churchward, although keeping to the extreme length and width, constructed a carriage which had passenger doors to each compartment. These doors, being flat with no tumble home, created an in and out effect against the full sides, which resulted in the concertina effect and so the **soubriquet.**

On page 35 *figure 42* shows the ten compartment all-3rd, built under *lot 1110* in 1906, running number 3601, photographed in 1947 at Thingley Junction, in the late Great Western livery. *Figure 40* is an official photograph of a 'Concertina' brake compo as originally built and in the 1906 livery. This vehicle is *E.80* built under *lot 1121*, and is of the same series as that shown in *figure 41*, in B.R. livery. The number of this carriage was 7656. Finally, top right of these pictures *figure 39* is a composite, shown standing in Bristol Temple Meads in 1951. Built under *lot 1119* to *diagram E.81*, running number 7675.

The brake 3rd of the 'Concertina' series is illustrated on this page, in the official drawing, which gives all the necessary dimensions for model-making. Constructed in 1906 under *lot 1112*, the classification was *D.43*. There were fourteen carriages built with running numbers 3479-92. When first put into stock the lighting was by gas, but later this system was changed for electricity.

—

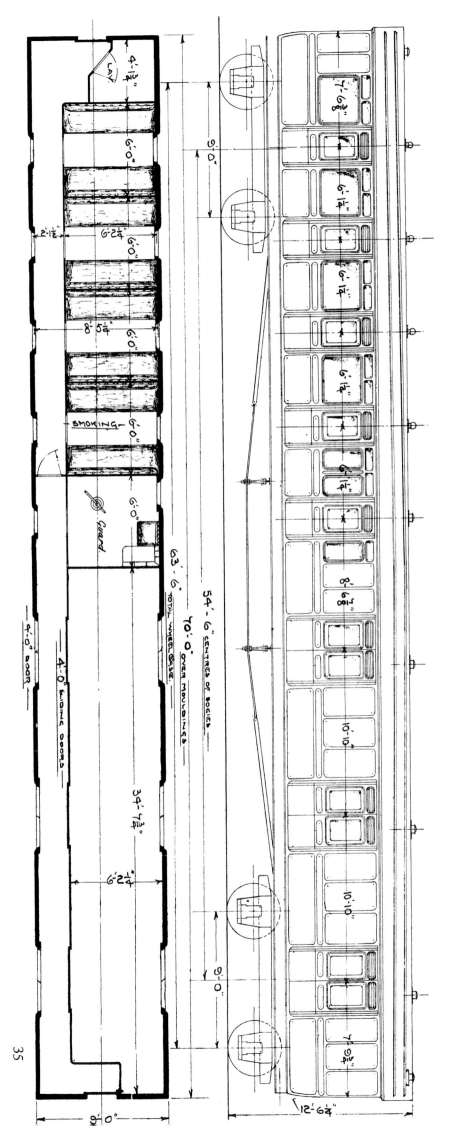

SMOKING

Guard

FIG 43

FIG 45

LOT.1112
DIA.D.43

FIG 44

It will have been noticed from the last few photographs that these carriages were fitted with hammered glass lights over the side windows, but as time passed and the coaches were shopped, many of the toplights were covered over with steel panels. On this page an example is depicted in *figures 43 and 44* and shows No.3479 in B.R. days so treated. *Figure 45* shows the van end of No.3498 with the toplights still in situ. There were only two batches of brake 3rds built to the 'concertina' outline. The first *Lot 1112* contained fourteen carriages and the second series in 1907 consisted of ten similar coaches. The trussing under these carriages was in quadruple form, the queen posts mounted on two transverse beams and forming the fulcrum to the flat bars, which were drilled to accept the threaded ends of the queen posts, thus allowing adjustment.

LOTS.1114, 1115, 1118,
DIA.H.13.H.14

Also in the 'Concertina' programme were three lots of Second Class diners, made to diagrams *H.13* and *H.14* under *lot numbers 1114, 1115,* and *1118,* all in 1906. Unfortunately I have no pictures or drawings of these vehicles as made, but only as rebuilt, first in 1936 and later just before the second World War when some were fitted with six wheeled bogies. *Figure 46* is the official picture of No.9527 demoted to 3rd class diner and finished in the 1935 livery. The vehicles' original numbers were 401—412. Renumbered 9522—33.

In the lower photograph is seen No.9526, in British Railways maroon livery, running on the six wheeled bogies mentioned. On page 223 of Part I can be seen the original interior of this carriage, which was number 8/405. *Figure 47*.

FIG 46

FIG 47

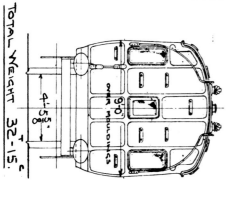

TOTAL WEIGHT 32-15ᵗᶜ

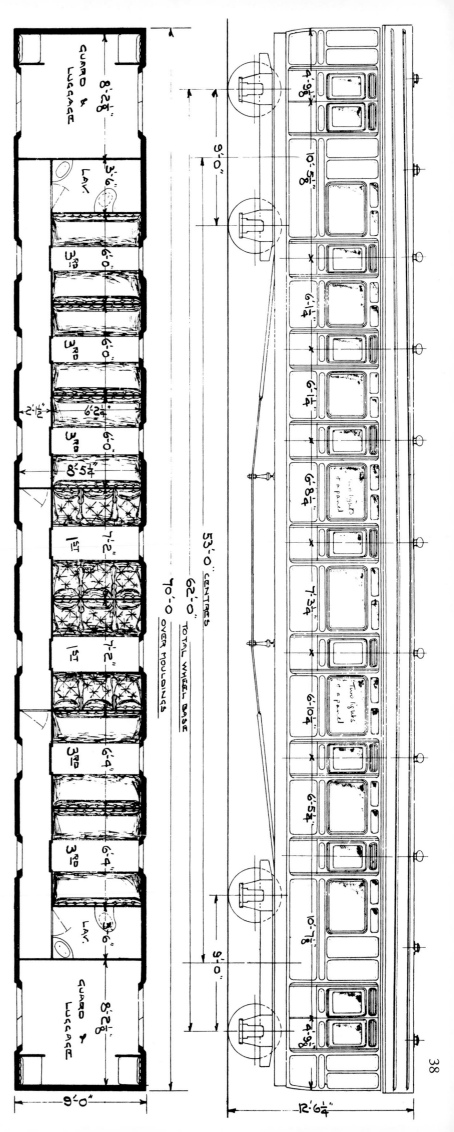

Perhaps the best known and remembered vehicles in the 'Concertina' series were the slip coach versions, one of which was still being rostered on the Bicester slip in 1959. Not bad for a carriage built fifty-three years before! The official drawing shows the layout of these double-ended slips well, and the photograph, figure 49 below, which I took at Faringdon in 1947, shows the end details. After this particular coach, number 7691, had been relegated to branch line duties the slip gear was removed, although the vacuum reservoirs are still in place between the queen posts, as are the toplights. Diagram was F.13 and fifteen carriages were constructed, numbering 7685 - 99 under Lot 1117 in 1906.

LOT.1117
DIA.F.13

Figure 49, showing No.7691 at Faringdon with slip gear removed. In the two lower photographs two more F.13's are shown, on the left No.7687 pictured at Swindon, complete with toplights, and on the right figure 51, No.7699 with the toplights panelled over, still used on slip duties. The small detail picture in figure 48 shows the slip in position with warning gong and slip-coupling still in place.

FIG 49

DIA.F.13

FIG 50

FIG 51

FIG 48

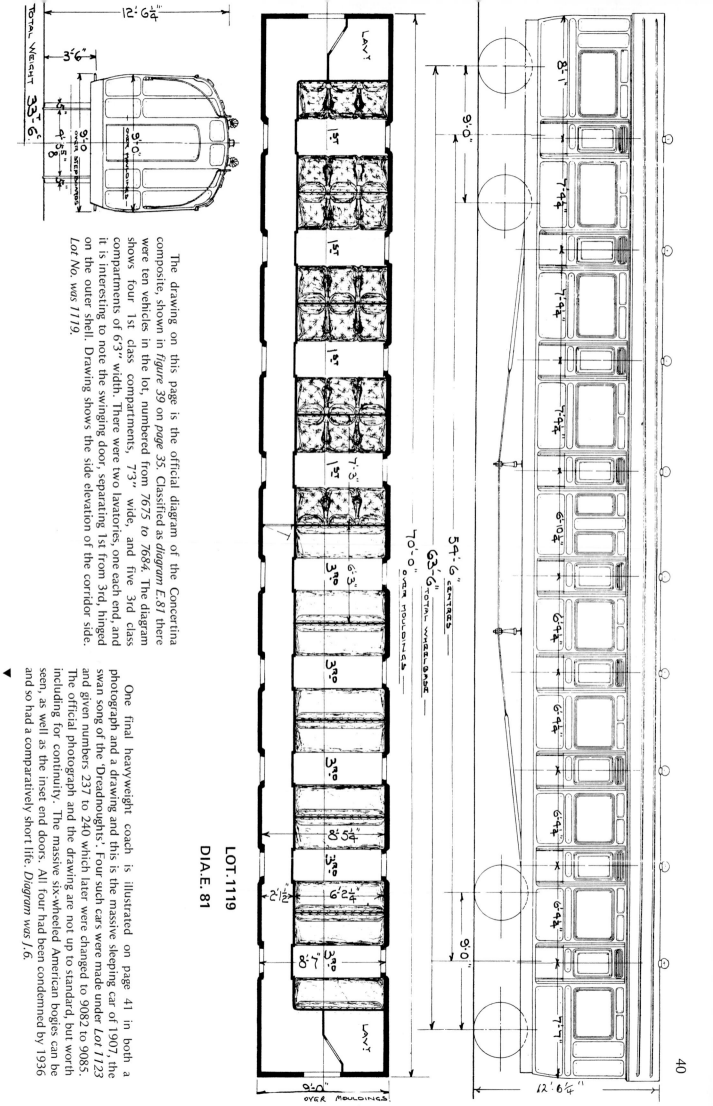

The drawing on this page is the official diagram of the Concertina composite, shown in *figure 39* on *page 35*. Classified as *diagram E.81* there were ten vehicles in the lot, numbered from *7675 to 7684*. The diagram shows four 1st class compartments, 7'3" wide, and five 3rd class compartments of 6'3" width. There were two lavatories, one each end, and it is interesting to note the swinging door, separating 1st from 3rd, hinged on the outer shell. Drawing shows the side elevation of the corridor side. *Lot No. was 1119.*

LOT.1119

DIA.E. 81

One final heavyweight coach is illustrated on *page 41* in both a photograph and a drawing and this is the massive sleeping car of 1907, the swan song of the 'Dreadnoughts'. Four such cars were made under *Lot 1123* and given numbers 237 to 240 which later were changed to 9082 to 9085. The official photograph and the drawing are not up to standard, but worth including for continuity. The massive six-wheeled American bogies can be seen, as well as the inset end doors. All four had been condemned by 1936 and so had a comparatively short life. *Diagram was J.6.*

▼

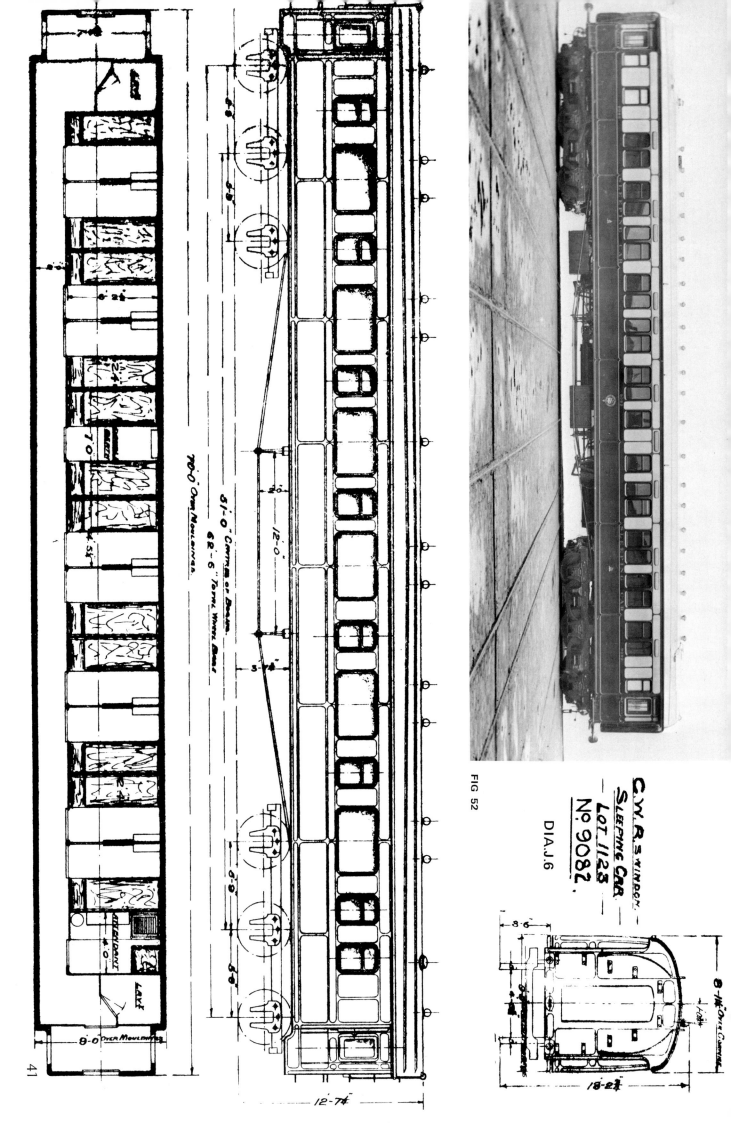

FIG 52

G.W.R. SWINDON.
SLEEPING CAR.
LOT 1123
No. 9082.

DIA.J.6

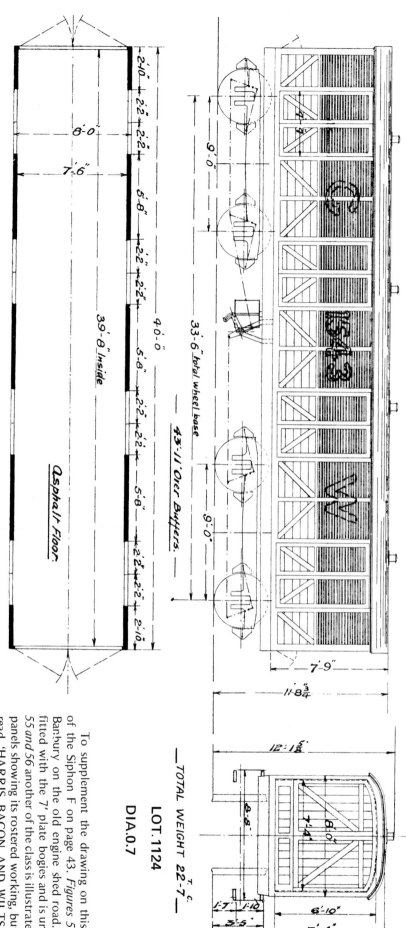

LOT. 1124

DIA. 0.7

— TOTAL WEIGHT 22-7 T.C. —

Asphalt Floor.

Siphon F was the code name for this ventilated 'brown' vehicle. Built in 1906 under *lot 1124* there were only six constructed, numbering from 1543 to 1548. The *diagram* was O.7, being in the passenger carriage series. Originally 9' volute bogies were fitted, but later after shopping some emerged with American 9' bogies and others, as shown, with the 7' plate bogie. An old official photograph in the M.R.N. of November 1931 shows the painting and lettering with the large 24" G.W. painted on the louvres midway on the fifth upright and the thirteenth upright respectively, whilst the number (1543) was in 18" high numerals, also on the louvres each side of the central upright.

For the benefit of modellers I have sketched in lightly the placing of these letters and numbers.

To supplement the drawing on this page are four photographs of the Siphon F on page 43. *Figures 53 and 55* show No.1545 at Banbury on the old engine shed road. Note that this specimen is fitted with the 7' plate bogies and is unbranded, whereas in *figures 55 and 56* another of the class is illustrated, bearing not only the side panels showing its rostered working, but also the roof boards which read 'HARRIS BACON AND WILTSHIRE SAUSAGES CALNE AND NEWCASTLE VIA BANBURY'. This van used to work regularly through and I can recall it going to the north on the 9.05p.m. Swindon every other day and returning on the 10.00p.m. York alternatively.

Jim Whittaker, who has made a model of this vehicle, tells me that the drawing is quite accurate, except for the diagonal frames on the end elevation, which are shown too wide. He has actually measured an existing prototype and the diagonal frames are (or were!) 3" wide at the body face tapering to 2⅞" and sometimes 2⅜" on the outside face of the framing. Jim suggests all diagonal frames be about 0.042" wide on a 4mm scale model.

A couple of final notes; there was only one vacuum cylinder on these vans of the old type, of course, and being gas lit the reservoir tanks were mounted transversely in pairs just in front of the brake handle. The number of the vehicle was usually painted in the centre triangle, alongside the label clip, and the Great Western roundel was situated on the upper triangle above the number.

FIG 54

DIA.0.7

FIG 56

TO WORK BETWEEN
CALNE AND
NEWCASTLE
VIA BANBURY

FIG 57

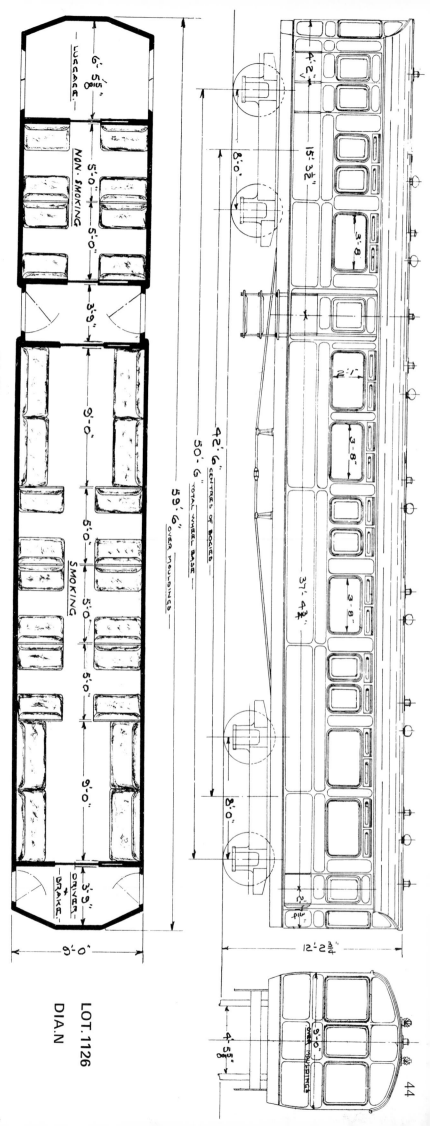

Having dealt briefly with the steam rail cars, it follows that the trailers which accompanied them, which were converted from them, and, finally superseded them, should be described in their various forms. At the time that the steam rail car was being developed, namely 1904, an alternative system was put into operation. This consisted of a trailer car, built on similar lines to the S.R.M. but without the motive unit, coupled to, and propelled by, one of the small '517' class of 0—4—2T engines. As time went by it was found that the steam cars, successful as they were, could not cope with more than one extra trailer, which imposed a limit not only on passengers', but also restricted the traffic department, tacking extra vehicles on to the tails of the branch trains. Therefore the arrangement of separate trailer and engine, which could handle even two bogie trailers on each end, plus a horse box or two, finally proved so successful that this form of light train overtook and finally eclipsed the steam cars, and indeed, the system survived right into British Railways days. The idea was more flexible in maintenance, also, than the S.R.Ms as the trailers were always ready for use, even if the locos were changed for washing out, etc. Although perhaps out of context it is perhaps of interest to note here that upwards of 100 engines were fitted with auto-gear, so that they could be driven from the front end of the trailers, again avoiding the need of running round at termini. Indeed, it is perhaps not well known that some of the 517 class were even painted crimson lake or brown to match up with the trailers they served, and two 0—6—0T's, No.533 and 833, went further and had a dummy coach shell fitted over them to look even more like their carriages! (*See page 80*)

However, back to the construction of the trailers themselves. The official drawing on *page 44* is of one of the short 59'6" cars, built to *diagram N* under *Lot 1126* in 1907. There were six built to this design with numbers 36 to 41. Note that these cars were fitted with end windows at both ends. Entry was effected through the central doors to a vestibule which led to a small non-smoking saloon at one end, and a large smoking compartment at the other. The small picture gives close-up detail of the movable steps, but it should be pointed out that this particular set is shown on a *'P' diagram* trailer and not the one in the drawing.

LOT. 1126
DIA.N

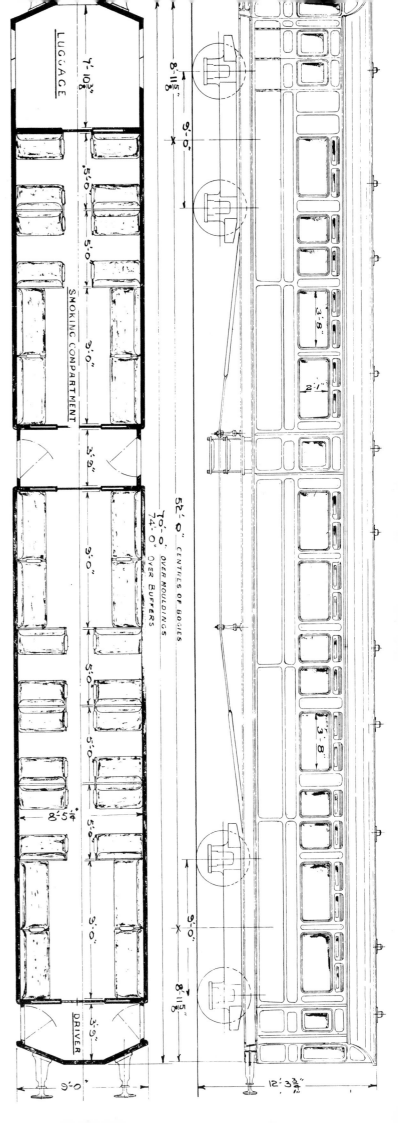

LOT.1127
DIA.L

FIG 58

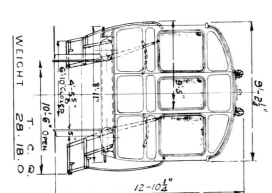

WEIGHT T. C. Q.
28. 18. 0

This drawing depicts the trailer design classified as 'L' on the diagram. Vehicles built to this outline numbered thirty in various lots and there were slight variations amongst each batch. For instance, some, like the drawing, had corridor connections at one end; some did not even have a driver's compartment; and yet others had all large windows in the sides with no droplights save the driver's, guard's and luggage compartments. Lot 1127 included Nos.42 to 47; Lot 1141 Nos.53 to 58; Lot 1143 Nos.59 to 70; and Lot 1108 Nos. 29 to 34, which has been described on page 28.

The small photograph, figure 58, shows the auto gear on the end of a 'P' class trailer and contains many other details. The telescopic square shaft on the left is the universal coupling which connected the regulator in the trailer to the regulator on the engine. The electric cables are for the bell communication between driver, fireman and guard, and the dangling wire was for connecting with the locomotive's whistle. Note the large buffers, necessary because of the extreme length of the vehicle, 74' over buffers.

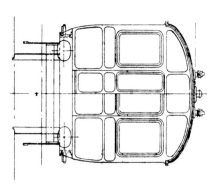

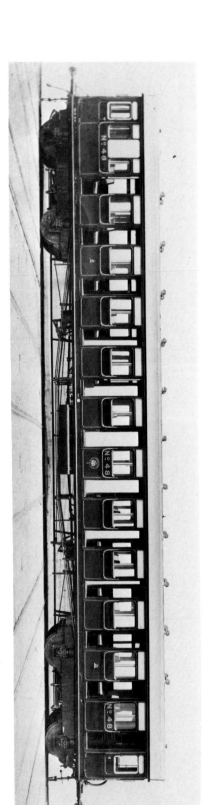

FIG 59

LOT.1128
DIA.0

This drawing and photograph illustrate the unusual trailer car No.48. Built in 1907, the idea was to try to get speedy entry and exit for passengers on the suburban service. As can be seen, the seats were placed centrally, and the doors which slid sideways like the modern Tube trains were operated by a large lever (later a hand wheel) by the guard. However, the scheme did not prove successful, as some of the travelling public got trapped in these doors! *Figure 59* shows the coach with the doors open, but these were later fixed and passenger entrances made at each end. (See also 'Coaches 1'.)

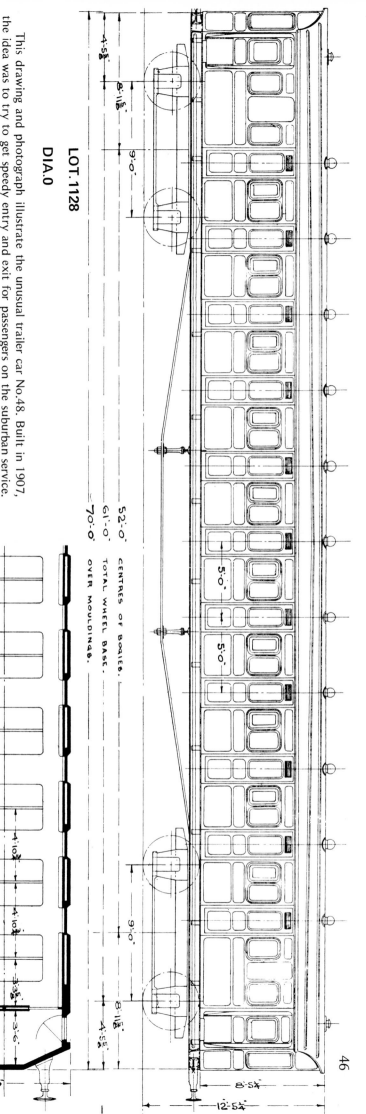

52'-0"   CENTRES OF BOGIES.
61'-0"   TOTAL WHEEL BASE.
70'-0"   OVER MOULDINGS.

4'-5½"
8'-11½"
9'-0"
5'-0"
5'-0"
9'-0"
8'-11½"
4'-5½"
8'-5¼"
12'-5¼"

Sliding Doors
— G.W.R. SWINDON —
— TRAILER CARRIAGE —
— TOTAL SEATS. 96. —

4'-10½"
4'-10½"
3'-6"
3'-6"
5'-0" CENTRES
9'-0"

Doors mechanically operated from inside at this end.

46

The next three pages cover those interesting and long-lived restaurant cars, the 70' vehicles classified as *H.15*. First built in 1907, some of the original twelve were still working on main line expresses in 1961, albeit rather face-lifted, but still recognisable.

On this page is shown an official photograph of No.9544 and one can see what massive vehicles they were. Fitted with the American 9' bogie, the lighting was by electricity, but the stoves were heated by gas, as witness the battery boxes and gas tanks slung underneath the car. Note also that the Churchward vacuum cylinder has been fitted, and although this particular vehicle is roof-boarded for South Wales expresses, the stock served all main line routes on the system. *Figure 60*. The drawing is the official Swindon one of 1936 and shows the modernisation which took place on ten of these 70' cars.

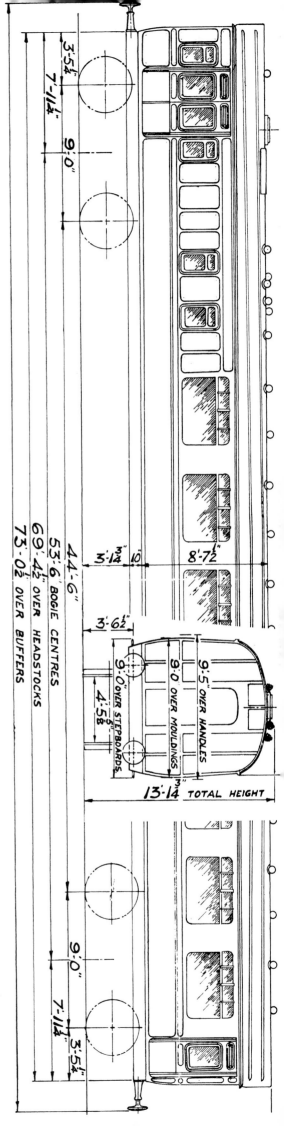

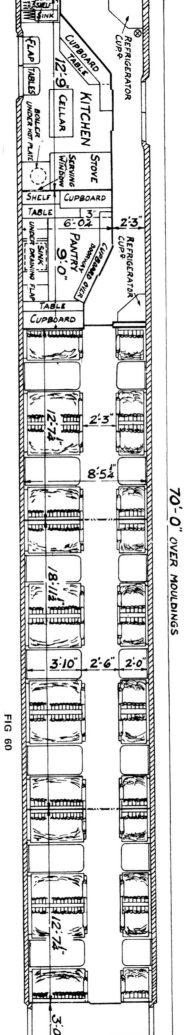

FIG 60

_G. W. R_
RESTAURANT CAR
SWINDON. _APRIL 1936._
LOT 1131.

Nos 9535 to 9542
9544 & 9545.   DIA.H.15

47

FIG 61

DIA.H.15

Here we show some excellent detail pictures of car No.9542 of the *H.15 diagram*, taken by Roye England in British Railways days at Swindon. *Figures 61 and 62* show the kitchen end of the car, and it can be seen that this vehicle still retains some of the original panelling, but the bogies have been changed for

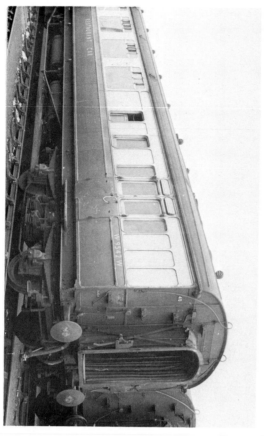

FIG 62

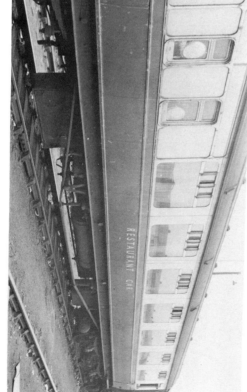

FIG 64

the modern pressed steel pattern. Note that the two sides are completely different in layout to allow for the corridor. *Figure 63* shows the modern seating and upholstery, whilst *figure 64* shows the large flush windows fitted in the late thirties.

FIG 63

48

FIG 65

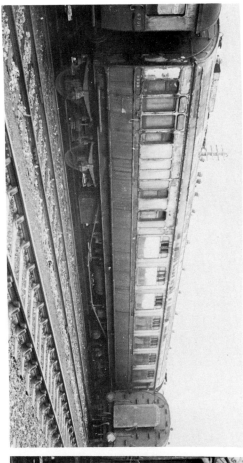

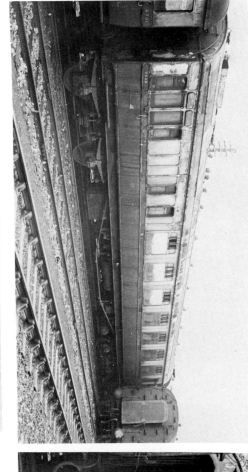

FIG 66

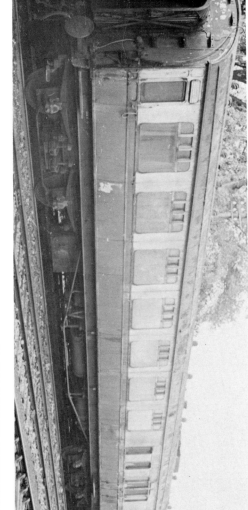

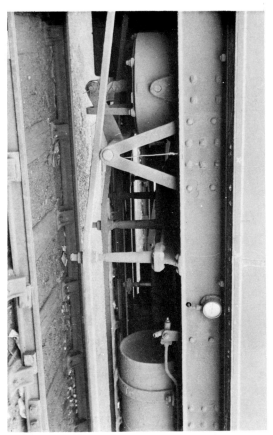

FIG 67

DIA.H.15

FIG 68

More examples of the *H.15* diners are illustrated on this page. Top left, (*figure 65*) is No.9539 at Henley-on-Thames sidings in 1948, prior to shopping, and top right is a sister car No.9541 at the same place, also awaiting a major refit (*figure 66*). At the bottom left is car No.9542 again, this time shown marshalled in a down express at Swindon station. (*figure 67*) On the lower right is an excellent close-up of the queen posts

trussing, vacuum and gas cylinders on coach No.9542. The small gauge is recording the amount of gas in the tanks, and the small inlet valve just below this gauge is where the gas supply hose was attached when recharging the reservoirs. (*figure 68*)

FIG 69

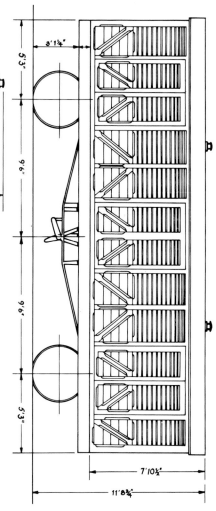

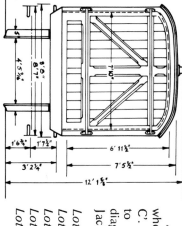

Also in 1907 were produced the short four wheeled milk vans which bore the code name 'Siphon C'. Built under five separate lots over the years 1906 to 1910 there were fifty of these vans and the diagrams were O.8 and O.9. Details kindly given by Jack Slinn are as follows:-

Lot 1125 Nos. 1515 - 18   Dia. O.8 - 1907 8' wide
Lot 1133 Nos. 1525 - 42   - 1906 8' wide
Lot 1133 Nos. 1519 - 24   Dia. O.9 - 1906 8'6" wide
Lot 1162 Nos. 1503 - 24   - 1909 8'6" wide
Lot 1183 Nos. 1482 - 1501   - 1910 8'6" wide

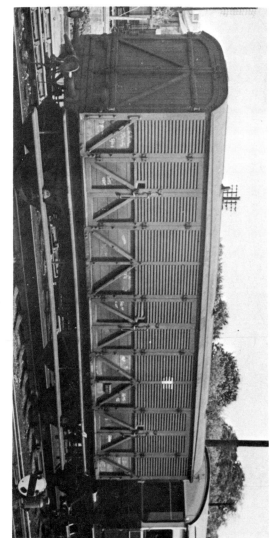

The official drawing leaves much to be desired. The measurements are accurate, but the chamfered diagonals are much too wide and the door hand holes have been omitted. In figure 69, which is No.1506 standing at Banbury North in 1949, one can see the roof board brackets which seem to be the only difference in this O.9 design to that of O.8 shown bottom right of No.1520 at Weymouth. (Figure 71)

The six wheeled Siphon in the photograph bottom left, figure 70, is a one-off job, and I can find out little about it. It was pictured at Kensington Addison Road, in 1946, by Mike Longridge, who always termed it a Siphon D! but this is only pure conjecture. If anyone can throw any light on this vehicle, I would be indebted. I think it is a rebuilt Siphon C as the framing is similar, although the number 1777 doesn't fit. Diagram O.4.

LOT.1133   DIA.0.8 0.9

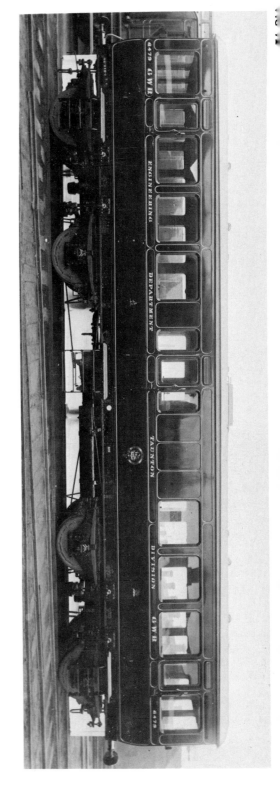

Two departmental vehicles feature on this page. At the top, is No.6479 whose under-frame was originally built for the M & M Rly, and rebuilt in 1910 for use as an inspection saloon. The lower plate is of the famous dynamometer car. A drawing for this can be found in Part 1. Both these vehicles are preserved on the Dart Valley Line. The pictures show an interesting comparison in liveries.

FIG 73

Bullion vans feature on this page, and in particular the broadside official photograph of 878 is interesting as it shows the vehicle in the crimson lake livery of the 1912 period, whereas the two lower photographs show No.819 and 820 at Old Oak Common 1947 in the post-war chocolate and cream. These interesting vehicles were made especially for the transport of gold bullion to the United States, via Plymouth, and the vans 36' x 8' were mounted on heavy bogies to carry a load of 16 tons. Some of them had doors on one side only, and these were locked by keyholes in the door handles themselves. The drawing I have seems to be wrong in respect of the vacuum cylinder position; according to the photographs the two cylinders were not on the centre line, but about 1' aft of C/L and exactly abreast and not staggered as with most coaches. Note in the older vehicles 819 and 820 the old communication chain eyelets are still in place along the edge of the roof. Details are as follows:-

LOT.1220
DIA.M.17

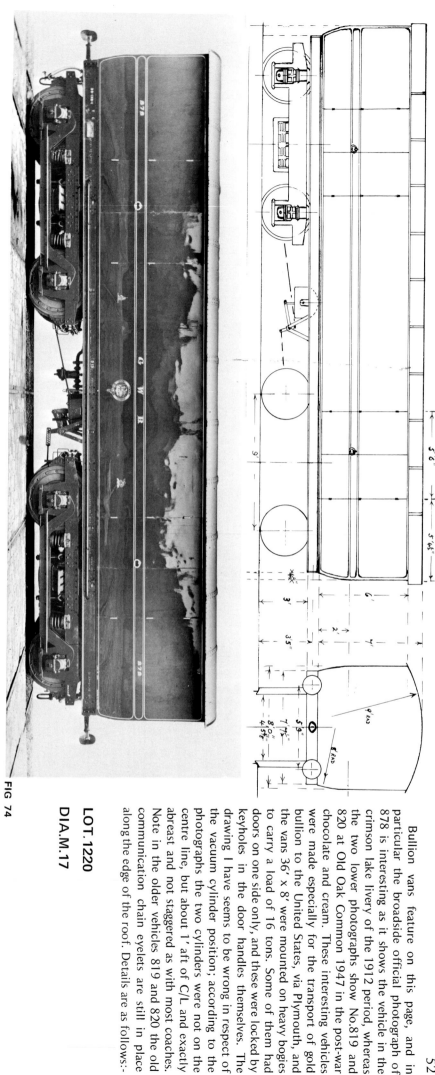

FIG 74

Lot 996	of 1903	running numbers 791 - 792	Diagram M.16
Lot 1139	of 1907	"	819 - 820	M.17
Lot 1220	of 1913	"	878	M.17

FIG 75A

FIG 75

FIG 77

Both ends and sides of No.88 Steam Rail Car are shown in these three pictures, kindly loaned by David Lee. As can be seen these cars were larger than the previous *diagram Q*, being 70' long instead of 59'6", seating 61 passengers against the 45 of the shorter carriage. There were seven S.R.Ms built to *Lot 1140* in 1908 to the *diagram R*, and a couple of months later nine more were constructed to the same classification, an example being shown on the next page.

Several details of interest include the American 9' bogie fitted at the trailing end, the Great Western type single large door in the centre, and the double doors for the additional luggage compartment. This series was the heaviest of all the steam rail cars, scaling 45 tons plus, as can be seen by the small cast figures fixed to the top left of the driving cab. Of this weight 29 tons was carried on the engine bogie to give maximum adhesion.

The pictures show the 1927 style of painting and it is interesting to note the white roofs and the pedal gong at the trailing end in *figure 77*. More details of this filment can be seen on *page 28*.

LOT.1140

DIA.R.

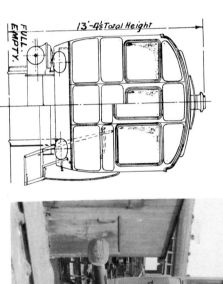

13'-4½ Total Height
FULL.
EMPTY.

FIG 78

FIG 76

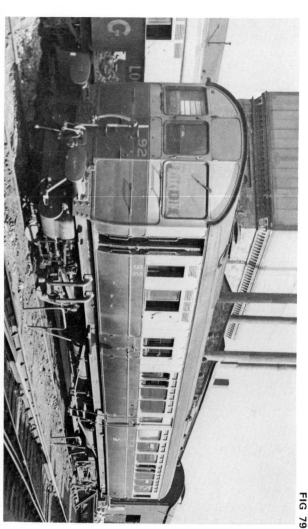

FIG 79

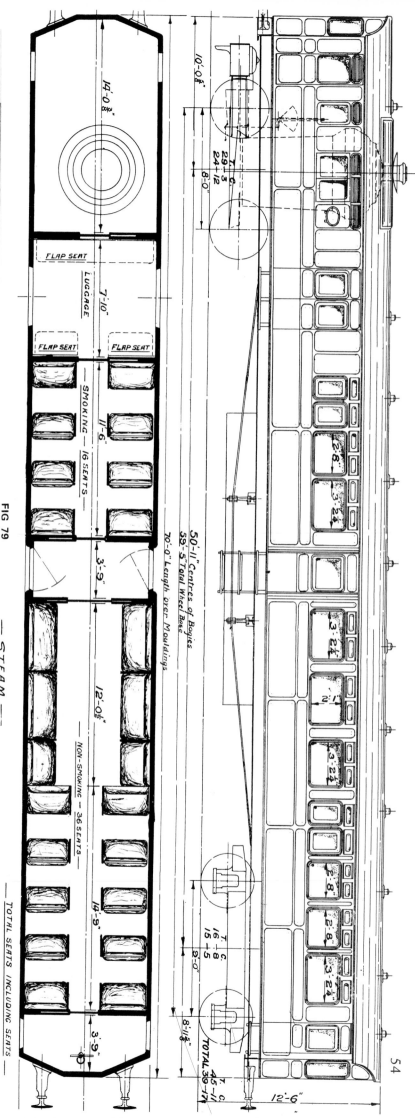

— STEAM —
— MOTOR CAR —
— LOT.1140 Nºs 84 TO 90 —
— " 1142 " 91 TO 99 —

LOT.1142
DIA.R.

— TOTAL SEATS INCLUDING SEATS —
— IN LUGGAGE COMPARTMENT 61 —

FLAP SEAT

LUGGAGE

FLAP SEAT   FLAP SEAT

SMOKING — 16 SEATS

NON-SMOKING — 36 SEATS

50'-11" Centres of Bogies
59'-5" Total Wheel Base
70'-0" Length over Mouldings

14'-0⅜"

7'-10"

11'-6"

3'-9"

12'-0½"

14'-9"

3'-9"

10'-0⅝"
8'-0"

2'-8"

3'-2¼"

2'-8"

12'-6"

54

Lot 1142 of February 1908 was the last order for Steam Rail Cars to be constructed for the Great Western Railway and the *diagram R*, seemingly having proved itself, was again used for these last nine vehicles. The photograph at the foot of the page illustrates how similar the last lots were, and the only difference I can notice is that of the panelling on the front end. It is also perhaps of interest to mention here that the driver's doors and side lights were of the sliding type and not swing and drop respectively. This can be seen clearly in this picture. No.92 is shown at Slough and standing alongside is a loco coal wagon from which the car has obviously being coaled up. One final point of note, it was always the practice with these rail cars to use locomotive department headlamps for the end which was leading, and traffic department tail lamps for the trailing end. This is the reason for the two brackets, the higher one for headlamp and the lower for a tail lamp.

This ends my coverage of these fascinating vehicles, and if any reader would like further information, I would suggest you refer to Part VI of the R.C.T.S. series "*Locomotives of the Great Western Railway*", published in 1956.

The next development in the coach building was the 'Toplight' series, so called because of the hammered-glass small lights situated over the main side windows. There were two types, the 56' - 57' short bodied type, and the larger 70' design. On this page are shown four examples of composites. *Figure 81* is No.7547 of *Lot 1138* to *diagram E.83*, showing the compartment side. *Figure 82* is of a 70' E.84 compo, No.7551 of *lot 1145*, whilst *figures 82A* and *80* illustrate the E.85 56' vehicle, corridor side of No.7715 and compartment side of No.7717. The respective lots and numbering were thus:-

Lot 1138	E.83	1907	Nos. 7533 — 47
Lot 1145	E.84	1908	Nos. 7548 — 53
Lot 1147	E.85	1909	Nos. 7712 — 27

FIG 81

LOT.1138
DIA.E.83

FIG 82

FIG 82A

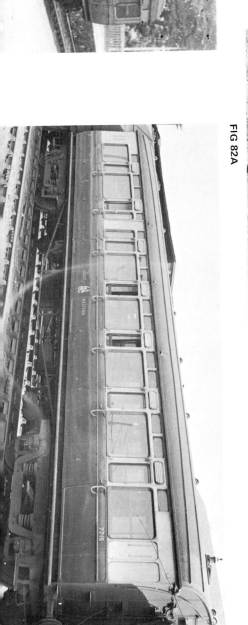

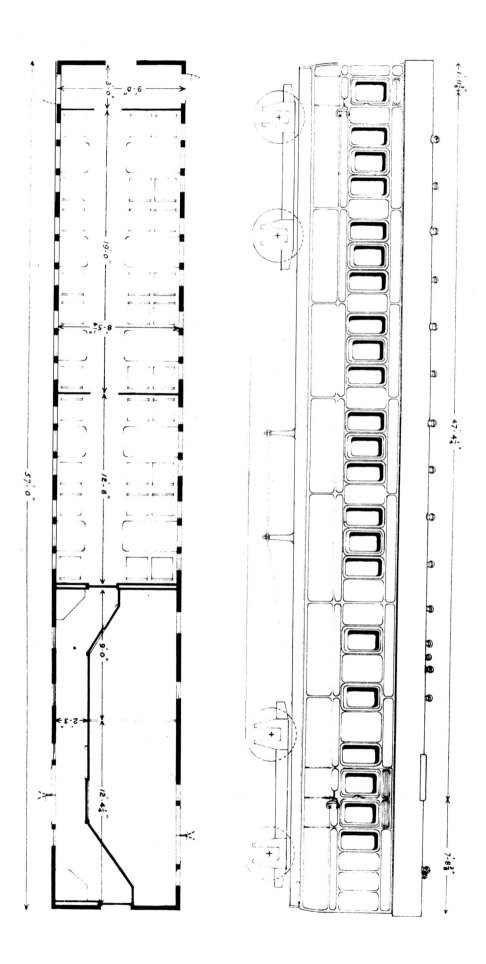

Drawing and photograph showing before and after modernisation. This restaurant car was constructed in 1908 under *Lot 1149* and was one of six numbering 9546 to 9551. They were all 57' long and contained two separate saloons, one large and one small with the kitchen in the usual place for the period, at the end. They were contemporaneous with the 'toplight' series, but did not have this feature.

When modernised in the late thirties, the small side windows with drop lights were changed for large single windows with sliding toplight openings. Also the American 8' bogies were replaced with pressed steel type, 9' in length. *Figure 83* shows 9551 in British Rail ownership.

FIG 83

LOT.1149   DIA.H16

Diagram 39 shows the opposite side of *H.16* restaurant car described on page 56. Important to modellers, as the two sides were different.

Two single-ended slip coaches were made in 1908 to the 'Toplight' design, and *figure 84* shows one of these as originally constructed. The lot number was *1150* and running numbers were 7101 and 7102, (*diagram F.14*). This example is shown mounted on the 8' American bogies and the five large vacuum reservoirs can be seen clearly mounted transversely under the centre of the vehicle. These single-ended slips were useful carriages, as the gangwayed end could be coupled to one of two extra coaches and so form a self-contained slip section, through which passengers and staff could move. The maximum number of vehicles allowed to be slipped was fixed at four and Banbury often used to see such a portion off the 7.10 p.m. Paddington – Birmingham express. Perhaps I should clarify this by stating this rule only applied after 1910, as before this date as many as five vehicles have been slipped at one station.

FIG 84

LOT.1150

DIA.F.14

FIG 85

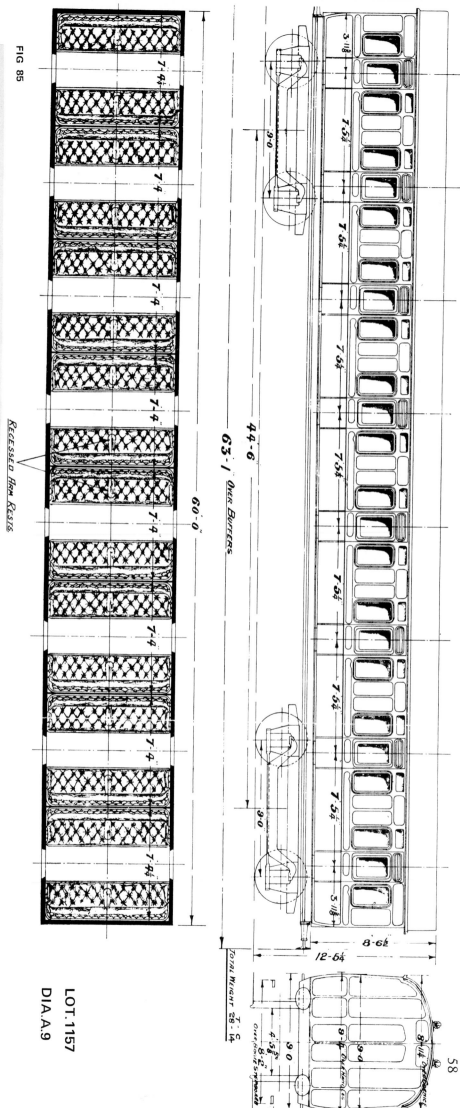

RECESSED ARM RESTS

LOT.1157
DIA.A.9

'Toplight' suburban stock built in this period consisted of sets of stock which formed the suburban trains for the Birmingham and London areas. One exception, however, was a batch of 20 large sumptuous 'Firsts', constructed under *Lot 1157* in 1908 to the *diagram* A.9, Nos. 8197 to 8216. The drawing shows the massive proportions for a non-corridor carriage, the length being 63'1" over buffers with an overall width of 9'4". There were eight compartments, each 7'4" wide with recessed arm rests in the centre of each seat, which seems to suggest that the compartments were designed for four passengers in extreme comfort, but by folding the arm rests up six seats could be made available.

When new, the vehicles were fully panelled, with a mock corridor door panel at the ends, I could never see the reason for this, no doubt for easy fitting of gangway at later date. Roye England's picture shows number 8203 in B.R. days.

58

Diagram F.15 was allotted to the 57' double ended slips which were produced under Lot 1166 in 1909. There were fourteen constructed, numbering 7103 to 7109, and 7994 to 8000. Of the first series of 'Toplights', known as BARs 1 due to the configuration of the underframe trussing, these carriages formed the backbone of the slipping programme for many years, where one coach was sufficient for the traffic, such as Bicester, Westbury and Princes Risborough, etc. Some of the first batch to be built were unusual in that the interior followed the same pattern as the 'Dreadnoughts'; the corridor changed sides in the middle of the carriage, so that the 1st class had the corridor on one side and the 3rds on the other, with two small lavatories in the centre vestibule. This arrangement, however, was superseded in the second series, and in the official drawing it can be seen that the corridor is on one side only, and has one large lavatory which was shared between the two classes. Notice also, that here, as with the majority of slip coaches, the passengers could not get through to the guard's compartment, or vice versa. A vital consideration, when the slip guard was concentrating on the slip operation!

F15, No's 7105-8 have staggered corridors
F16, No's 7103/4/9, 7994-8000 straight corridors

LOT.1166

DIA.F.15 & 16

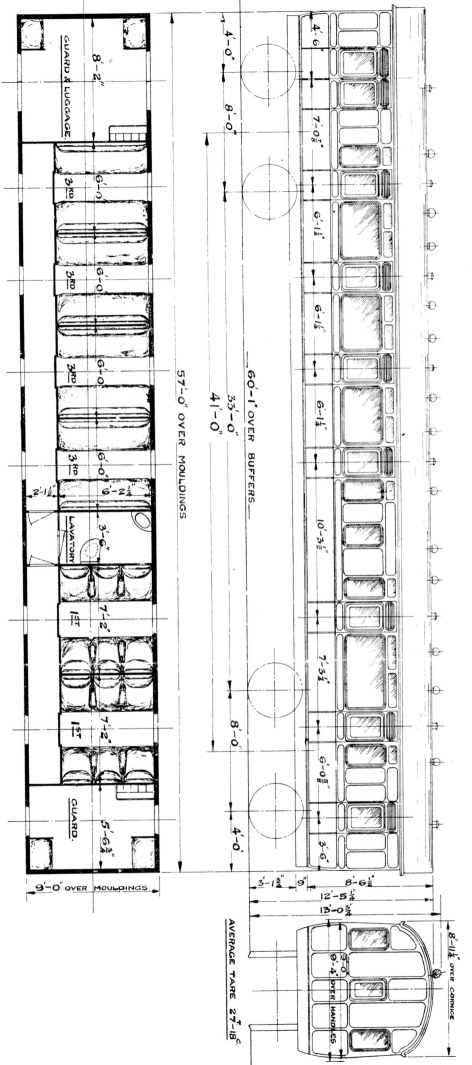

FIG 86

This whole page is devoted to photographs of ex-slip coach No.7109 of the *F.16* classification to the drawing on *page 49*, taken in the carriage sidings at Swindon by Roye England in B.R. days. Both sides of the carriage are shown at the top of the page, *figures 86 and 87*, whilst below are two excellent detail pictures of the vacuum cylinder, Bars 1 trussing, queen posts and vacuum reservoirs. The small star painted on the body's lower edge is to locate the vacuum release cord to shunters. *Figure 88 showing* one side of the coach and *figure 89* the opposite.

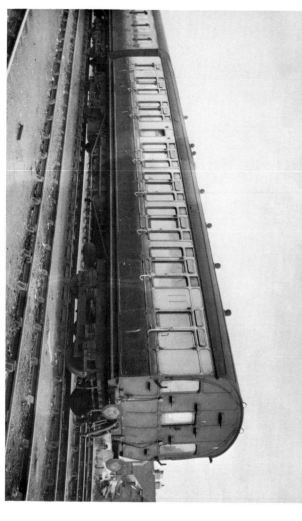

FIG 88

DIA.F.16

60

FIG 87

FIG 90

FIG 91

LOT.1165
DIA.M.13

Accumulator boxes nearside

AC box nearside

Dynamo farside

12'11⅛" total height

4'5⅝"

3'3¾"

8'11¼"

2'5½"

I always find one-off jobs fascinating, and this large 70' parcels van which was put into stock in 1908 is one of these. It was made under *Lot 1165* to *diagram M.13* and numbered 833. Just why it had the framing outside I cannot say, but it certainly did make an unusual vehicle. My friend Jim Whittaker has made a model of this van and has painted it in the original chocolate and cream, which looks most odd, as one usually associates outside framing with the brown bogie Siphons, etc.

The chassis was trussed by four sets of bars, in the Toplight style, and originally ran on 9' bogies, being changed to the 7' plate type shown in the photographs in the late twenties. The van's main duties, when I knew it, were for the conveying of parcels, hence the sliding doors. The pictures show the van at Oxford, *figure 90* and Banbury station, *figure 91*. It should be noted that the guard's compartment was offset in this vehicle so that the two sides were not identical. The modellers drawing above is included as it shows position of steps and vacuum cylinders.

DIA.M.13

FIG 91A

This official diagram of No.833 shows the plan where the offset end can clearly be seen. Also in the photograph (*figure 91a*), note the guard's door on this side in a different placing to the opposite side shown in *figure 90*. I would add that doubts have been expressed about this vehicle being painted in chocolate and cream, but I have photographs to prove this was so in the 1930's.

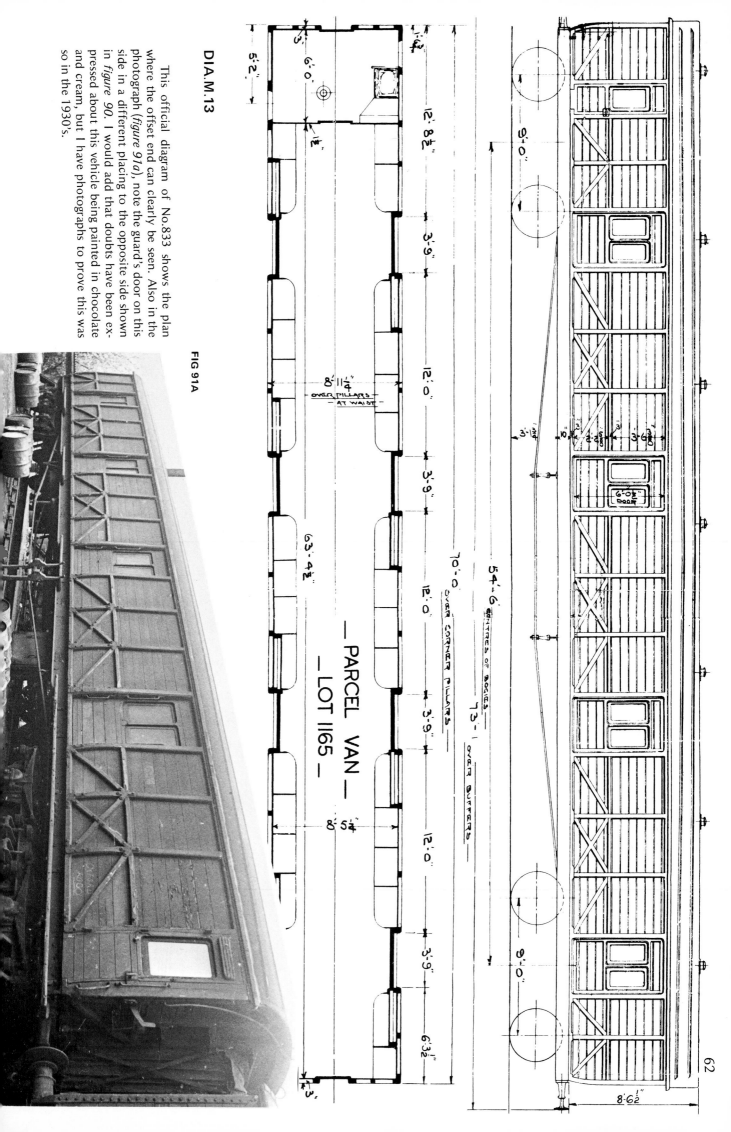

— PARCEL VAN —
— LOT 1165 —

6'-0" DOOR

OVER CORNER PILLARS

OVER BUFFERS

OVER PILLARS AT WAIST

CENTRES OF BOGIES

FIG 92

FIG 93

LOTS.1168,
1172

DIAS.C.31

D.46

Four photographs of the short 'Toplight' carriages of the BAR 1 series feature on this page. The close-up in *figure 92* shows many constructional details, although no doubt taken especially to show stowage of the coach batteries. Note the full panelling and the early livery. The vehicle concerned is one of the full 3rds to *diagram C.31*, and *figure 93* shows the corridor side of the same class of carriage. This particular vehicle is No.2446 of the series built to *Lot 1172* which included Nos.2436 to 2455. *Figure 94*, lower left, shows one of the brake composites in the same series, running in B.R. days but still with most of the panelling still visible. Classification was *E.87* to *Lot 1169*; Running Nos. 7732 to 7737, (example shown is No.7733.)

Figure 95, bottom right, is one of the brake 3rds, No.2343, which I photographed at Hereford in 1947, again with nearly all panelling still on the sides. Diagram was *D46* to *Lot 1168*; Nos.2342 to 45; and *Lot 1174* Nos.2356 to 65 in 1910 and 1911 respectively.

FIG 94

Note all these carriages are mounted on the lighter bogies, one on the 9' Fishbelly, and two on the 8' American type.

FIG 95

FIG 96

A vehicle well known to all Great Western railwaymen was the 'whitewash' coach. This was a carriage which was coupled on to the end of a regular express and was used to indicate to the Engineering Department, bad spots in the track. It is said to have originated from tests carried out when experimenting with new bogies, when staff aboard vehicles fitted with these prototype bogies threw whitewash down the loo when getting extreme oscillation on any particular section of track. Be that as it may, in my day this vehicle, which was a converted 'Brake 3rd Toplight', was much more sophisticated and the equipment was connected to the bogies direct. White liquid was automatically released when passing over a rough patch of track, and the movement and location was recorded on a graph in the coach. The permanent-way staff received prior notice of the passing of this test car, and one could see all the local gangers right along the route with their men, looking to see if their particular section had received a dollop from the Valkyries as they swept past!

The two pictures show the vehicle in Great Western colours at Snow Hill station, figure 96, and on the turntable at Swindon in B.R. maroon, figure 97, and at the bottom left an example of the brake 3rd from which it was converted. (This one is No.2363, figure 98).

FIG 97

FIG 98

LOT.1174

These five large vans are of great interest as they show the large 'Churchward' proportions applied to Mail and Baggage vans. Although slightly out of order in the Lot numbers and building dates, they have been shown together here, so that good comparisons can be made.

First to be described is that on the top right, figure 99 No.821, one of a series of four which were some of the first elliptical roofed, main line stock to be built by the Great Western in 1904, under Lot 1062, 70' in length, with side gangways, there were three large sliding doors on each side and four large windows. My picture was taken at Old Oak Common in the late forties. At the bottom of the page on the right is another one-off

On page 65 appear the 70' passenger vans of the 'M' series.

LOTS.1061	DIAS.M.10
1062	M.14
1185	M.15

vehicle, No.837 of *Lot 1061*. This was the Ocean Mails slip van which is shown and described on *page 10* as built. This picture was taken at Old Oak Common in 1947, when the slip apparatus had been removed and the bogies changed for American 9' type. *Figure 101* centre right, is a 12 wheel version of Ocean Mails van, No.1205, built under *Lot 1185* to *diagram M.15*. This carriage had three sliding doors each side, and not only a guard's compartment but also a lavatory was provided for the staff.

The two other vans, No.876 and 877 were built under *Lot 1178* to *diagram M.14* and were used for the Fishguard Boat trains. That in *figure 100* shows No.876 standing in the old dock at Banbury station in 1947, and *figure 102* shows No.877 at Weymouth in 1950 in wartime brown livery. The two pictures show each side, so will be useful to modellers. One point to note is that in the early vans of *M.8* classification some of the protective bars at the window were horizontal, whereas in the *M14's* the bars are all vertical.

FIG 100

FIG 99
FIG 101

FIG 102

FIG 103

FIG 100

vehicle, No.837 of *Lot 1061*. This was the Ocean Mails slip van which is shown and described on *page 10* as built. This picture was taken at Old Oak Common in 1947, when the slip apparatus had been removed and the bogies changed for American 9' type. *Figure 101 centre right*, is a 12 wheel version of Ocean Mails van, No.1205, built under *Lot 1185* to *diagram M.15*. This carriage had three sliding doors each side, and not only a guard's compartment but also a lavatory was provided for the staff.

The two other vans, No.876 and 877 were built under *Lot 1178 to diagram M.14* and were used for the Fishguard Boat trains. That in *figure 100* shows No.876 standing in the old dock at Banbury station in 1947, and *figure 102* shows No.877 at Weymouth in 1950 in wartime brown livery. The two pictures show each side, so will be useful to modellers. One point to note is that in the early vans of *M.8* classification some of the protective bars at the window were horizontal, whereas in the *M14's* the bars are all vertical.

FIG 99
FIG 101

FIG 102

FIG 103

FIG 104

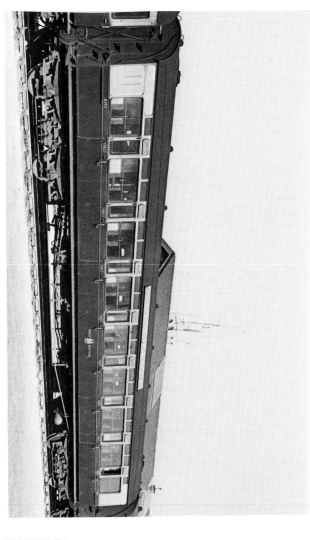

The next first class carriages to be made were the 70' Toplights constructed in 1910, to the *diagram A10*. Three examples are shown on this page. *Figure 104* is of No.8192 photographed at Worcester, in the Cheltenham Flyer rake. *Figure 106* is of 8185 at Swindon carriage sidings, and *figure 105* shows the compartment side of the design on No.8186. There were fifteen vehicles made to this design, running numbers being from 8181 to 8196.

LOT.1176

DIA.A.10

FIG 105

Page 67 shows No.2366, another one-off carriage. A brake 3rd with only three compartments and a huge 40'7½" luggage van, it was supported on 12 wheeled bogies and was of the 'Toplight' Bars 1 series. Its lot number was *1181* to *diagram D.48* and it was completed in late 1910. Roye England's picture shows the vehicle under the ownership of British Railways but still painted chocolate and cream. Note that there was no separate corridor in the luggage compartment as in the later design.

FIG 106

66

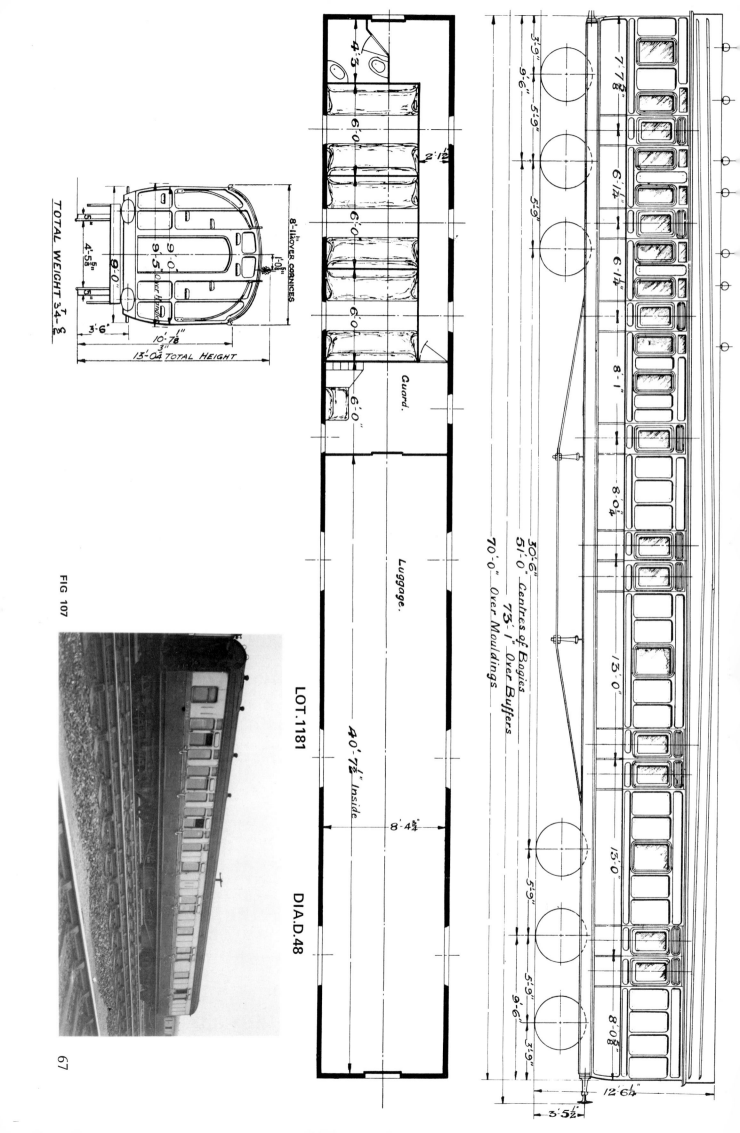

FIG 107

LOT.1181

DIA.D.48

TOTAL WEIGHT 34-8 T

8'-11" OVER CORNICES
9'-5" Over Handles
9'-0"
9'-0"
1'-08"
5"
4'-58"
5"
3'-6"
10'-78"
3"
13'-08" TOTAL HEIGHT

4'-3"

6'-0"

2'-1½"

6'-0"

6'-0"

6'-0"

Guard.

6'-0"

Luggage.

40'-7½" Inside

8'-4¾"

3'-9"
9'-6"
5'-9"
5'-9"
7'-8"
6'-7¼"
6'-7¼"
8'-1"
8'-0¼"
13'-0"
13'-0"
8'-0½"
5'-9"
5'-9"
9'-6"
3'-9"

30'-6"
51'-0" Centres of Bogies
73'-1" Over Buffers
70'-0" Over Mouldings

12'-6¼"
3'-5½"

67

FIG 108

LOT.1177   DIA.H.19

LOT.1182   DIA.A.11

FIG 110

LOT.1188
DIA.D.49

FIG 109

Top left on this page, *figure 108*, is restaurant car No.9555, one of the four built in 1911 to *diagram H.19* under *Lot 1177*. Although shown modernised, standing in Swindon station, this vehicle was originally constructed for the Fishguard Boat train stock and comes in the 'Toplight' period. Other numbers were 9552, 9553 and 9554.

Above, *figure 109*, is a photograph I took at Henley in 1960. It shows one of the 'Toplight' Brake 1sts which again, like the *H.19s*, were made for the Fishguard Boat trains. These trains, which were put on in early 1911, consisted of eight 1st class carriages (*A.10s*), one of the restaurant cars just described above (*H.19*), with a 70' luggage car at one end (*M.74*), and one of these brake 1sts at the other. Ironical that after getting into top gear like this for the Transatlantic traffic, the First World War put a stop to the Cunarders calling at Fishguard, and so this superb stock was put to other uses. Diagram was *A.11* and three were made, Nos.8178-79 and 80. *Figure 110*, bottom left, shows one of the brake 3rds of the 'Toplight' non-corridor suburban stock, which were formed at both ends of four coach sets, running in the Birmingham area. This particular set was No.5 and photographed by me at Banbury Loco in 1948. At that time the set was painted in the war-time all-over brown. The other two coaches which made up the set were composites of the *E.89 diagram*. The vehicle depicted is No.2389 *diagram D.49 of Lot 1188* of 1911.

FIG 111

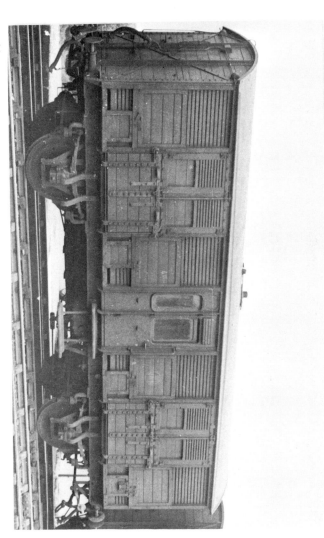

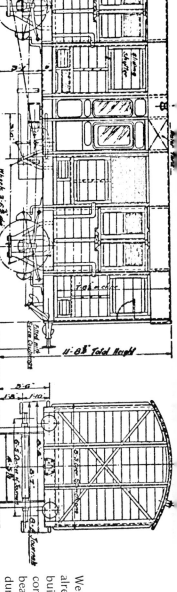

LOT.1186
DIA.W.7

A vehicle for conveying cattle for passenger trains on the Great Western was code named 'Beetle' and one of the earlier variety has already been described in *Part I*. A development of this van was to build a similar carriage, with two sections divided by an attendant's compartment in the middle. This enabled a cowman to travel with the beasts and to be able to feed them and generally keep an eye on them during the journey. This was often necessary with prize stock going to a show or sale. The two examples on this page show how little the design changed over the course of years, once evolved.

Bottom left is No.992 of *Lot 1186* which would have been built in 1911, and on the right is No.219 of *lot 1380* which would be circa 1928, the only differences being in the end bracing. Notice that nearly all the louvres had sliding shutters, which could close off the ventilators. The official diagram was *W7* and numbers ran from 981 to 1000.

FIG 112

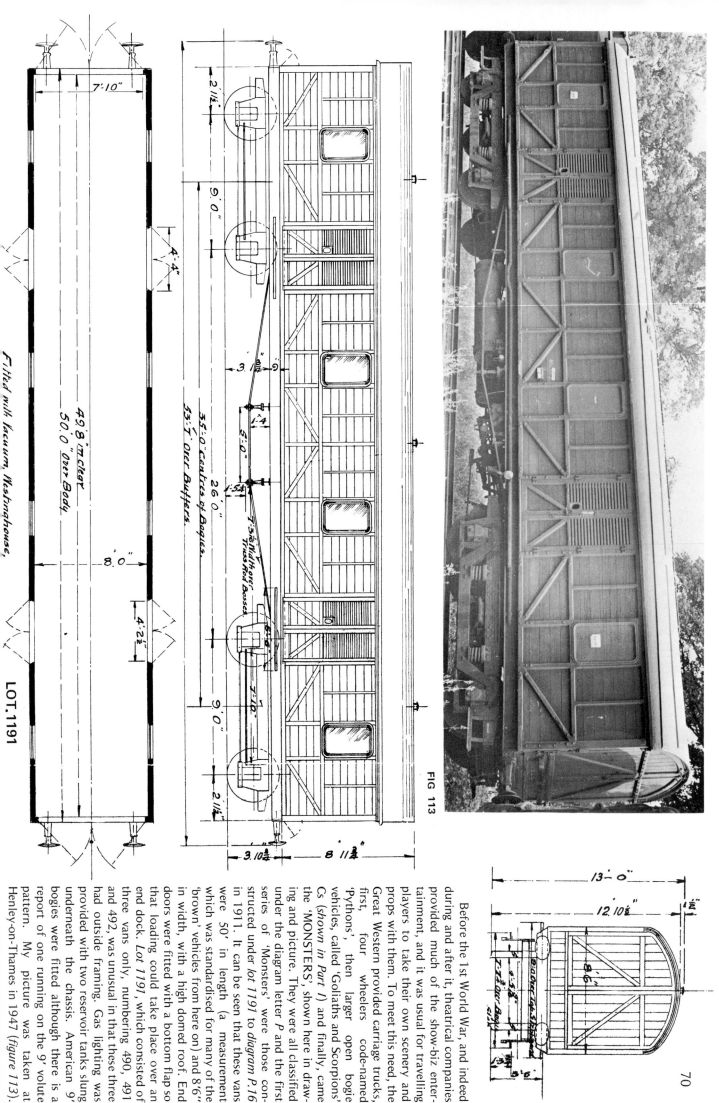

FIG 113

Before the 1st World War, and indeed during and after it, theatrical companies provided much of the show-biz entertainment, and it was usual for travelling players to take their own scenery and props with them. To meet this need, the Great Western provided carriage trucks, first, four wheelers code-named 'Pythons', then larger open bogie vehicles, called 'Goliaths and Scorpions' Cs *(shown in Part I)* and finally, came the 'MONSTERS', shown here in drawing and picture. They were all classified under the diagram letter *P* and the first series of 'Monsters' were those constructed under *lot 1191* to *diagram P.16* in 1911. It can be seen that these vans were 50' in length (a measurement which was standardised for many of the 'brown' vehicles from here on) and 8'6" in width, with a high domed roof. End doors were fitted with a bottom flap so that loading could take place over an end dock. *Lot 1191*, which consisted of three vans only, numbering 490, 491 and 492, was unusual in that these three had outside framing. Gas lighting was provided with two reservoir tanks slung underneath the chassis. American 9' bogies were fitted although there is a report of one running on the 9' volute pattern. My picture was taken at Henley-on-Thames in 1947 *(figure 113)*.

LOT.1191

Fitted with Vacuum, Westinghouse,

7'·10"

4'·4"

49' 8" in clear

50' 0" over Body

8'·0"

4'·2½"

9'·0"

2'·1½"

35'·0" Centres of Bogies.

53'·7" over Buffers.

3'·1¾"

3'·0"

1'·4"

1'·5½"

26'·0"

7'·3¾ Mid over Truss Rod Bosses.

9'·0"

2'·1½"

3'·10¾"

8'·11¾"

13'·0"

12'·10½"

9'·6"

70

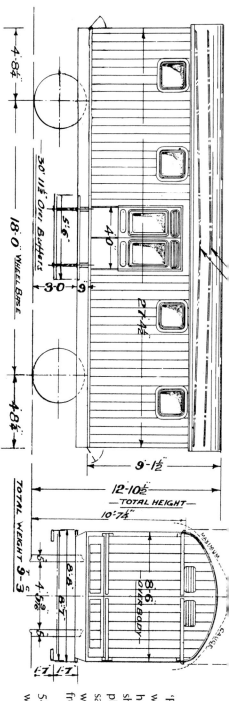

LOT.1197
DIA.P.14

FIG 114

Covered Carriage Trucks (four wheeled) were always known as 'Pythons', this being the code name given to this class of vehicle. They were large vans for a four wheeler, the wheelbase being 18', and the height going up to the limit of the loading gauge. The offical drawing shows the type with the small square windows, which ties up with the photo of No.5361 took at Caerphilly in 1947. (figure 114). For interest sake only, I also show a picture of No.70, a similar Python but one which did not originate from Swindon, but which was absorbed from one of the Welsh railways (figure 115).

There were two lots of P.74s built, one batch to lot 1134 Nos.531 to 540, and the other to lot 1197, Nos.541 to 560, the latter being fitted with two braking systems, vacuum and Westinghouse.

FIG 115

71

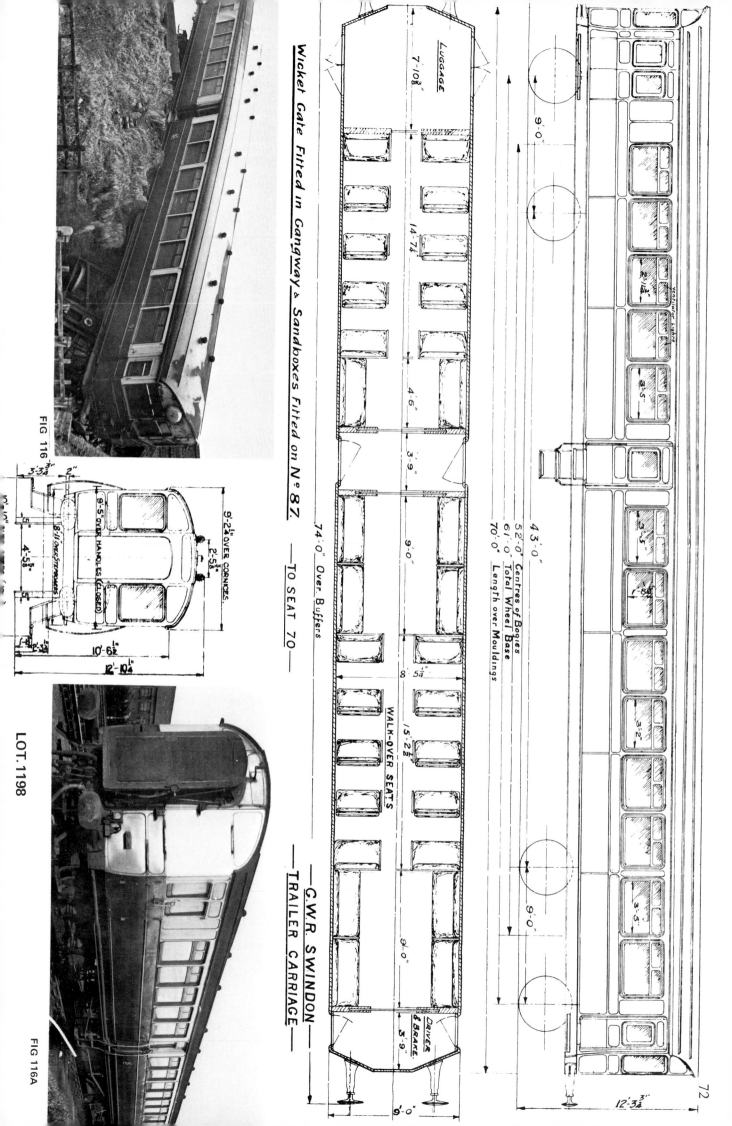

FIG 116

FIG 116A

LOT. 1198

Wicket Gate Fitted in Gangway & Sandboxes Fitted on Nº 87.

— TO SEAT 70 —

— G.W.R. SWINDON —
— TRAILER CARRIAGE —

LUGGAGE

7-10¾"

14-7¼

4'-6"

3'-9"

9'-0"

8'-5¼"

WALK-OVER SEATS

15'-2½

9'-0"

DRIVER & BRAKE

3'-9"

9'-0"

74'-0" Over Buffers

43'-0"

9'-0"

52'-0" Centres of Bogies
61'-0" Total Wheel Base
70'-0" Length over Mouldings

9'-0"

9'-5" OVER HANDLES (CLOSED)
9'-2¼" OVER CORNICES.
8'-11" OVER STREAMERS
3'-3¾"   2"
2'-5⅝"
4'-5¾"
10'-6½"
12'-10¼"

Ventilator Light

3'-5

3'-5

8½

3'-2"

3'-5

12'-3¾"

72

Two Banbury trailers shown on page 72, No.83 in the loco sidings and No.91 off the road at Cropredy, *figure 116*. Both of the same class, namely *diagram U*, the lot number was *1198 of 1912* and there were twelve built numbering from 81 to 92. The drawing indicates windows in the luggage end, but when I knew them, and as the photos testify, this end had a gangway but no windows. In the picture of the derailment one can see an unusual view of an American 9' bogie showing the cup in which the pivot-pin sits.

FIG 117

Brake 3rd No.35/6 shown in the two photographs on the left of this page, *figures 117 and 117a* is an example of rebuilding and shows how easily it is to be led astray by modelling solely from pictures. This long 70' vehicle started life in 1912 as a BAR 2 Toplight and about the only thing remaining of the original coach is the underframe, all the windows and panelling being fitted years later.

At the bottom of this page is a picture of the 'Siphon Gs', *Figure 118*. The example shown is one of the early ones, built in 1913, No.1479 under *lot 1211* to *diagram 011*. There were many orders for these Siphon Gs, in fact there were six different lots as under:-

	running numbers	1462 to 1481 of 0.11
Lot 1211 of 1913	"	1442 to 1461 "
Lot 1264 of 1916	"	1345 to 1364 "
Lot 1316 of 1923	"	1290 to 1309 "
Lot 1347 of 1925	"	1271 to 1289 "
Lot 1368 of 1926	"	1240 to 1269 "
Lot 1378 of 1927		

LOT.1211   DIA.0.11

The line drawing gives a good representation of the planking, but an official drawing can be found on page 123.

FIG 118

FIG 117A

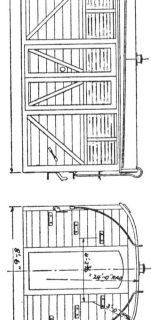

57'-0"

8'-6"   24'-0"RAD

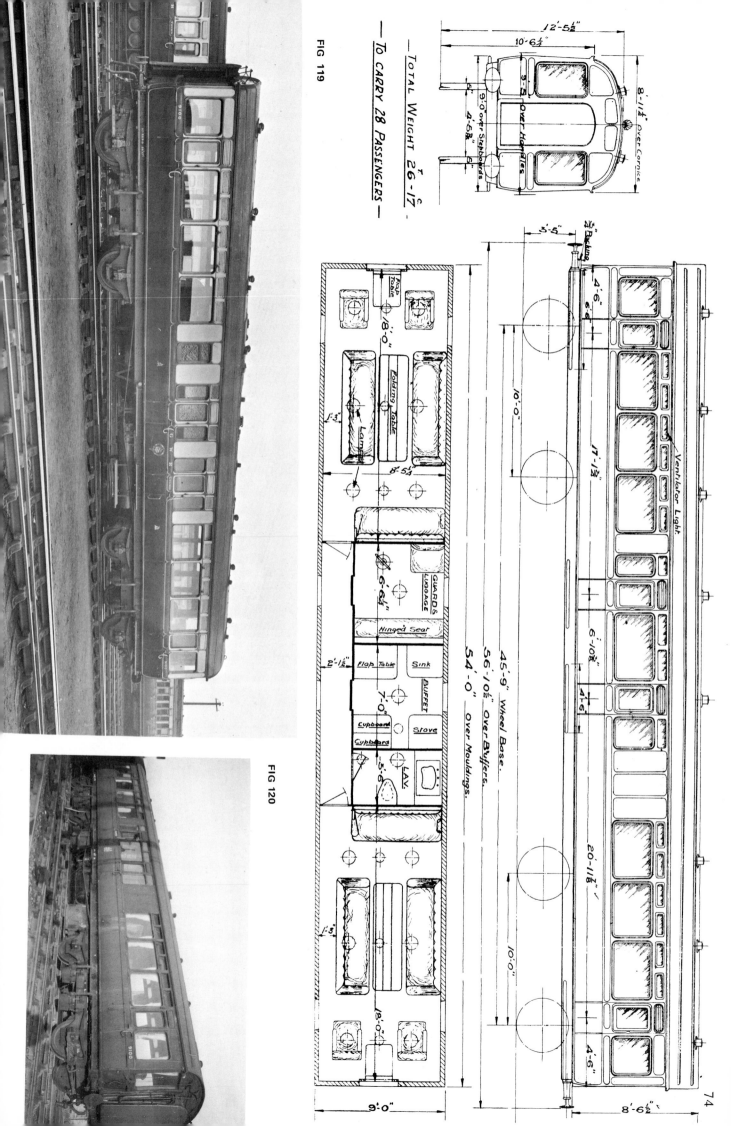

FIG 119

FIG 120

— TOTAL WEIGHT 26-17 —

— TO CARRY 28 PASSENGERS —

12'-5½"
10'-6¼"
8'-11½" Over Cornice.
9'-5" over Handles.
9'-0" over Stepboards.
5"
4'-5⅝"
5"

3'-5"
3" Packing.
4'-6"
6'-6"
17'-1½"
Ventilator Light.
6'-10⅜"
4'-6"
20'-11⅝"
4'-6"
8'-6½"

45'-9" Wheel Base.
56'-10½" Over Buffers.
54'-0" Over Mouldings.
10'-0"
10'-0"

Trap Table
18'-0"
Folding Table
Lamp
8'-5½"
1'-5"

GUARD & LUGGAGE
6'-6¼"
Hinged Seat
Flap Table   Sink
2'-1½"
7'-0¾"   BUFFET
Cupboard   Stove
Cupboard
3'-6"   LAV.

1'-5"
10'-0"
18'-0"
9'-0"

74

Page 74 illustrates another one-off job, the conversion of the old Royal carriage into a modern 'Toplight' saloon. This was achieved by using the old chassis and Dean bogies of the ancient nineteenth century Royal, and fitting onto this a specially constructed 1st class saloon for the use of Mr. Churchward on official journeys. The official drawing illustrates the layout of the interior, and gives the essential dimensions of the outline. The official photograph *figure 119*, shows the coach when first converted, and the small picture, *figure 120*, shows it at the end of its life. Note that the vacuum cylinder is of the Churchward pattern, as the old Dean type has been removed. In its last days the saloon was used as an inspection coach.

Lot 1212 of 1913 was an unusual order in that of the seventeen brake composites built under the *diagram E.95*, three were outshopped as single-ended slips. This official drawing shows the design as a slip composite whereas the photograph, *figure 121* taken at Banbury in 1948 illustrates the carriage as it was first planned. The main differences, apart from the slip gear, were the fitting of gangways at the van end only, and access to the guard's compartment from the corridor in the E.95 series. Running numbers were 6945 to 6961, three being taken out of sequence for the slip carriages. The slips were given *diagram F.20* and numbers 6962–4.

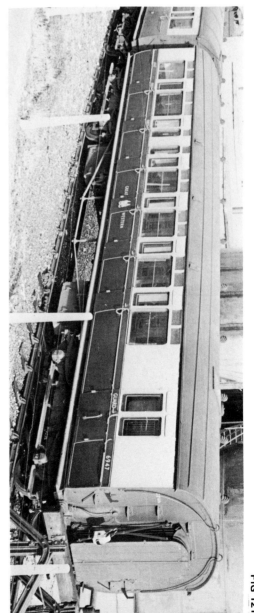

FIG 121

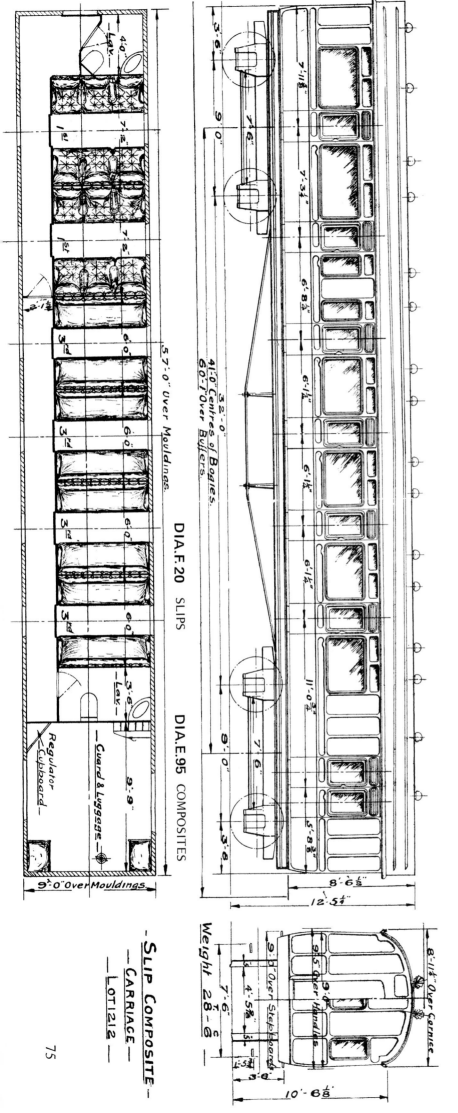

DIA.F.20 SLIPS

DIA.E.95 COMPOSITES

— SLIP COMPOSITE —
— CARRIAGE —
— LOT 1212 —

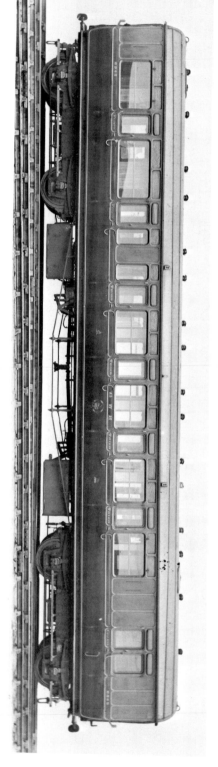

FIG 122

LOT. 1212

E95
F.21

FIG 123

These two official photographs illustrate *lot 1212* well. *Figure 122* at the top of the page shows No.6945, similar in every way to No.6947 on the previous page, except that this vehicle is in the crimson lake livery of the period. The lower photograph, *figure 123* is of the single ended slip constructed to the drawing on *page 75*. Note the number 6963.

FIG 124

The open carriage truck, code name 'Scorpion' illustrated on this page in the upper photograph, *figure 124*, is actually Scorpion D as it is of the 21' dual braked variety. It was used for the transport of road vehicles by passenger train, provided the load was not too high or did not exceed 8 tons. Many such vehicles were built between 1908 and 1916. A list of details is as follows:

1908	*lot 1158*	running numbers	443 to 452		*Diagram P15*
1913	*lot 1217*	"	453 to 467		" "
1914	*lot 1245*	"	468 to 482		" "
1912	*lot 1206*	"	110/1/3-6/9/22-5/8-30/1/4-7/42		" "
1915	*lot 1244*	"	121/39/40/1/6/7/53/64/6/83/6/78/9-81		" "
1913	*lot 1216*	"	145/9-52/5/8/7/61/3/5/8/9/71/5		" "
1916	*lot 1255*	"	187/8/9-91/3-5/8/200/2/4/5/8/9		" "

No.9091 is the 'Toplight' version of the sleeping car built under *lot 1218* of 1914. This photograph shows the 57' 1st class vehicle constructed to diagram J8; there were only two vehicles on the order, Nos. 9090 and 9091. The

FIG 125

livery shown is the crimson lake. Notice that these carriages were steel sheeted, the panels being painted in. Accommodation consisted of one double berth and eight singles, with a small attendant's compartment at one end, and a stove provided for light meals, *figure 125*.

FIG 126

FIG 127

More pictures of sleeping car No.9091 in later days, *figure 128* shows the vehicle after a major refit in the late forties, on six wheeled bogies, painted in the last style of Great Western livery. The accommodation is now composite 1st and 3rd as can be seen by the transfers on the waist line. *Figures 126 and 127* show the final phase in B.R. ownership, returned to 1st class standard and painted British Railways maroon.

LOT.1218   DIA.J.8

The next pattern of covered carriage truck in the 'Monster' series was the inside-framed variety shown in the pictures on page 79. As with the *P.16*s, only three were made — Nos. 483 and 484 and 485 under diagram *P.18* to *lot 1223* in 1913. The vehicle on the left, *figure 129*, is No. 484 and that on the right in *figure 130* is No. 485.

The official drawing gives all the leading dimensions, and marks a further batch on *lot 1265*, which was 581 to 595 in 1920.

FIG 128

FIG 129

FIG 130

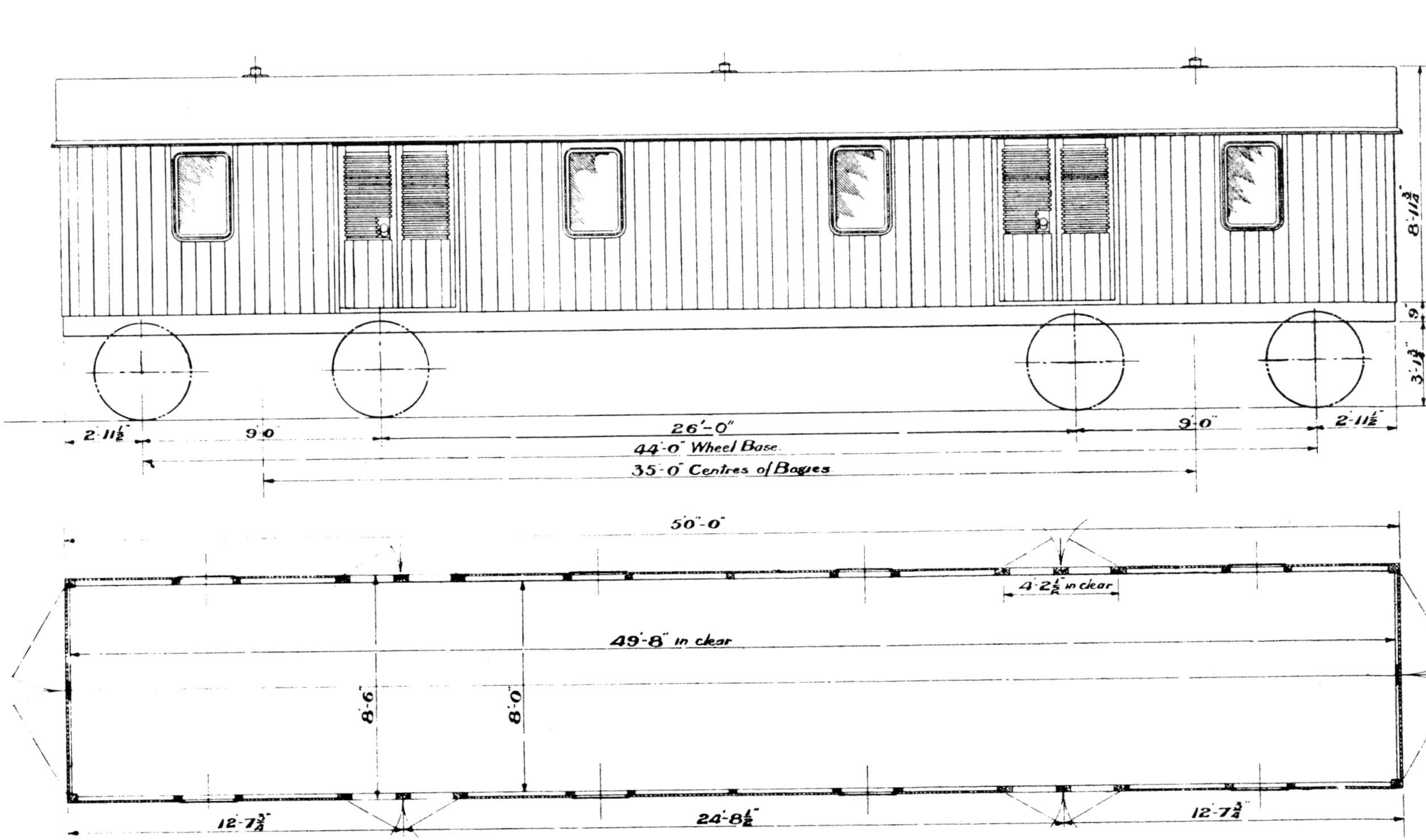

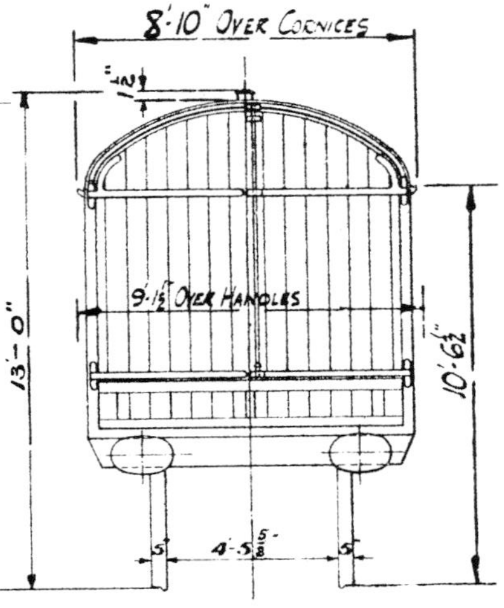

12'-7¾"

8'-6"

8'-0"

49'-8" in clear

50'-0"

24'-8½"

12'-7¾"

4'-2½" in clear

2'-11½"

9'-0"

26'-0" Wheel Base.

44'-0"

35'-0" Centres of Bogies

9'-0"

2'-11½"

3'-1¾"   9"   8'-11¾"

12'-10½"

13'-0"

8'-10" OVER CORNICES

9'-1" OVER HANDLES

4'-5½"

10'-6½"

	T.	C.
LOAD TO CARRY	10 -	0
TARE	23 -	6

LOT.1223

DIA.P.18

— CWR —
— COVERED SCENERY VAN —
— SWINDON — AUGUST 1913 —
— LOT 1223 —
— " 1265

— "MONSTER" —

79

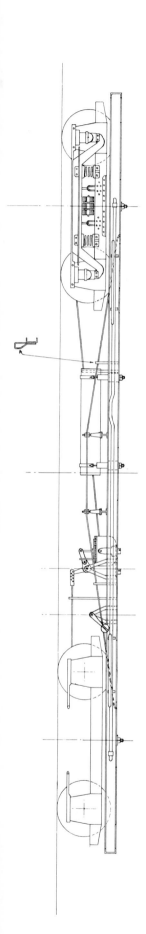

G W

483

MONSTER

FIG 131

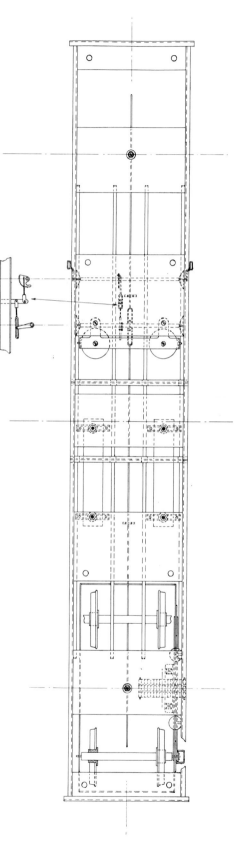

Page 80 shows Jim Whittaker's work again. The picture illustrates the superb model of a *P18* Monster, made by this super-detail modeller, and if one compares this picture with the prototypes on the previous page, it will be seen and appreciated just how fine this small miniature really is. To help other modellers, Jim has prepared a plan and elevation of a chassis to suit these Monsters, and they are reproduced here to 4mm scale.

Just room on this page to illustrate briefly the coach which was an engine! The auto-car movement had reached such proportions that several locos were so camouflaged to run with several trailers on each end but the experiment did not last, and the covering was removed, more details in the Great Western Engine book now being compiled.

Figure 133 illustrates No.94, one of the largest single saloon trailers made. Constructed under *lot 1224* in 1913, there were three vehicles, Nos.93, 94 and 95. Being gangwayed, these trailers often worked in pairs, giving through access for the conductor-guard to check and issue tickets. *Diagram was Q.*

LOT.1224
DIA.Q.

FIG 133

FIG 136

FIG 134

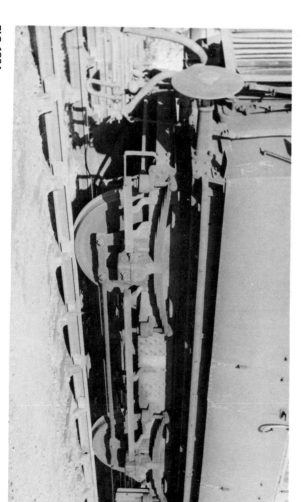

FIG 136A

LOT.1234

DIA.C.32

FIG 135

no toplights, were steel panelled, and the later series had trussing consisting of rigid angle irons, cantilevered.

Lot 1234 of 1914 was for twelve 57' corridor 3rds, figures 134 and 135 show both sides of No.2572 one of this series, diagram C.32. The two bottom shots give many details of the 'fishbelly' 9' bogie, and of the coupling gear. Note the large round-head buffers with the oblong shanks in figure 136a.

FIG 137

Two other examples of the C.32 design are shown at the top of this page, that in figure 137 being No.3888 of lot 1269, and the example below being No.2570 of lot 1234. Note that these two carriages differ from that on the previous page in still having their toplights in place; also note that the drawing does not show the windows which were in the lavatories. Running numbers were as follows:-

Lot 1234	Nos. 2569 to 80	1914
Lot 1246	Nos. 3913 to 47	1915
Lot 1269	Nos. 3879 to 3900	1920
Lot 1286	Nos. 3631	1922
Lot 1312	Nos. 2463/4/6-71/6	1922 " ex-Ambulance

It should be noted that several of these coaches were repurchased from the War Department after World War I, and reconverted from their use as ambulance trains.

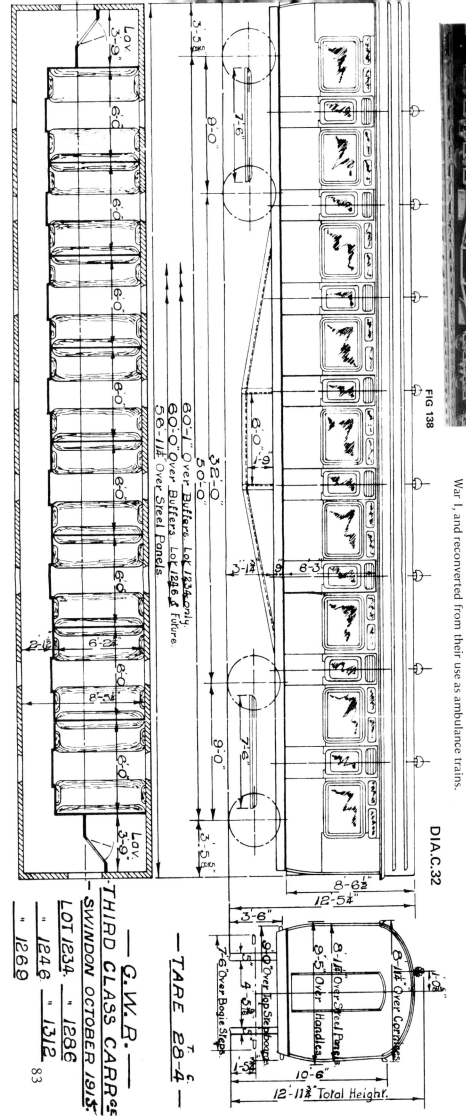

FIG 138

DIA.C.32

Lav. 3'-9"
6'-0"
6'-0"
6'-0"
8'-0"
8'-0"
8'-0"
8'-0"
8'-0"
Lav. 3'-9"

7'-6"
9'-0"
3'-5"
3'-5½"

6'-0"
6'-0"
9'-0"
7'-6"
3'-5½"
3'-5"

8'-3"
9"
3'-1¼"

2'-1½"
6'-2¼"
8'-5¼"
8'-0"

60'-1" Over Buffers, Lot 1234 only.
60'-0" Over Buffers, Lot 1246 & Future.
58'-11¾" Over Steel Panels
52'-0"
50'-0"

— G.W.R. —
— THIRD CLASS CARR^GE. —
— SWINDON OCTOBER 1915. —
LOT 1234. — " 1286
" 1246 — " 1312
" 1269

— TARE 28-4 —
T. C.

8'-6½"
12'-5¼"

3'-6"
7'-6" Over Bogie Steps.
9'-0" Over Top Steps
9'-0" Over Stepboards
8'-1¼" Over Steel Panels
9'-5" Over Handles.
8'-1¼" Over Cornices
5"
4'-5⅛"
5'-5"
10'-6"
12'-11¾" Total Height.

83

FIG 139

FIG 141

FIG 142

FIG 140

The other form of 'Toplight' undertrussing known as 'Multibar' consisted of round rods, the diagonals being single and the horizontals being in pairs, and figure 142 shows this form in good detail. At the top left, figure 139, is one of the Brake 3rds 57', No.3598, built under lot 1235 to diagram D.56. This picture was taken at Bristol Temple Meads in 1951, whereas the other three photos on this page are detail shots of one vehicle, namely a 10 compartment 3rd No. 2592 which was constructed under the next consecutive lot No. 1236 to diagram C.33.

LOT.1236

DIA.C.33

FIG 143

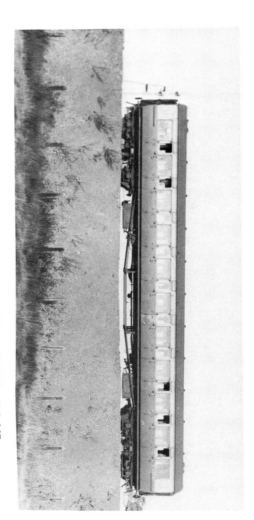

FIG 145

FIG 144

These three photographs below illustrate again the 10 compartment 3rd in the 'Toplight Multibar' design. The official photo in figure 145 shows the coach as made, with the appropriate livery and white roof; this is No. 2588. The other two pictures by Roye England depict No.2592 and show both sides of the same vehicle. There were twenty vehicles in this batch, all 69'11¼" in length, running numbers 2581 to 2600.

85

Lot 1238 of 1914 was for 20 Covered Carriage Trucks to the diagram P.19, but this order was modified to include one last vehicle, which was to be specially strengthened for the carriage of elephants. This may sound odd, but these were the days of travelling circuses and menageries, and so provision had to be made for elephants. No.580 was built to diagram P.20 and was always branded "specially strengthened". The drawing is the offical Swindon diagram of P.19 and links with the picture of No.569 in the bottom right-hand, figure 148. The other two photographs show No.580 when new, (figure 147), and in 1949 at Banbury Jct. (figure 146). Running numbers were 561 to 579 as P.19.

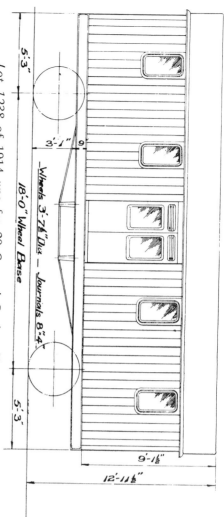

_G.W.R_

COVERED CARRIAGE TRUCK

—SWINDON, APRIL 1914 SCALE ⅛=1FOOT—

Lot 1238. First 19.

FIG 146

—Wheels 3'-7½"Dia — Journals 8"×4"—

5'-3"

3'-1"

18'-0" Wheel Base

5'-3"

9'-1½"

12'-11½"

Tare 9. 14. T.C.
Load to carry 16-6

8'-6"

4'-5⅝"

5'

10'-8¾"

8'-10" Over Cornices

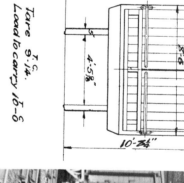

LOT.1238
DIA.P.19

FIG 147

FIG 148

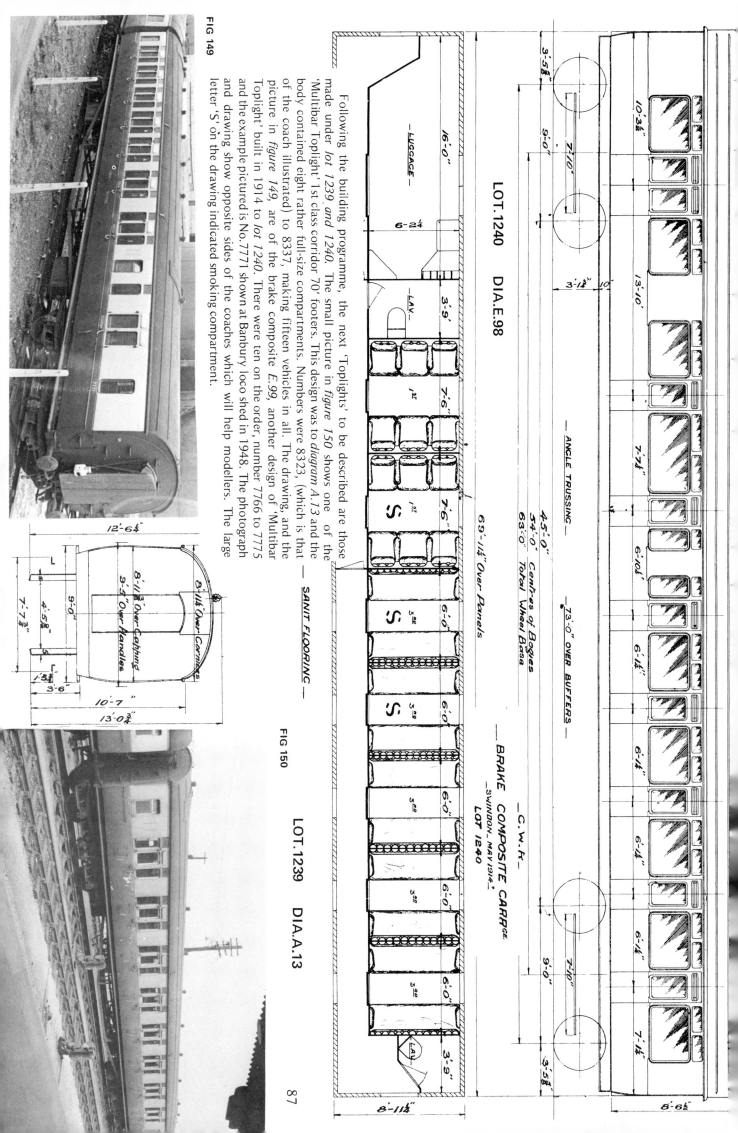

Following the building programme, the next 'Toplights' to be described are those made under *lot 1239* *and 1240*. The small picture in *figure 150* shows one of the 'Multibar Toplight' 1st class corridor 70' footers. This design was to *diagram A.13* and the body contained eight rather full-size compartments. Numbers were 8323, (which is that of the coach illustrated) to 8337, making fifteen vehicles in all. The drawing, and the picture in *figure 149*, are of the brake composite *E.99*, another design of 'Multibar Toplight' built in 1914 to *lot 1240*. There were ten on the order, number 7766 to 7775 and the example pictured is No.7771 shown at Banbury loco shed in 1948. The photograph and the drawing show opposite sides of the coaches which will help modellers. The large letter 'S' on the drawing indicated smoking compartment.

FIG 149

FIG 150

LOT.1240   DIA.E.98

LOT.1239   DIA.A.13

— ANGLE TRUSSING —

— SANIT FLOORING —

— C.W.R. —

— 73'-0" OVER BUFFERS —

45'-0" Centres of Bogies

63'-0" Total Wheel Base

69'-11½" Over Panels

— BRAKE COMPOSITE CARRIAGE —
— SWINDON – MAY 1914. –
LOT 1240

The next Horse Box to be described is the N.12 of 1915 and 1918. The drawings taken from the offical diagram are to the scale of 7 mm to 1 ft (0 gauge) which enables detail to be drawn clearer. The photograph shows one of the class No.192 in the horse dock at Aynho Station. Details of numbers are as follows:

FIG 151

Lot 1242 N.12 304/19/23/8/41/8/55/6/70/4/6/7/405/9/11 of 1915

Lot 1243 N.12 198/204/7-9/32-4/61/78/87/9/90/6/7 of 1916

Lot 1254 N.12 7/9/20/6/8/31/9/131/4/5/43/50/4/62/6/73/4/5/7/8 of 1918

Lot 1245 N.12 184/8/92-5/242/384/414/415/

LOT.1242
DIA.N.12

12'~7⅞"

4'10"
1'8"

3'~1"

9'~0"
8'~6"
12'~1"

G.W.R. Horse Box

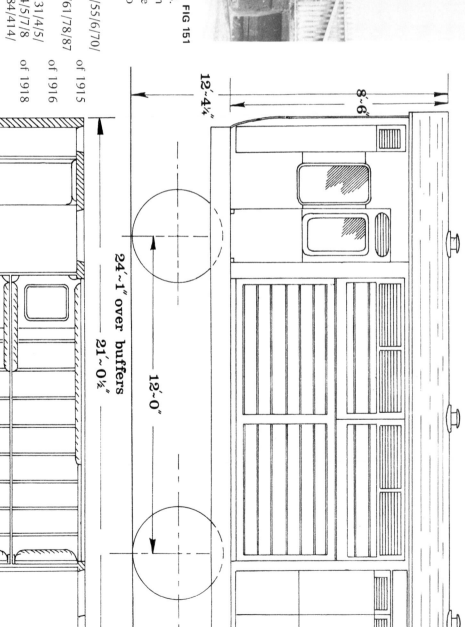

12"
0
1'
2'
3'
4'
5'
6'
7'
8'

12'~4¼"
8'~6"

24'~1" over buffers
21'~0½"
12'~0"

Lots 1242, 1243, 1254.

88

It is worth noting that the numbers of these horse boxes were painted on the bottom right of the right hand partition doors.

LOT.1247   DIA.D.56

A short version of the 'Multibar Toplight' Brake 3rd in picture and drawing. The picture was taken of No. 3774 at Oxford North in 1947, (*figure 152*), and shows the compartment side, and the official drawing gives the side elevation of the corridor, which runs the full length of the vehicle, the luggage space being partitioned off. Running numbers and dates are as follows:— Diagram was D.56 of 1914 et seq.

Lot 1235 — Nos. 3593 to 3598	Lot 1247 — Nos. 3763 to 3777 of 1919
Lot 1257 — Nos. 3778 to 3786	Lot 1270 — Nos. 3787 to 3792 of 1920
Lot 1279 — Nos. 3805 to 3810	Lot 1291 — Nos. 3503 of 1921
Lot 1293 — Nos. 3505 to 3506	Lot 1315 — Nos. 3515 of 1922
Lot 1339 — Nos. 4243 of 1925	

FIG 152

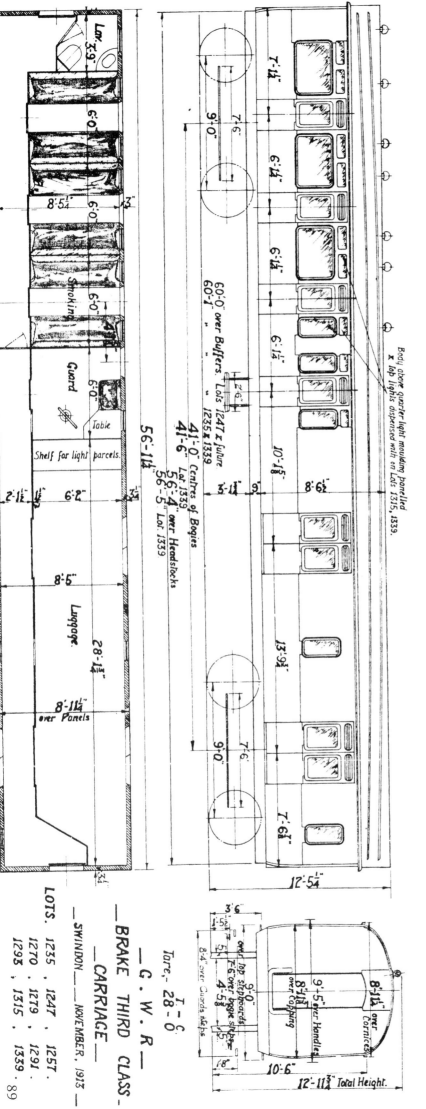

G.W.R. — BRAKE THIRD CLASS — CARRIAGE — SWINDON — NOVEMBER, 1913 —

LOTS. 1235 , 1247 , 1257 ,
       1270 , 1279 , 1291 ,
       1293 , 1315 , 1339 .

89

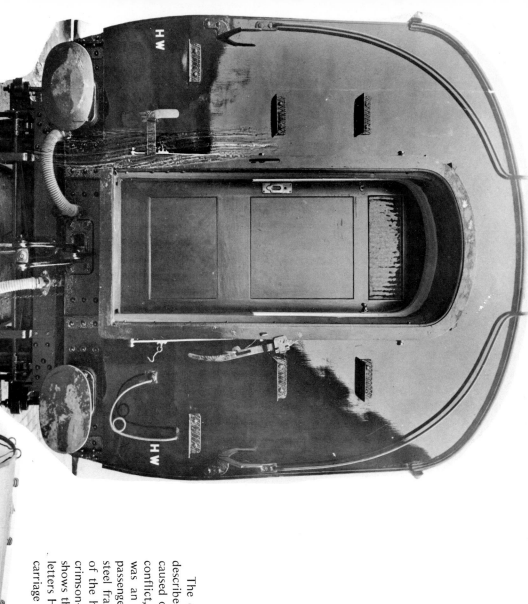

FIG 153

LOT.1248

DIA.C.39

FIG 154

The date sequence here takes a leap forward to 1921 as, although the next vehicle to be described was planned and designed in 1914, it was not outshopped until 1921. This delay was caused of course by the First World War, and although vehicles were made during the years of conflict, the programme was severely curtailed. The carriage shown on this page is No.3948, which was an experimental vehicle, constructed under *lot 1248* to *diagram C.39*. It was the first passenger-carrying coach to be made which was completely fireproof. The body was built with steel framing instead of wood, and both sides and ends were covered with steel panels. Also, much of the hitherto timber flooring was replaced with asbestos. *Figure 155* shows the carriage in the crimson-lake livery as built, with *figure 154* illustrating the steel-panelled ends. The smaller picture shows the vehicle in B.R. time painted chocolate and cream at Newbury station (*figure 153*). The letters H.W. indicated hot water supply in the toilets, which had to be noted and dealt with by the carriage and wagon department during frosty weather (see fuller details later).

FIG 156

FIG 157

The restaurant car shown on this page is one of the large almost 70' series, which were built in 1922 under *lot 1249* to *diagram H.24*. As can be seen, they were rather severe slab-sided carriages, with no tumble-home whatsoever. The example shown in the small photograph, *figure 157*, (taken, incidentally, leaving No.1 platform at Paddington), is No.9557, and the large official picture of the interior, *figure 156*, is of vehicle No.9561 taken as built. Five of these diners were later retrimmed inside by Messrs. Hamptons, but this was not until after the second World War. Running numbers were 9556, 9557, 9558, 9559, 9560 and 9561.

The top picture shows another variety of the open carriage trucks, code named Scorpions. This example is one of the *P.15 diagram*. No.480 and *P.15* was dual fitted. One can just see the letters G and W painted on the side of the floor. (*figure 158.*) There were many built under several lots. Running numbers of *lot 1245* were 468 to 482.

Four long double-ended slips of the last Toplight design were completed in 1916, being Nos.7990-93. Constructed under *lot 1252*, their *diagram was F.21*. The lower official photograph, *figure 160*, shows No.7993 as outshopped in the crimson lake livery. In the early nineteen-forties, these carriages had their slip apparatus removed, and they were demoted to full 3rd class vehicles, but restored to their slip rosters between 1947 and 1950. (Note the unusual bogie). *Figure 159* illustrates one of the 57' 'Toplight' passenger brake vans built during the First World War. This coach, No.256, is one of the steel panelled type, with no toplights, and the heavy angle-iron trussing. Only two were in this lot, No.255 and 256. (*diagram K.22*) Note the American bogies which remained on the vehicle from first till last.

FIG 158

LOT.1245
DIA.P.15

92

LOT.1252   DIA.F.21

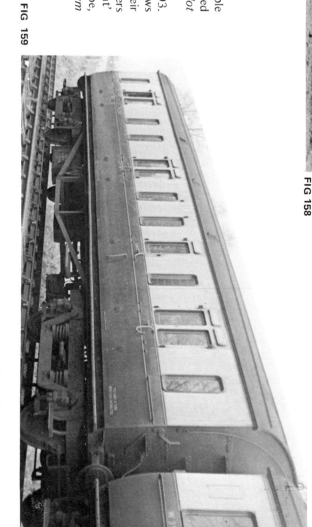

FIG 159

DIA.K.22

Another example of Great Western similarity is shown here. In the top picture, *figure 161*, we have an eight compartment 3rd class corridor coach No.3981, which was made as a 'Multibar Toplight', under *lot 1256 of 1919*, *diagram C.35*. In the lower offical photograph, *figure 162*, is seen No.9093, which was built a *J.9* composite sleeper, and was used originally on the Paddington-Neyland night service. Later this carriage was rebuilt as a seven-berth 1st class sleeper and formed part of the Wartime 'ALIVE' train. Original numbers were 7596, 7600, later 9092, 9093

LOT.1256

DIA.C.35

FIG 161

LOT.1251

J.9

Later J.16

FIG 162

93

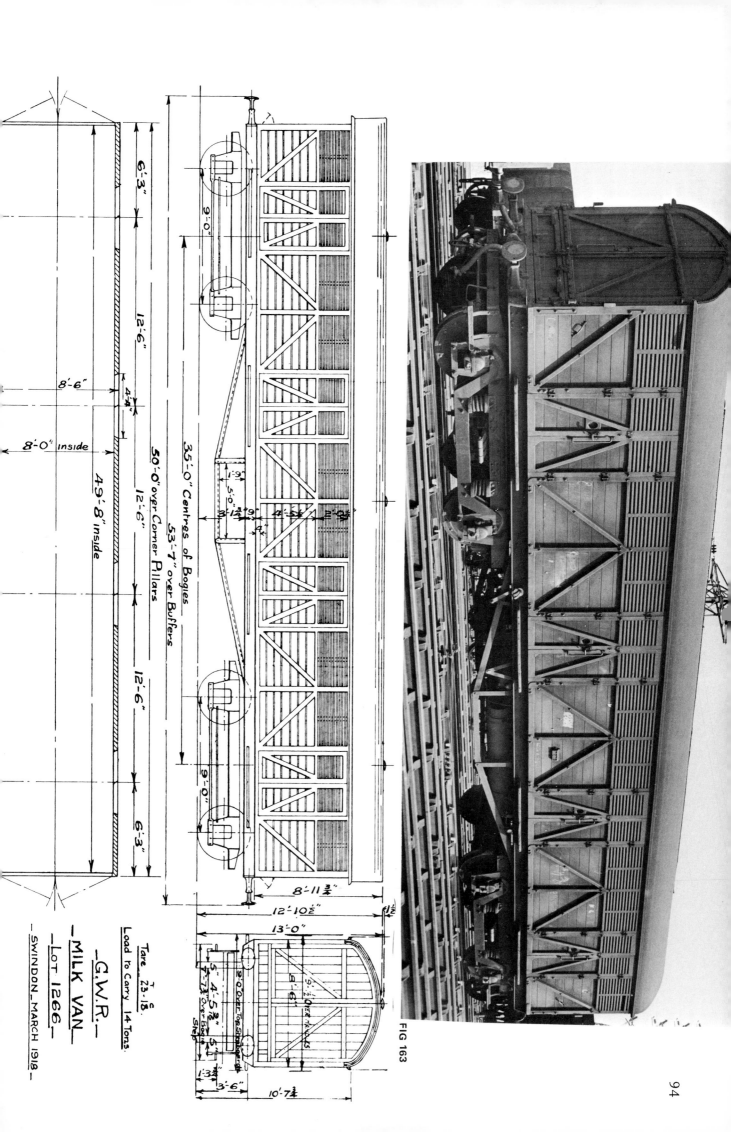

FIG 163

— G.W.R. —
— MILK VAN —
— LOT 1266 —
— SWINDON, MARCH 1918 —

Load to Carry 14 Tons.

Tare 23·18.

35'-0" Centres of Bogies
50'-0" over Corner Pillars
53'-7" over Buffers

49'-8" inside

8'-0" inside

6'-3"   12'-6"   12'-6"   12'-6"   6'-3"

8'-6"

9'-0"   9'-0"

8'-11¾"
12'-10½"
13'-0"

3'-6"
10'-7¾"

94

A cross between the 'Monsters' (P.16) and Siphon Gs (O.11) would be a reasonable way to describe the next vehicle. Another 50' 'brown' van using the high roof profile of the 'Monsters' and with end doors, but with the outside framing and louvres of the bogie Siphons.

This vehicle was code named Siphon H and was built in 1919 under *lot 1266* to *diagram O.12*. Running numbers were from 1422 to 1441. Although described on the offical drawing as a 'Milk Van', by virtue of the end doors, it could be used for scenery or motor vehicles, and I have seen light aircraft stowed in one! However, I should point out that inside there were no moveable wheel chocks like those fitted in the *P* series. They were not quite so useful in traffic as the Siphon G, as they were not gangwayed, so train staff could not pass through for sorting, etc. It might be of interest to mention that one prototype Siphon H was made to *diagram O.10* which was similar in all respects, except in roof profile which was low, following the Siphon G shape. This odd vehicle was No.1502 to *lot 1164* of 1908. The photograph on page 94 is another example of Maurice Earley's art. Taken by Sonning Box it illustrates the Siphon H very well.

FIG 164

FIG 164A

DIA. 0.12

FIG 165

FIG 166

This page highlights the Siphon H by means of four more photographs. The top two, *figures 164 and 164a* are both sides of No.1432, taken at Thingley Junction in 1947. The centre shot, *figure 165*, is of No.1428 at Reading, and the lower picture, *figure 165*, is of No.1440 taken on a moving train at Taunton in 1948. Note they all have the contemporary heavy angle-iron trussing, and American type 9' bogies.

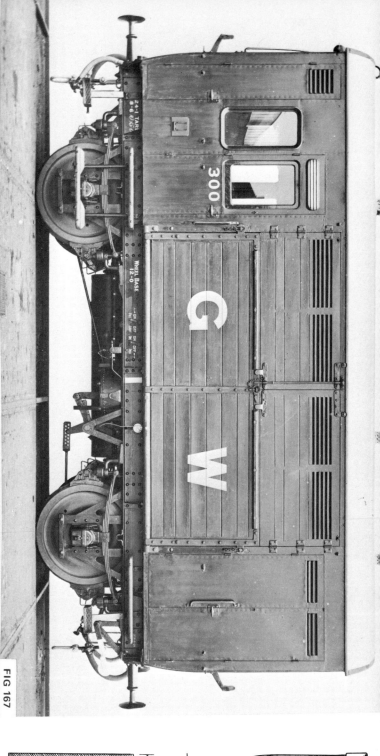

FIG 167

The most numerous of the Horse Box diagram was the *N.13* design. They were built over a period of years from 1921 until 1930, under seven lots. Numbers are given below with approximate dates. From the offical drawing (to 4mm sacle) it will be seen that the sides are flat, with no curvature whatsoever, although the ends have a slight tumblehome. The two photographs show the outside (with the 1930 livery) (*figure 167*) and also the interior illustrating the removable partitions. These were stowed in the narrow compartment on the left, whereas the larger cabin on the right was for bales of hay, straw and possible tack. (*figure 168*). Some of these boxes were lit by pot oil lamps, but the majority had gas lighting. Three horses could be carried side by side.

Lot 1267	303/5/7/10/3/7/21/2/5/30/3-6/42/4/6/9/57/8 /63/7/71/2/373/5/8/80/1-3/5/7/96/97-401 /403/4/7/8/10/2/6/7-20/2/4/425/7-39	built 1922
Lot 1268	223/5/36/7/9/40/228	built 1922
Lot 1379	147-8/176/80/1/3/6/9/90/9	built 1926
Lot 1367	144/6/52/3/6/7-61/3/4/8/9/892-927	built 1925
Lot 1386	241/4/7-9/53/5/6/8/9	built 1928
Lot 1397	263-7/271/4/6/83-5/8/91-5/8-300	built 1928
Lot 1408	273/394/5/421/3/6/40-8/50/2/3/60/76	built 1930

LOT 1267

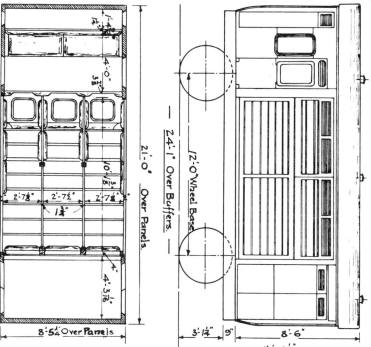

DIA N.13

DIA.C.37

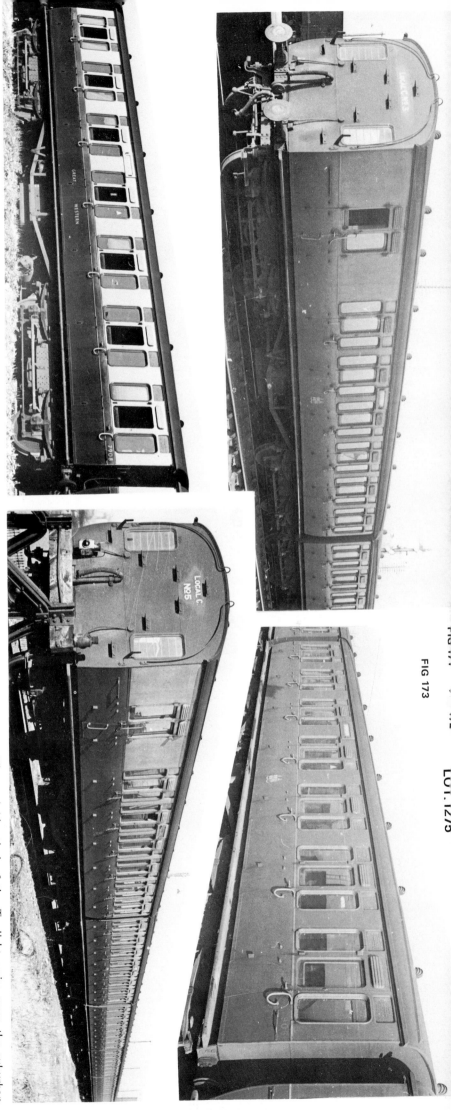

FIG 173

The real 'shorties' of the Toplight series were the suburban coaches, planned in 1913, but delayed until 1921-22, because of wartime restrictions. There were three designs, the full 3rds being diagram C.37, brake 3rd D.62, and composites which were E101. They were all only 48' in length, and were made up in trains of six coaches, usually two 3rds, two Compos., and a brake 3rd at each end, van outward. With the exception of the two ends, all the buffers were the very short type, as each set was close-coupled. My pictures show these interesting vehicles in three different liveries. The official picture in figure 173 shows the crimson lake period, figures 169 and 170 the brown all over style of the Second World War, and the centre photographs, figures 171 and 172, the post-1945 chocolate and cream. Coach numbers are, top left No.3752 diagram D.62; top right No.7905, diagram E.101; centre left No.7908 diagram E.101; centre left No. 3755 (this vehicle is preserved on Dart Valley line); lower photograph No.3902 diagram C.37.

97

FIG 174

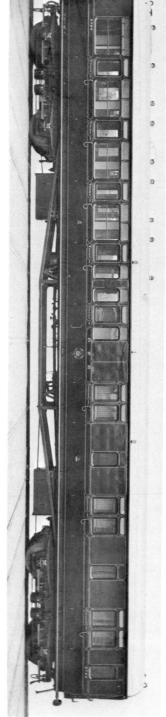

DIA.D.69

FIG 175

DIA.E.102

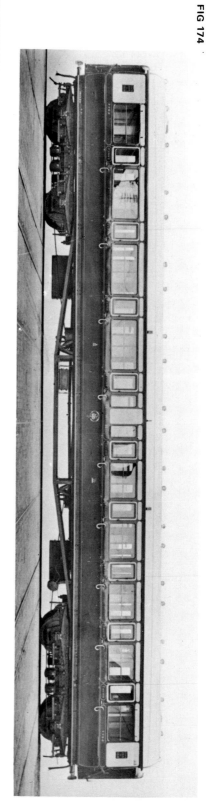

Three of the larger 'Toplights' are shown here, all of the 'Multibar' series but to different designs and in progressive liveries. *Figure 174* is the *70'* composite No.7782 built in 1921 to *diagram E.102*. Twelve vehicles were made, numbering 7776 to 7787. The livery here is the 1920 chocolate and cream panelled. In *figure 175* is No.3794 as built, in the crimson lake livery. This was one of twelve built under *lot 1278* to *diagram D.69*. The brake composite in the lower picture, *figure 176*, is one I photographed in 1947 at Henley-on-Thames No.7791, it is one of a series of ten numbering from 7788 to 7797 which were built to *diagram E.104* under *lot 1280* in 1922. The livery here is the post-war chocolate and cream with double waist lining.

LOT.1280

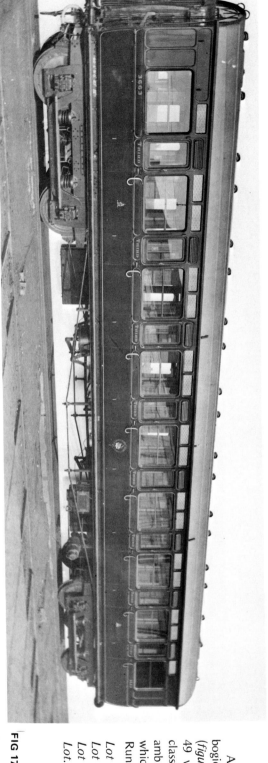

FIG 177

A full third, running on the lightweight 8' American bogies, features in this official photograph of No.3663, (figure 177). This 57' Toplight of Bars 1 design was one of 49 vehicles built under four separate lots to the same classification of C.35. Many of these vehicles were used in ambulance trains and re-converted in the early twenties, which brings them in here slightly out of sequence. Running numbers and lots were as follows:-

Lot 1256 Nos. 3949 to 3981   of 1917
Lot 1290 Nos. 3645 to 3652   of 1921 (converted)
Lot 1295 Nos. 3662 to 3667   of 1921 (converted)
Lot. 1313 Nos. 3668   of 1922 (converted)

99

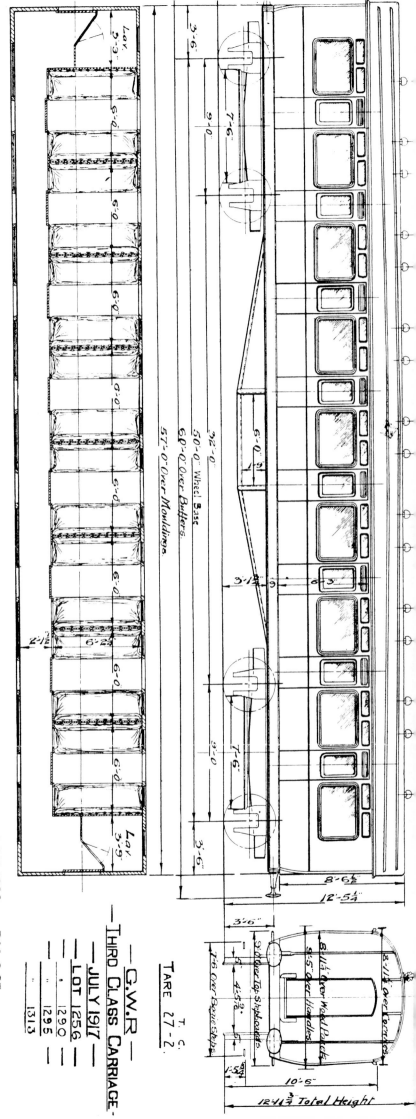

LOT.1290   DIA.C.35

— G.W.R —
— THIRD CLASS CARRIAGE —
— JULY 1917 —

	LOT 1256	
	” 1290	
	” 1295	
	” 1313	

TARE 27 - 2.

T. C.

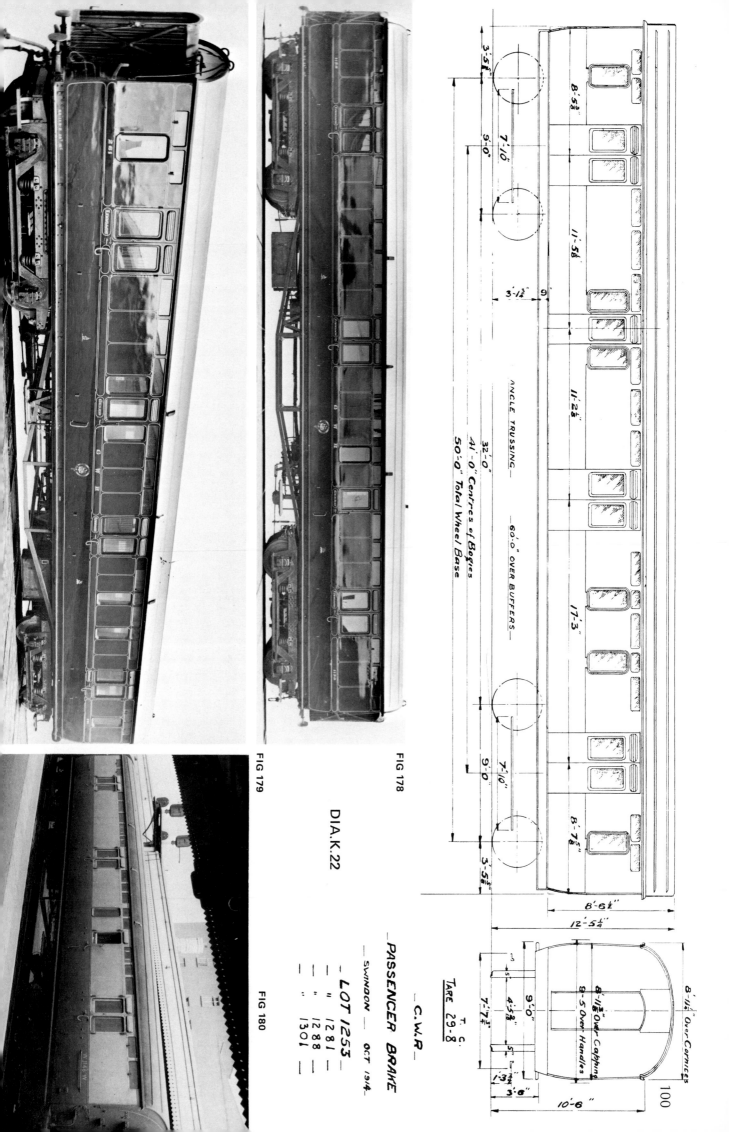

FIG 179

FIG 178

FIG 180

DIA.K.22

— C.W.R —

PASSENGER BRAKE

— SWINDON — OCT 1914

LOT 1253
— " — 1281 —
— " — 1288 —
— " — 1301 —

ANGLE TRUSSING

60'-0" OVER BUFFERS

32'-0"

41'-0" Centres of Bogies

50'-0" Total Wheel Base

TARE 29-8

3'-5⅛"
9'-0"
7'-10"
11'-5⅝"
8'-5⅝"
3'-1¾"
9
11'-2⅜"
17'-3"
7'-10"
9'-0"
8'-7⅝"
3'-5⅝"

8'-6¼"
12'-5¼"

8'-1⅛" Over Capping
9'-5 Over Handles
8'-11¾" Over Cornices

9'-0"
7'-7¾"
4'-5⅛"
3'-6"
10'-6"
100

War ambulance trains, there were also some 1 Toplight luggage vans, and this page illustrates the type used. They were built to the *diagram K.22* and were in four lots as follows:-

Lot 1253   Nos. 255 and 256
Lot 1281   Nos. 257 to 266
Lot 1288   Nos. 267   (Ambulance use)
Lot 1301   Nos. 1129 to 1153

Modellers should note that the sides are unequal, there being eight windows on the van side, and thirteen on the corridor side, not shown on the official drawings! *Figures 178 and 179* illustrate this point well.

Saloons were coaches which were specially constructed for families or invalids, so that the private parties could have sole use of the vehicle. This picture is of a rebuilt saloon, No.9366, which I pictured at Thingley Junction in 1947 as a 3rd class *diagram G.54*. (*figure 181*). It is a mixture of two eras, Dean and Churchward, the chassis being of 1904 vintage and the body 1922 period.

The drawing illustrates one of these ex-Ambulance saloons, which started life as a clerestory invalid saloon in 1904 to *diagram G.33* (*see Part 1*). In 1915 four of these vehicles were adapted for use on the ambulance trains, being used as sleeping quarters for medical orderlies and their stores. After the war three of these carriages were stripped of their bodies and rebuilt with a special short Toplight body with eliptical roof and reclassified as *diagram G.54*, becoming the 3rd class saloon shown in the Swindon drawing.

FIG 181

LOT.1284   **DIA.G.54**

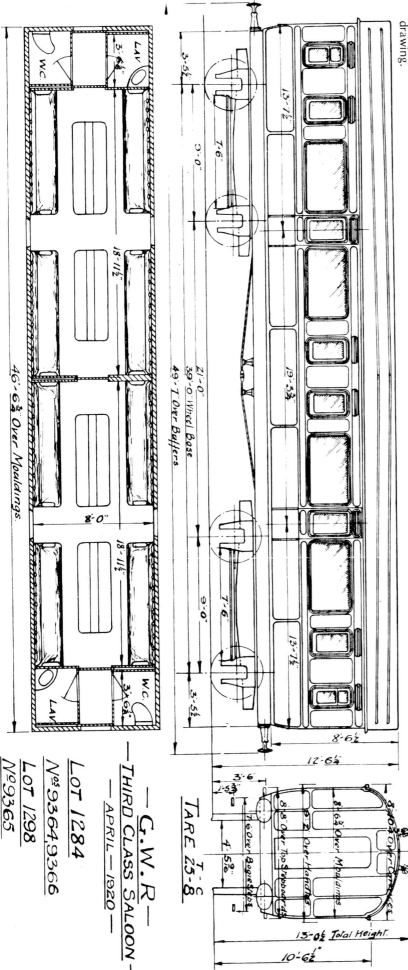

— G.W.R —
— THIRD CLASS SALOON —
— APRIL — 1920 —

LOT 1284   Nos 9364 9366
LOT 1298   Nº 9365

TARE 25-8

46'-6¾ Over Mouldings.

49'1" Over Buffers
39'-0" Wheel Base

13'-0½ Total Height.

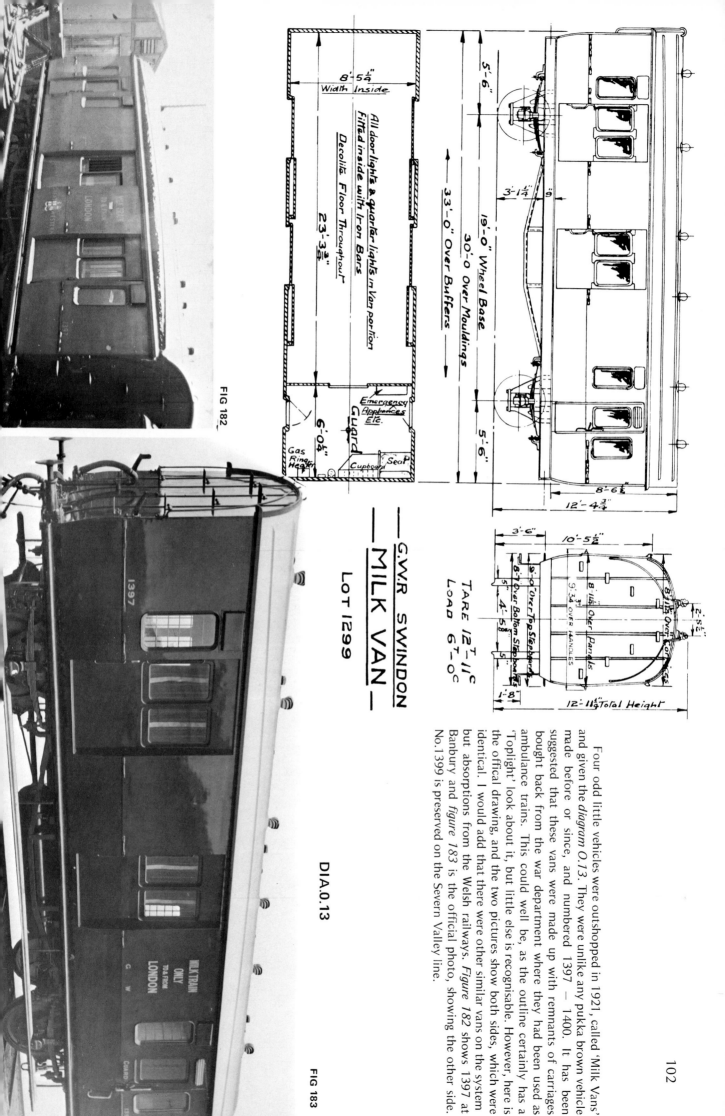

FIG 182

All doorlights & quarter-lights in Van portion
Fitted inside with Iron Bars

Decolila Floor Throughout

8'-5¼"
Width Inside

23'-3½"

6'-0¼"

19'-0" Wheel Base

30'-0 Over Mouldings

33'-0" Over Buffers

Emergency
Appliances
Etc.

Guard

Gas
Ring
Heater

Seat

Cupboard

5'-6"

3'-1¼"

5'-6"

8'-6½"

12'-4¾"

3'-6"

10'-5¼"

8'-1¼" Over Panels
9'-3½" OVER HANDLES

8'-9" Over Top Steps
8'-7" Over Bottom Stepboards

9'-3½" Over Handles

8'-1¼" Over Handles

2'-5¼"

12'-11⅛" Total Height

1'-8"

─── G.W.R. SWINDON ───
─── MILK VAN ───

LOT 1299

TARE 12ᵀ-11ᶜ
LOAD 6ᵀ-0ᶜ

DIA.0.13

Four odd little vehicles were outshopped in 1921, called 'Milk Vans' and given the *diagram O.13*. They were unlike any pukka brown vehicle made before or since, and numbered 1397 — 1400. It has been suggested that these vans were made up with remnants of carriages bought back from the war department where they had been used as ambulance trains. This could well be, as the outline certainly has a 'Toplight' look about it, but little else is recognisable. However, here is the offical drawing, and the two pictures show both sides, which were identical. I would add that there were other similar vans on the system but absorptions from the Welsh railways. *Figure 182* shows 1397 at Banbury and *figure 183* is the official photo, showing the other side. No.1399 is preserved on the Severn Valley line.

FIG 183

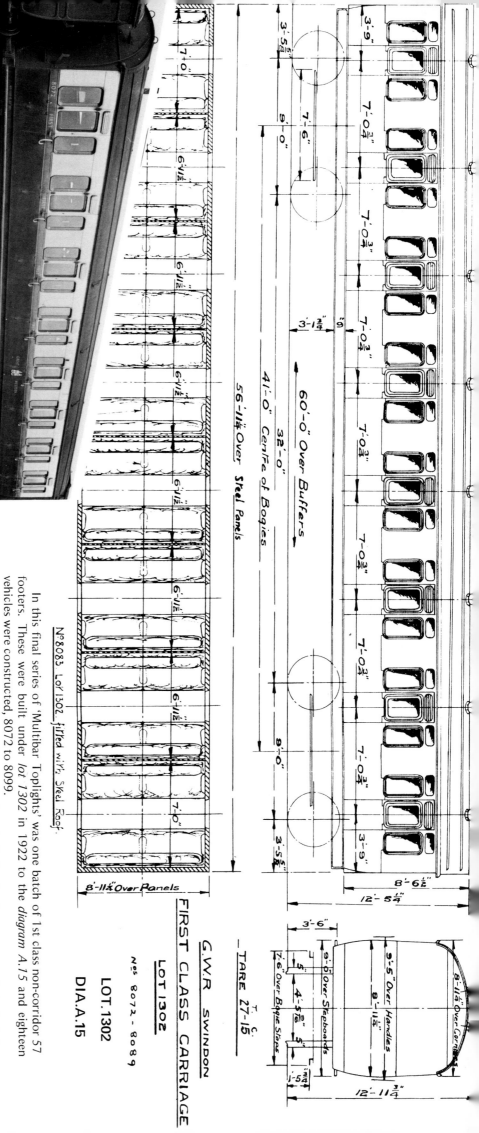

No 8083 Lot 1302 fitted with Steel Roof.

G.W.R SWINDON

FIRST CLASS CARRIAGE

LOT 1302

DIA.A.15

Nos 8072 - 8089

TARE 27-15

In this final series of 'Multibar Toplights' was one batch of 1st class non-corridor 57 footers. These were built under *lot 1302* in 1922 to the *diagram A.15* and eighteen vehicles were constructed, 8072 to 8099.

The drawing and photographs show the similarity to the gangwayed stock, being full-bodied and very roomy. A small oddity is that the two end compartments were ½" longer than the central ones! *Figure 185* shows No.8088 in original livery, and No.8072 in post 1945 chocolate and cream is seen in *figure 184*.

FIG 184

FIG 185

103

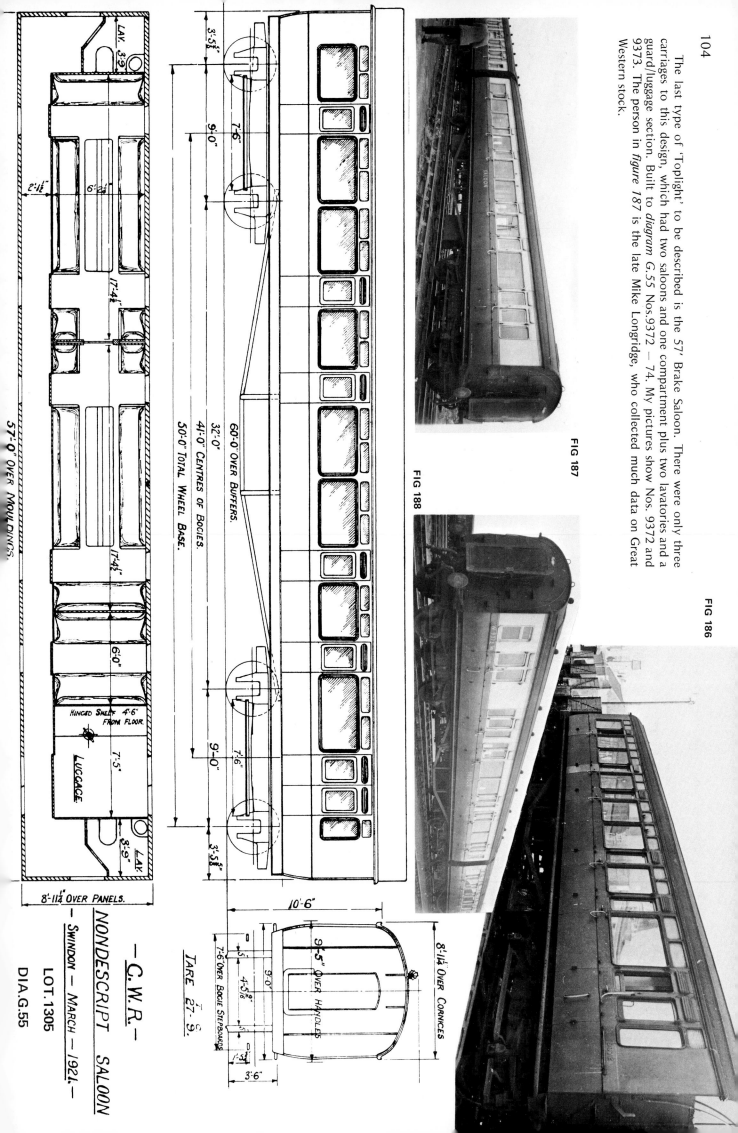

The last type of 'Toplight' to be described is the 57' Brake Saloon. There were only three carriages to this design, which had two saloons and one compartment plus two lavatories and a guard/luggage section. Built to *diagram G.55* Nos.9372 – 74. My pictures show Nos. 9372 and 9373. The person in *figure 187* is the late Mike Longridge, who collected much data on Great Western stock.

FIG 186

FIG 187

FIG 188

FIG 189

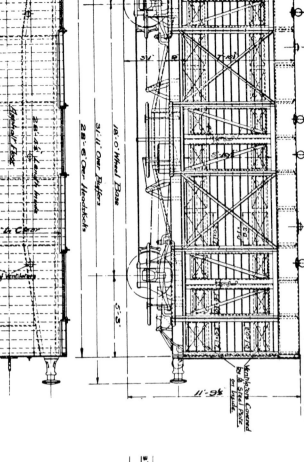

LOT.1258
DIA.S.9
DIA.S.8

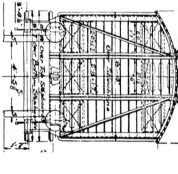

To cope with the fish traffic from South Wales and West Country ports, the Great Western had many very odd vehicles in service up to and during the 1914-18 War, some built as far back at 1880. As most of these wagons were quickly being condemned, a completely new design of fish wagon was planned, and between the years 1919 to 1923 one hundred and forty-seven vehicles were made to this diagram. The telegraphic code name was 'Bloater', but the *diagram was* S.8. To carry 10 tons their wheel base was 18'. They were fitted with three sliding doors on each side, which were in pairs, fastening in the centre. Equipped with gas lighting, they were also fitted later with six ventilators.

Fig. 190 shows 2277 of *lot 1307. Drawing is of Dia. S.9.*

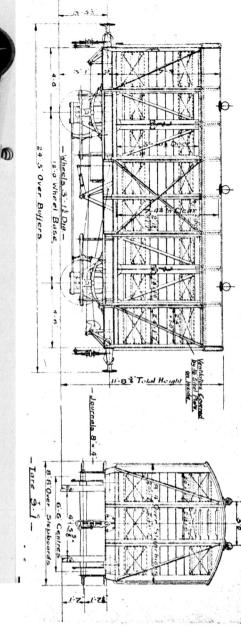

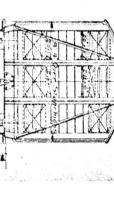

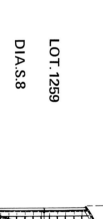

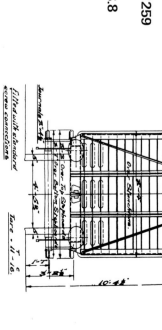

As can be seen in *figure 191* some had the long shank coach buffers (No.2177) and others the parallel self-contained pattern. With the decline of the fish traffic, many of these 'Bloaters' were fitted with flush doors, like the Fruit D's, and were available as parcel vans. Lot and number list as follows:

Lot 1258   Nos. 2139 to 2213   date 1919
Lot 1259   Nos. 2114 to 2138   date 1919
Lot 1307   Nos. 2268 to 2288, 2601 to 2629   date 1923

Converted to parcel vans later, Nos.2114 – 21, 2165 – 6, 2172 – 3, 2175/9/91/97-2200. *figure 192 shows the small fish van built to diagram S.6 of lot 700; the numbers were 2089 to 2113.*

FIG 191

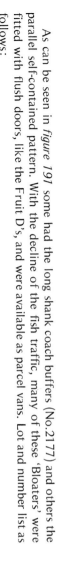

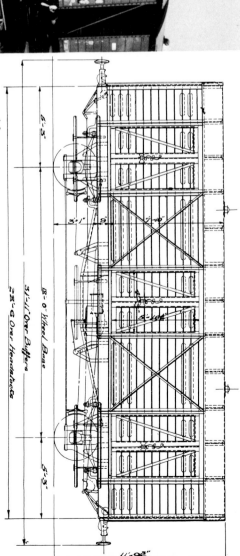

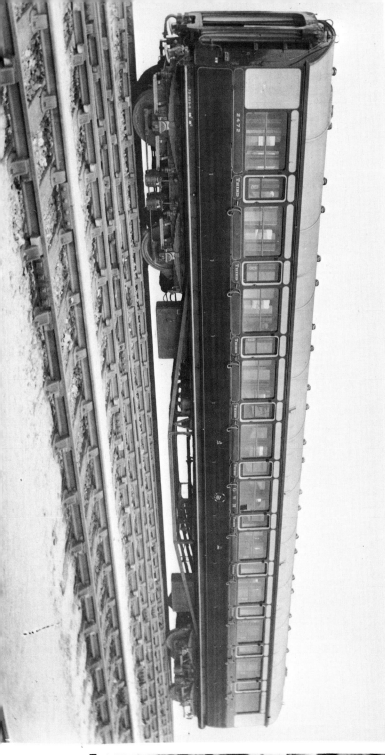

LOT. 1308   DIA.C.44   FIG 193

FIG 194

The vehicle shown in the offical photograph on this page, *figure 193*, is worthy of special note, as it was the beginning of the 'Bow-ended' carriage development, and the final phase of the 70' passenger coach on the Great Western Railway. The bow end design came about in an effort to improve the gangways at the ends of coaches. Hitherto, the long flexible gangways had always been a source of complaint from nervous passengers when moving from one coach to another. When considering the use of buck-eye couplers on modern stock, it was decided to use a very short corridor gangway, sprung at each corner to take the thrusts usually absorbed by the buffing gear, to drop the buffers out of the way, and use automatic couplers in place of the more usual screw-shackle and hook. So that the gangways could be very short, the ends of the vehicles were bowed out over the couplings in a single arc, and so resulted the 'Bow-ended' stock. When trials of the buck-eye system were running, the Great Western, always cautious and conservative, did not plunge headlong into the scheme but just fitted several trains to observe if results would justify the expenditure of the change. This vehicle, No.2472, was one on which the new system and bow-end was built into one end, whilst the other end was flat and completely standard so that extra vehicles could be added. The official photograph shows the buffers in the lowered position, and *figure 194*, the small picture, illustrates the detail on a dynamo for the period.

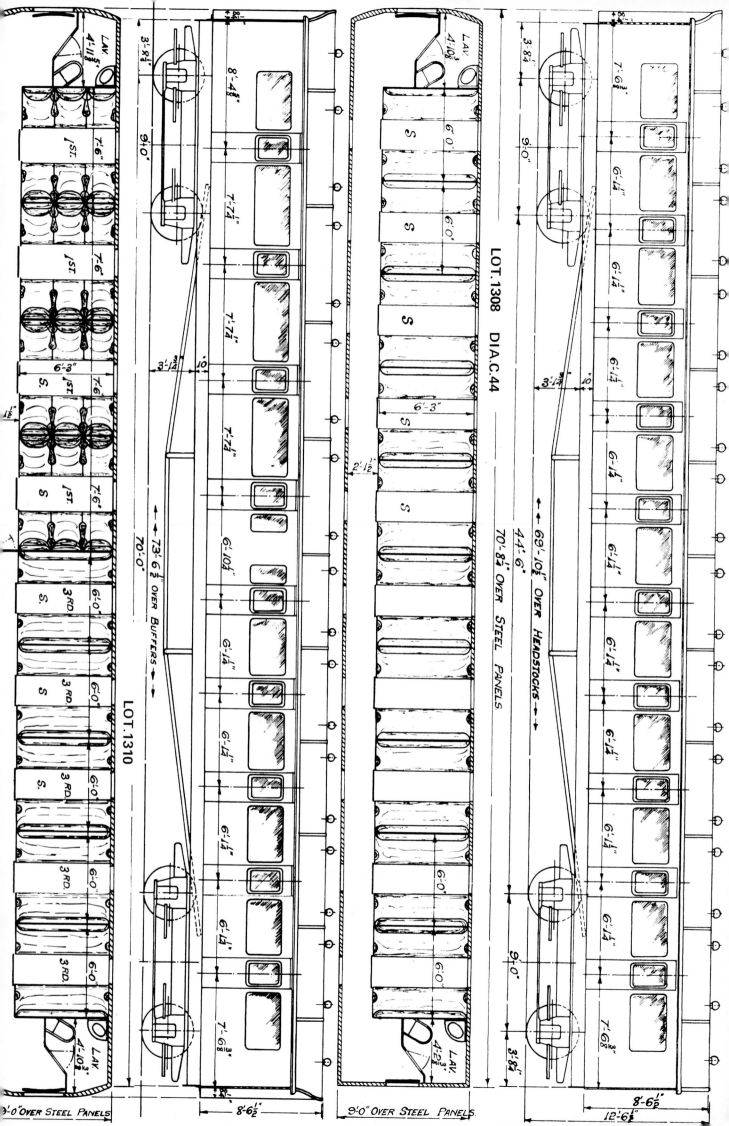

LOT.1308   DIA.C.44

70·8½" OVER STEEL PANELS.

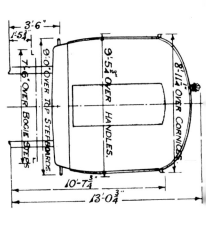

$\dfrac{\text{T. C.}}{\text{TARE } 36\text{-}19}$

— G. W. R. —
THIRD CLASS CARRIAGE.
SWINDON; DECEMBER, 1922.
LOT 1308.
NOS 2472, 2474.

8'-11¼" OVER CORNICE
9'-5¼" OVER HANDLES.
9'-0" OVER TOP STEPBOARDS
7'-6" OVER BOGIE STEPS
3'-6"
1'-5¼"
10'-7¼"
13'-0¾"

FIG 195

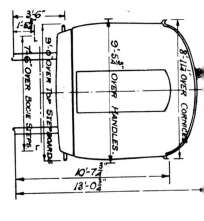

$\dfrac{\text{T. C.}}{\text{TARE } 37\text{-}11}$

— G. W. R. —
COMPOSITE CARRIAGE.
SWINDON; DECEMBER, 1922.
LOT 1310 NOS 7601 & 7604.
" 1319 " 7943, 5.

8'-11¼" OVER CORNICE
9'-5¼" OVER HANDLES.
9'-0" OVER TOP STEPBOARDS
7'-6" OVER BOGIE STEPS
3'-6"
1'-5¼"
10'-7¼"
13'-0¾"

DIA.E.110

FIG 196

The drawings on the previous *page 108*, show the outline and seating plan of the new 70' steel panelled bow-ended stock. That at the top of the page is one to *diagram C.44*, which had one bow-end and collapsible coupling gear, and one flat end and standard headstocks. The lot number was *1308* and running numbers were 2472 to 2475. Below this drawing is a similar 70' vehicle with two bow-ends, a composite built under *lot 1310* to *diagram E.109*, the painted numbers being 7601 to 7604. The end elevations are shown on this page, as it is impossible to get these drawings into the compass of the 12" page if they are to be to 4mm scale. The photograph of No.7604 was taken at Henley-on-Thames in 1947, (*figure 196*). The 7' bogie used for these vehicles is shown in detail in *figure 195*.

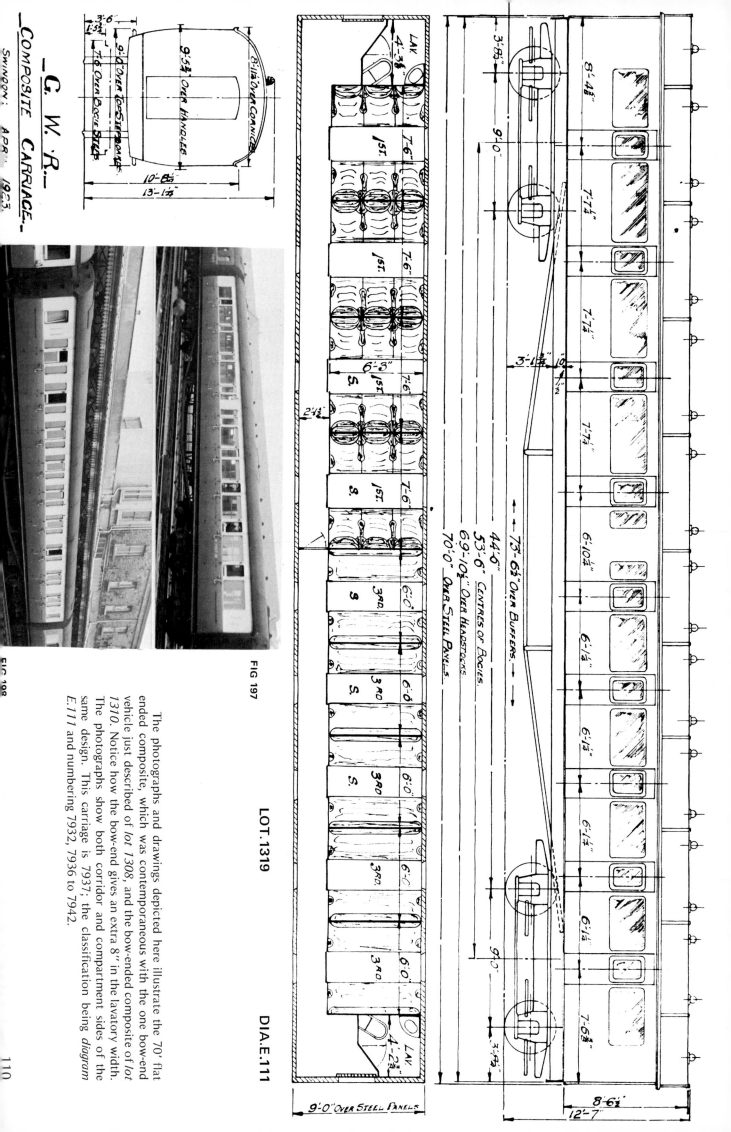

FIG 198

110

G. W. R.

COMPOSITE CARRIAGE.

SWINDON, APRIL 1923.

8'-1¼" OVER CORNICE.

9'-5½" OVER HANDLES

10'-8½"

13'-1¼"

9'-0" OVER TOP STEP BOARDS

7'-6 OVER BODY SIDES

3'-6

3'-3

1'-3½

FIG 197

LOT.1319   DIA.E.111

LAV.
4'-3⅛"

1ST.   7'-6"

1ST.   7'-6"

1ST.   6'-3"   7'-6"

S.

1ST.   7'-6"

S.
2'-4½"

1ST.

3RD.   6'-0"

S.

S.   6'-0"

3RD.

S.

3RD.   6'-0"

S.

3RD.

3RD.   6'-0"

3RD.

LAV.
4'-2⅜"

70'-0" OVER STEEL PANELS

69'-10½" OVER HEADSTOCKS

53'-6" CENTRES OF BOGIES.

44'-6"

73'-6¾" OVER BUFFERS.

3'-8¾"

9'-0"

7'-7¼"

7'-7¼"

3'-1¾"   10"

3"

7'-7¼"

6'-10¼"

6'-1¼"

6'-1¼"

6'-1¼"

6'-1¼"

9'-0"

7'-6⅜"

3'-3⅜

8'-4⅜"

9'-0" OVER STEEL PANELS

8'-6½"

12'-7"

The photographs and drawings depicted here illustrate the 70′ flat ended composite, which was contemporaneous with the one bow-ended vehicle just described of *lot 1308*, and the bow-ended composite of *lot 1310*. Notice how the bow-end gives an extra 8″ in the lavatory width. The photographs show both corridor and compartment sides of the same design. This carriage is 7937, the classification being *diagram E.111* and numbering 7932, 7936 to 7942.

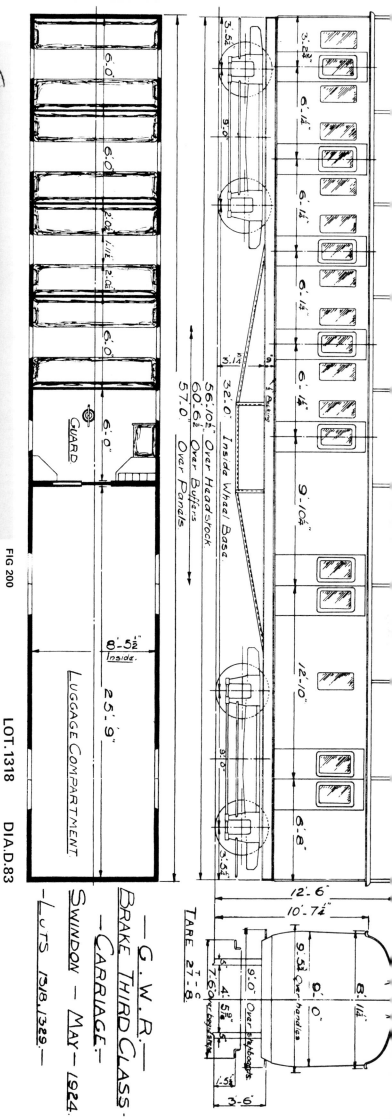

G.W.R.
BRAKE THIRD CLASS
CARRIAGE
SWINDON — MAY — 1924.
LOTS 1318, 1329.

TARE 27-8.

LOT.1318   DIA.D.83

LUGGAGE COMPARTMENT

GUARD.

FIG 199

FIG 200

The drawing of the brake 3rd shown here is of the first series of standard 57' stock which preceded the bow-ended stock proper. *Lot 1318* of 1924 was for ten of these vehicles, which had the same high-waisted sides of the bow-enders but with flat ends similar to the 'Toplights', and were fitted with 9' bogies. These carriages were used for short distance local trains, and really were the forerunners of a long line of suburban stock. Running numbers were 4399 to 4408, built to *diagram D.85*.

In contrast, bottom left shows a photograph of another ex-ambulance brake 3rd of the Toplight Bars 1 pattern, taken in B.R. days, *diagram D.52* and number 3508, *(figure 199.)*

The other official photograph, *figure 200*, is of a Siphon G, *diagram O.11 of lot 1316*, No.1359 shown as built, with white roof, it is worthy of inclusion as it shows the positioning of the 16" lettering on the sides.

111

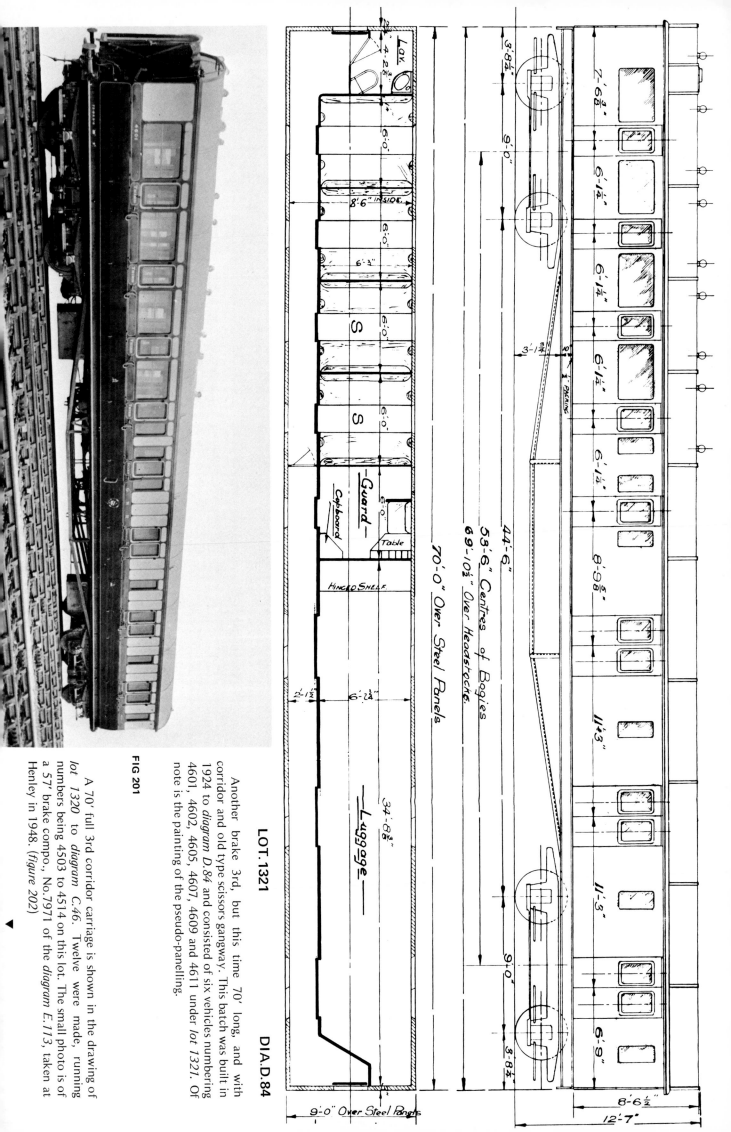

FIG 201

LOT.1321

DIA.D.84

Another brake 3rd, but this time 70' long, and with corridor and old type scissors gangway. This batch was built in 1924 to *diagram D.84* and consisted of six vehicles numbering 4601, 4602, 4605, 4607, 4609 and 4611 under *lot 1321*. Of note is the painting of the pseudo-panelling.

A 70' full 3rd corridor carriage is shown in the drawing of *lot 1320* to *diagram C.46*. Twelve were made, running numbers being 4503 to 4514 on this lot. The small photo is of a 57' brake compo., No.7971 of the *diagram E.113*, taken at Henley in 1948. (*figure 202*)

Lav.
4'2¾"
6'0"
8'6" INSIDE.
6'0"
6'3"
6'0"
S
S
6'0"
— Guard —
Cupboard
Table
Hinged Shelf.
2'1½"
6'2¾"
— Luggage —
34'8⅜"

70'-0" Over Steel Panels

69'-10½" Over Headstocks.

53'-6" Centres of Bogies

44'-6"

3'-8¼"
9'-0"
3-1¾"
9"
1" PACKING

7'-6¾"
6'-1¼"
6'-1¼"
6'-1¼"
6'-1¼"
8'-9⅝"
11'-3"
11'-3"
9'-0"
6'-9"
3'-8¼"
9'-0"

8'-6½"
12'-7"

9'-0" Over Steel Panels

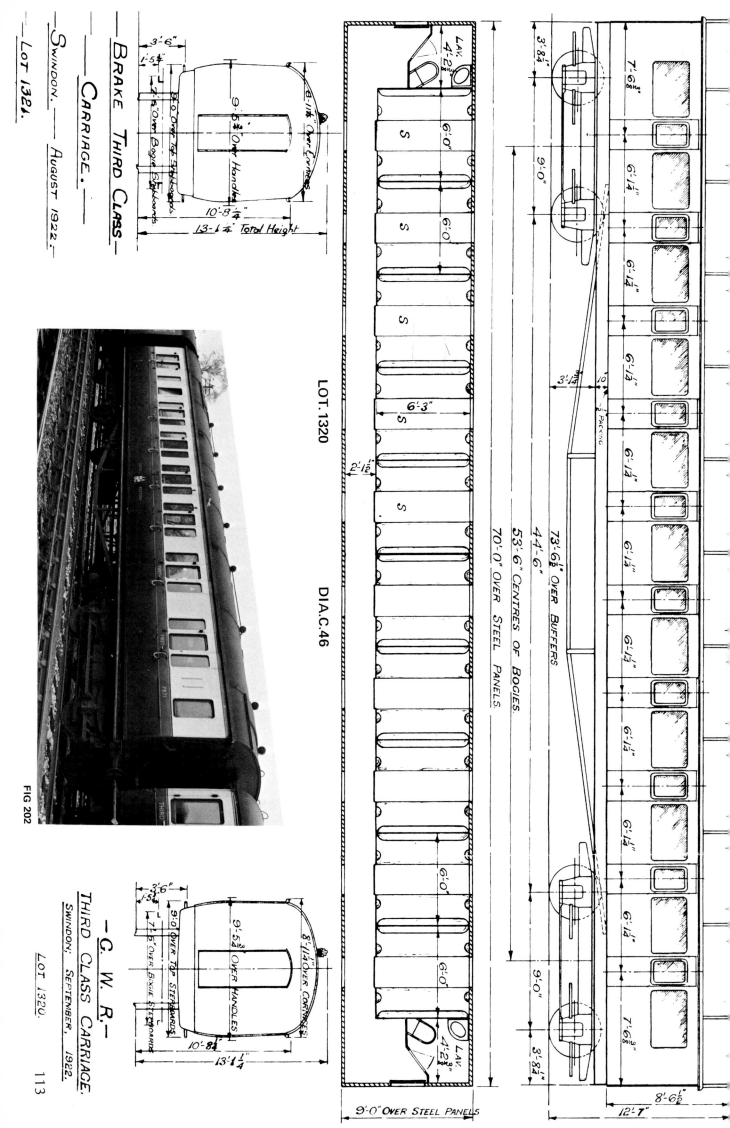

— BRAKE THIRD CLASS —
— CARRIAGE —
SWINDON. — AUGUST 1922. —
— LOT 1321. —

LOT.1320

DIA.C.46

FIG 202

— G. W. R. —
THIRD CLASS CARRIAGE.
SWINDON, SEPTEMBER, 1922.
LOT 1320.

113

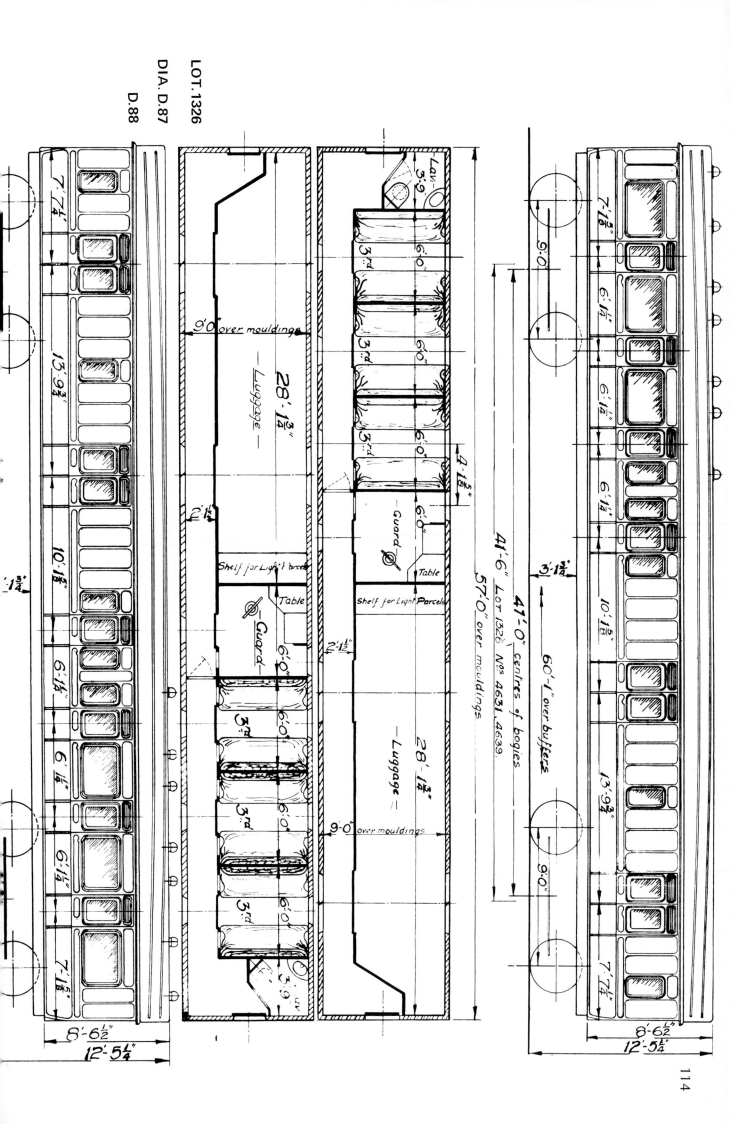

LOT. 1326

DIA. D.87

D.88

9'0" over mouldings

28'-1⅛"
— Luggage —

2'-1½"

Shelf for Light Parcels

Table

Guard

6'-0"

3rd

6'-0"

3rd

6'-0"

3rd

9'0" over mouldings

Lav.
3'-9"

3rd

6'-0"

3rd

6'-0"

3rd

6'-0"

4'-1½"

Guard

Table

Shelf for Light Parcels

28'-1⅛"
— Luggage —

4'-1½"

57'-0" over mouldings

41'-6" LOT 1326. Nᵒˢ 4631, 4639.

41'-0" centres of bogies

60'-1" over buffers

3'-1¾"

9'-0"

9'-0"

7'-7¼"

13'-9¾"

10'-1⅞"

6'-1¼"

6'-1¼"

6'-1¼"

7'-1⅝"

7'-1⅝"

6'-1¼"

6'-1¼"

6'-1¼"

10'-1⅞"

13'-9¾"

7'-7¼"

8'-6½"

12'-5¼"

8'-6½"

12'-5¼"

'-1¾"

114

FIG 203

In Part 1 it has been mentioned how some vehicles were made with right-hand vans and others with left-hand. The method of determining this feature is judged by the location of the van-end when viewing the coach from the corridor side. On this page and the next, we have good examples of this variation. The two drawings show two distinct versions of the 57' Toplight Bars 1, which were rebuilt in 1923 after serving an ambulance stock. The top drawing is to *diagram D.87* and is of the right-hand van type, and the photograph of No.4631 in *figure 204* shows an example of the pattern. The lower drawing is to the left-hand van design, and coach No. 4622 in the picture, *figure 203*, shows this construction. The diagram for left-handed, vans was *D.88*. Running numbers of this batch were 4622/4/6/8/30/2/4/6/8/40 and the *D.87's* were 4621/3/5/7/9/31/3/5/7/9. So it would seem that the even numbers were left-handed and the odd numbers reserved for the right-handed vans.

LOT.1326

DIA.D.87

— G.W.R. —
— BRAKE THIRD CLASS —
— CARRIAGE —

10'-6⅛"
3'-6"
9'0" over Top Slipboards
9'5" over handles
9'0"
7'-7¾" over bogie steps
4'-5½"
1'-5¾"
5"
5"
12'-11¾"

FIG 204

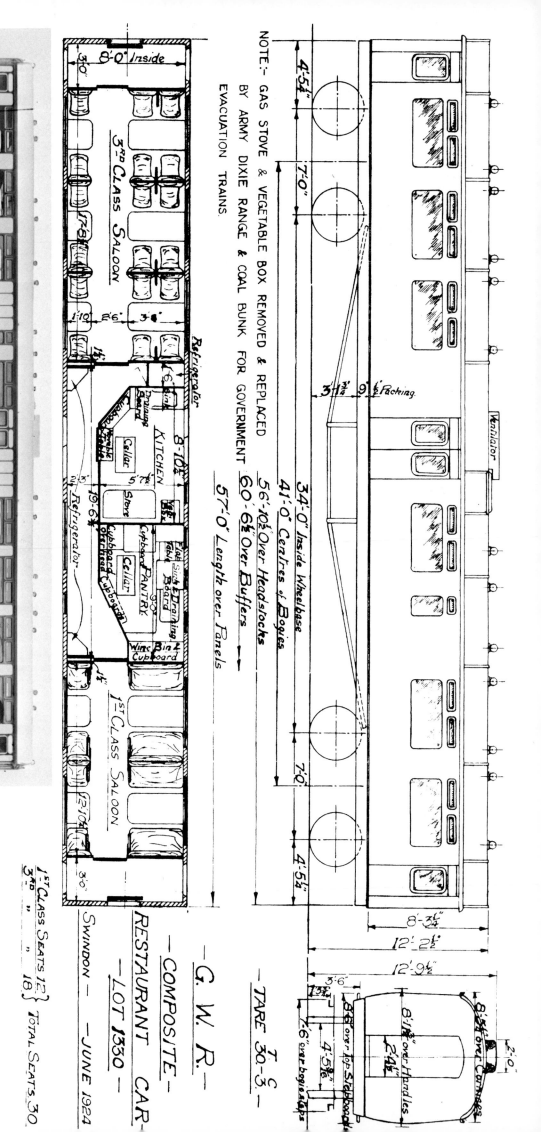

Two restaurant cars are shown here. The drawing illustrates one of the 57' vehicles, which were made for cross-country services other than main line duties. It can be seen from the plan what a comprehensive unit this design was. The kitchen is now situated in the centre with the pantry adjacent, and the 1st and 3rd class saloons are at each end of the carriage with a central gangway. Running on 7' plate bogies, the width was 8'6" over panels and the diagram was

were flat. A 70' version with bow ends is shown in the photograph at the bottom of the page. One of four, these bigger cars were for main line duties on the principal expresses and the one illustrated is No.9568. This diagram and lot were consecutive with the 57' footer, being H.26, lot 1331. Running Numbers 9568 to 71. The livery shown is the early-twenties style, where, although no panels existed, the paint shop has faithfully painted them on to the steel panels!

FIG 205

DIA.H.25

NOTE:- GAS STOVE & VEGETABLE BOX REMOVED & REPLACED BY ARMY DIXIE RANGE & COAL BUNK FOR GOVERNMENT EVACUATION TRAINS.

— G. W. R. —
— COMPOSITE —
— RESTAURANT CAR —
— LOT 1330 —
— SWINDON — — JUNE 1924 —
— TARE 30-3 —

1ST CLASS SEATS 12
3RD " " 18 } TOTAL SEATS 30

3RD CLASS SALOON

1ST CLASS SALOON

KITCHEN

PANTRY

Refrigerator

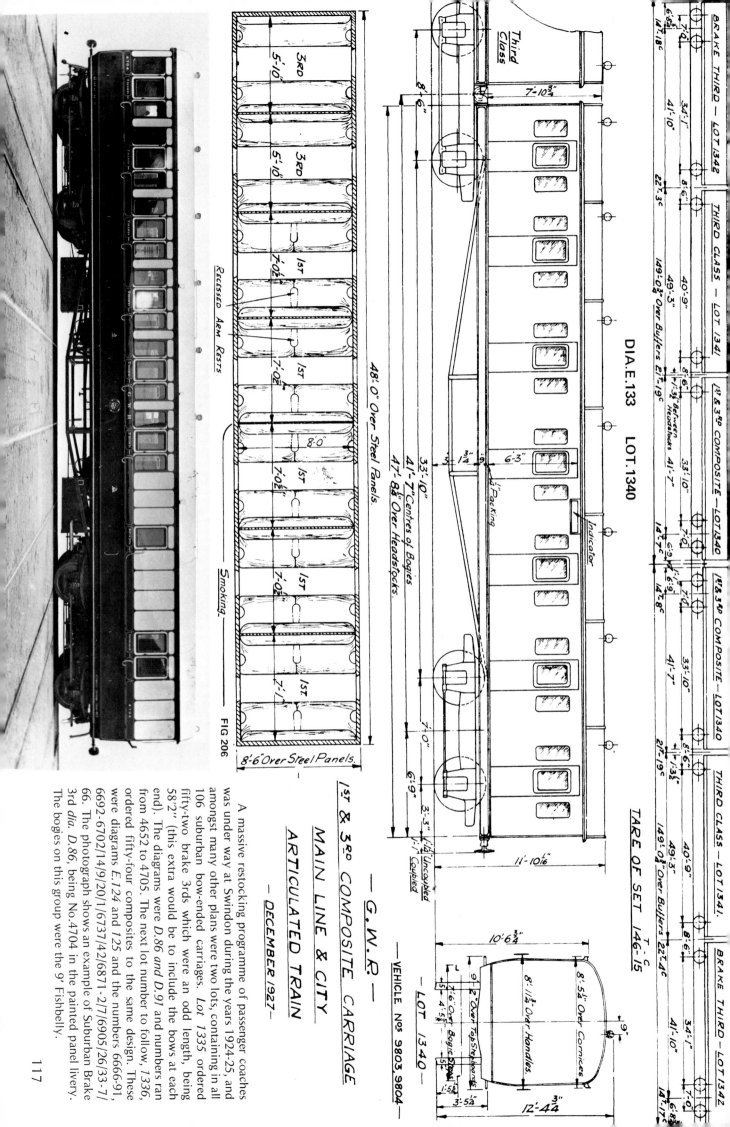

DIA.E.133 LOT.1340

Third Class

TARE OF SET 146-15

BRAKE THIRD — LOT 1342	THIRD CLASS — LOT 1341	1ST & 3RD COMPOSITE — LOT 1340	1ST & 3RD COMPOSITE — LOT 1340	THIRD CLASS — LOT 1341	BRAKE THIRD — LOT 1342

149'-0¾" Over Buffers 21'-19c

FIG 206

48'-0" Over Steel Panels.

8'-6" Over Steel Panels.

Recessed Arm Rests

Smoking.

3RD 5'-10" 3RD 5'-10" 1ST 7'-0½" 1ST 7'-0½" 1ST 7'-0½" 1ST 7'-0½" 1ST 7'-1½"

8'-0"

33'-10"
41'-7" Centres of Bogies
47'-8¼" Over Headstocks.

Indicator

— G.W.R. —
1ST & 3RD COMPOSITE CARRIAGE
MAIN LINE & CITY
ARTICULATED TRAIN
— DECEMBER 1927 —

— VEHICLE Nos 9803 9804 —
— LOT 1340 —

8'-5¼" Over Cornices
8'-11¼" Over Top Steelboards
12'-4¾"

A massive restocking programme of passenger coaches was under way at Swindon during the years 1924-25, and amongst many other plans were two lots, containing in all 106 suburban bow-ended carriages. *Lot* 1335 ordered fifty-two brake 3rds which were an odd length, being 58'2" (this extra would be to include the bows at each end). The diagrams were *D.86 and D.91* and numbers ran from 4652 to 4705. The next lot number to follow, 1336, ordered fifty-four composites to the same design. These were diagrams *E.124* and *E.125* and the numbers 6666-91, 6692-6702/14/9/20/1/6737/42/6871-2/7/6905/26/33-7/ 66. The photograph shows an example of Suburban Brake 3rd *dia. D.86*, being No.4704 in the painted panel livery. The bogies on this group were the 9' Fishbelly.

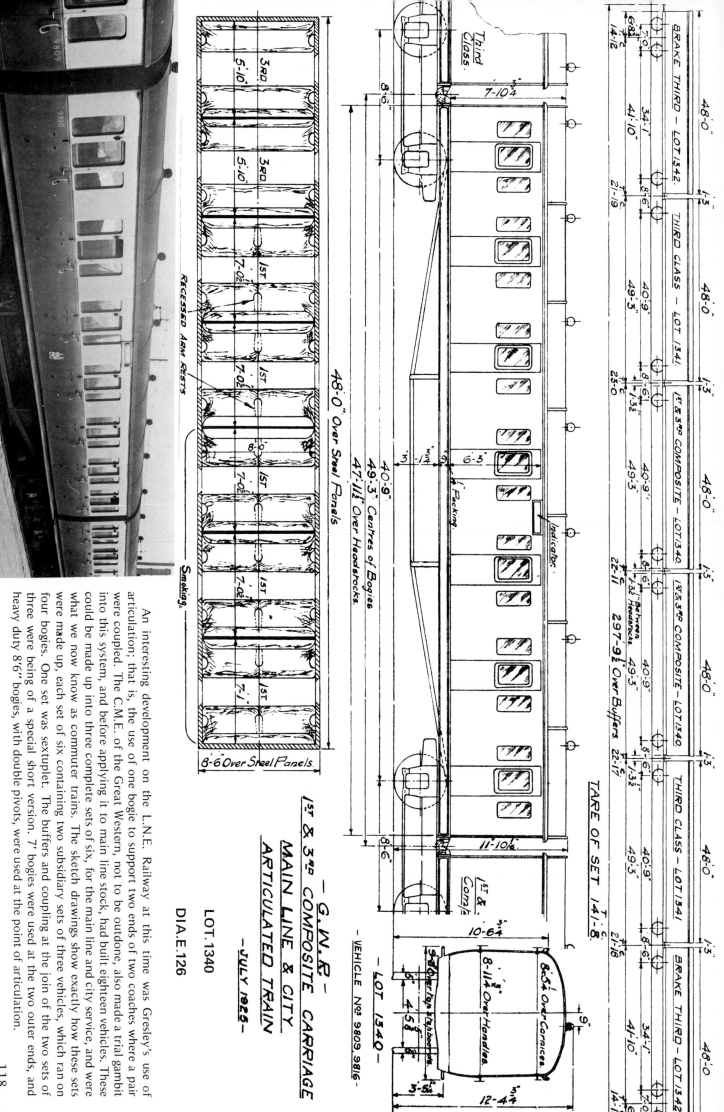

- G.W.R. -
1ST & 3RD COMPOSITE CARRIAGE
MAIN LINE & CITY
ARTICULATED TRAIN
- JULY 1925 -

LOT.1340

DIA.E.126

- VEHICLE Nos 9809, 9816 -

- LOT. 1340 -

TARE OF SET 141-8.

BRAKE THIRD - LOT 1342.

THIRD CLASS - LOT 1341

1ST & 3RD COMPOSITE - LOT 1340

1ST & 3RD COMPOSITE - LOT 1340

THIRD CLASS - LOT 1341

BRAKE THIRD - LOT 1342

Third Class.

1st & Comp.

Indicator

Packing.

8·6 Over Steel Panels.

48·0" Over Steel Panels

47·11½ Over Headstocks.

49·3" Centres of Bogies

40·9"

297·9½ Over Buffers

3RD 5·10½

3RD 5·10

1ST 7·02½

1ST 7·02½

1ST 7·02½

1ST 7·02½

1ST 7·1

8·0

RECESSED ARM RESTS

Smoking.

11·10⅝

10·6¼

12·4⅝

8·11¼ Over Handles.

8·5¼ Over Cornices.

9·6 Over Top Lightboards.

3·5½

An interesting development on the L.N.E. Railway at this time was Gresley's use of articulation; that is, the use of one bogie to support two ends of two coaches where a pair were coupled. The C.M.E. of the Great Western, not to be outdone, also made a trial gambit into this system, and before applying it to main line stock, had built eighteen vehicles. These could be made up into three complete sets of six, for the main line and city service, and were what we now know as commuter trains. The sketch drawings show exactly how these sets were made up, each set of six containing two subsidiary sets of three vehicles, which ran on four bogies. One set was sextuplet. The buffers and coupling at the join of the two outer ends, and three were being of a special short version. 7' bogies were used at the two outer ends, and heavy duty 8'6" bogies, with double pivots, were used at the point of articulation.

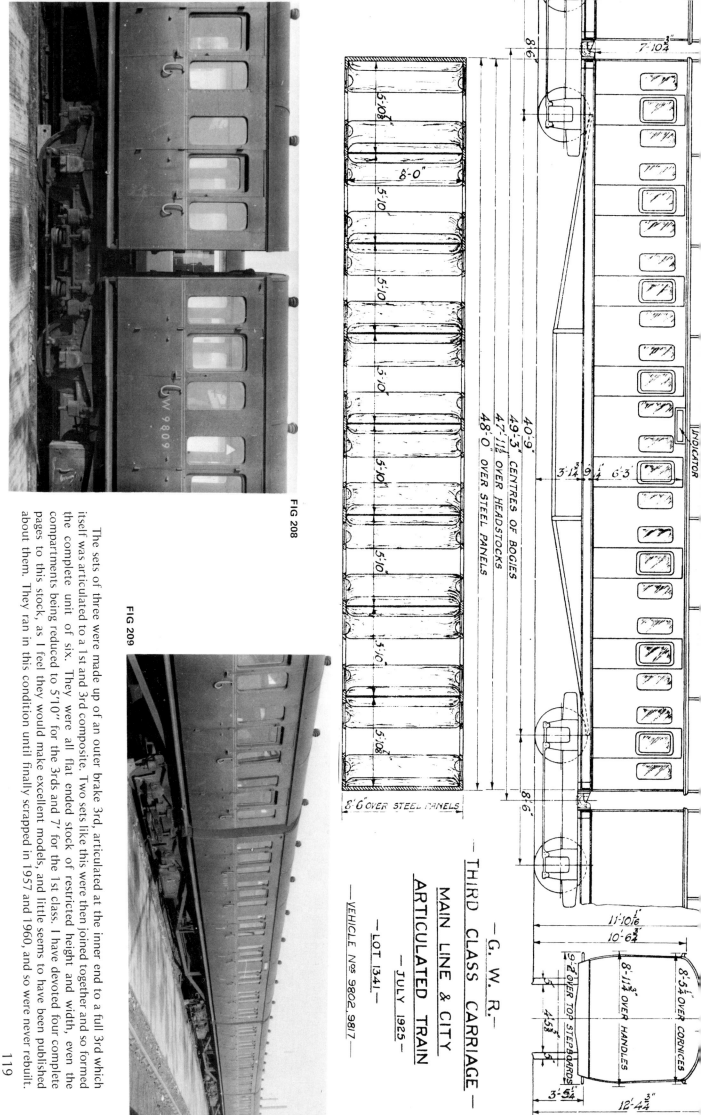

FIG 208

FIG 209

— THIRD CLASS CARRIAGE —
— MAIN LINE & CITY —
— ARTICULATED TRAIN —
— G. W. R. —
— JULY 1925 —
— LOT 1341 —
— VEHICLE Nos 9802, 9817 —

8'6"
7'-10¼"
40'-9"
4'-9'-3" CENTRES OF BOGIES
47'-11⅛" OVER HEADSTOCKS
48'-0" OVER STEEL PANELS
5'-10⅝"
8'-0"
5'-0"
5'-0"
5'-0"
5'-10½"
5'-0"
5'-0"
5'-10⅝"
8'6" OVER STEEL PANELS
INDICATOR
3'-1¼" 9¼" 6'-3"
8'6"
11'-10⅙"
10'-6¼"
8'-5¼" OVER CORNICES
8'-11¾" OVER HANDLES
9'-2" OVER TOP STEPBOARDS
4'-5½"
3'-5¼"
12'-4¾"

The sets of three were made up of an outer brake 3rd, articulated at the inner end to a full 3rd which itself was articulated to a 1st and 3rd composite. Two sets like this were then joined together and so formed the complete unit of six. They were all flat ended stock of restricted height and width, even the compartments being reduced to 5'10" for the 3rds and 7' for the 1st class. I have devoted four complete pages to this stock, as I feel they would make excellent models, and little seems to have been published about them. They ran in this condition until finally scrapped in 1957 and 1960, and so were never rebuilt.

119

Another ex-ambulance vehicle was the *diagram K.36* passenger brake van shown on page 121. The drawing shows the Toplight BARS 1 origin, and top left, *figure 212*, is No.1157 which is branded 'Paddington' and 'Bristol', and which has remained very much as built. Top right, *figure 213*, is another of the same batch, but changed into a medical unit van at Birmingham Snow Hill in 1948. This was No.1159. The lot number in 1925 was *1344* and running numbers were as follows:-

K.34 Nos. 1156/64; K.35 Nos. 2254/5; K.36 Nos 1157-63 *Lot 1344*. K.34 Nos. 116/8
K.37 Nos. 1165 *Lot 1345*

The design was never used again, although main line articulation was tried as will be described later. Lot and running numbers were as follows:-

Lot 1340 composite no's 9803-9804 *diagram C.133*.
No's. 9809/10/5/6 *diagram E.126*.
Lot 1341, Thirds no's 9802/5/8/11/4/7 *diagram C.53*
Lot 1342, Brake 3rds No's 9801/6/7/12/3/8 *diagram D.93*

FIG 210

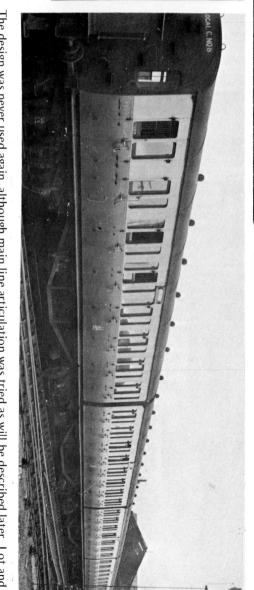

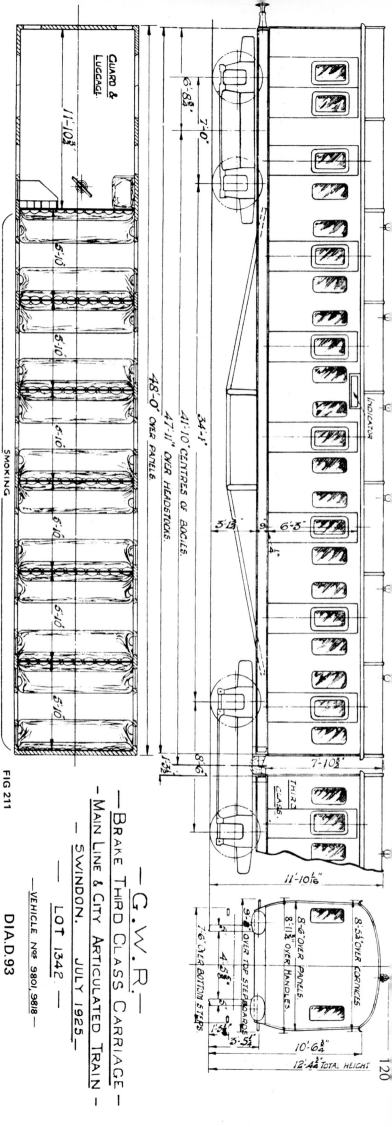

FIG 211

DIA.D.93

GUARD & LUGGAGE

SMOKING

11'-10½"

5'-0"

5'-10"

48'-0" OVER PANELS.

47'-11" OVER HEADSTOCKS.

41'-10" CENTRES OF BOGIES.

34'-1"

7'-0"

6'-8¾"

3'-1¼"

6'-3"

8'-6"

1'-3¼"

7'-10½"

INDICATOR

THIRD CLASS

11'-10¹⁵/₁₆"

7'-6" OVER BOTTOM STEPS

8'-4" OVER PANELS

8'-11½" OVER HANDLES

8'-5¼" OVER CORNICES

4'-5½"

1'-5¼"

3'-5¼"

10'-6¼"

12'-4¼" TOTAL HEIGHT

— G.W.R. —
— BRAKE THIRD CLASS CARRIAGE —
— MAIN LINE & CITY ARTICULATED TRAIN —
— SWINDON, JULY 1925 —
— LOT 1342 —
— VEHICLE Nos 9801, 9818 —

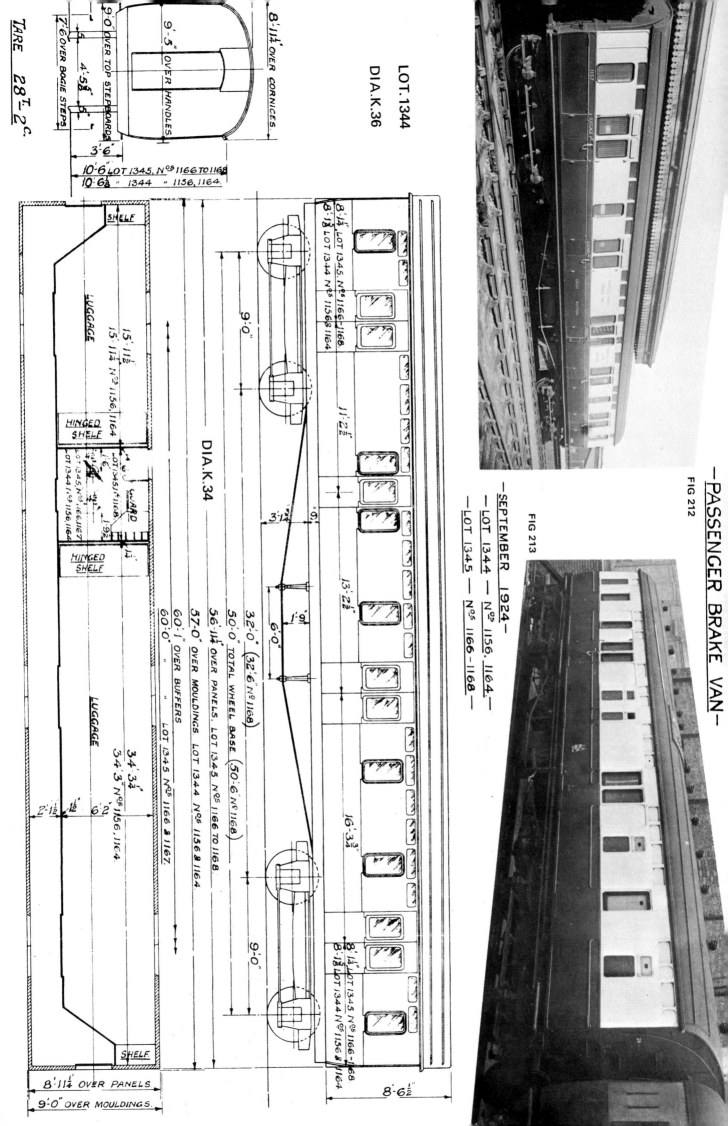

PASSENGER BRAKE VAN

FIG 212

FIG 213

— SEPTEMBER 1924 —
— LOT 1344 — Nᵒˢ 1156, 1164 —
— LOT 1345 — Nᵒˢ 1166 - 1168 —

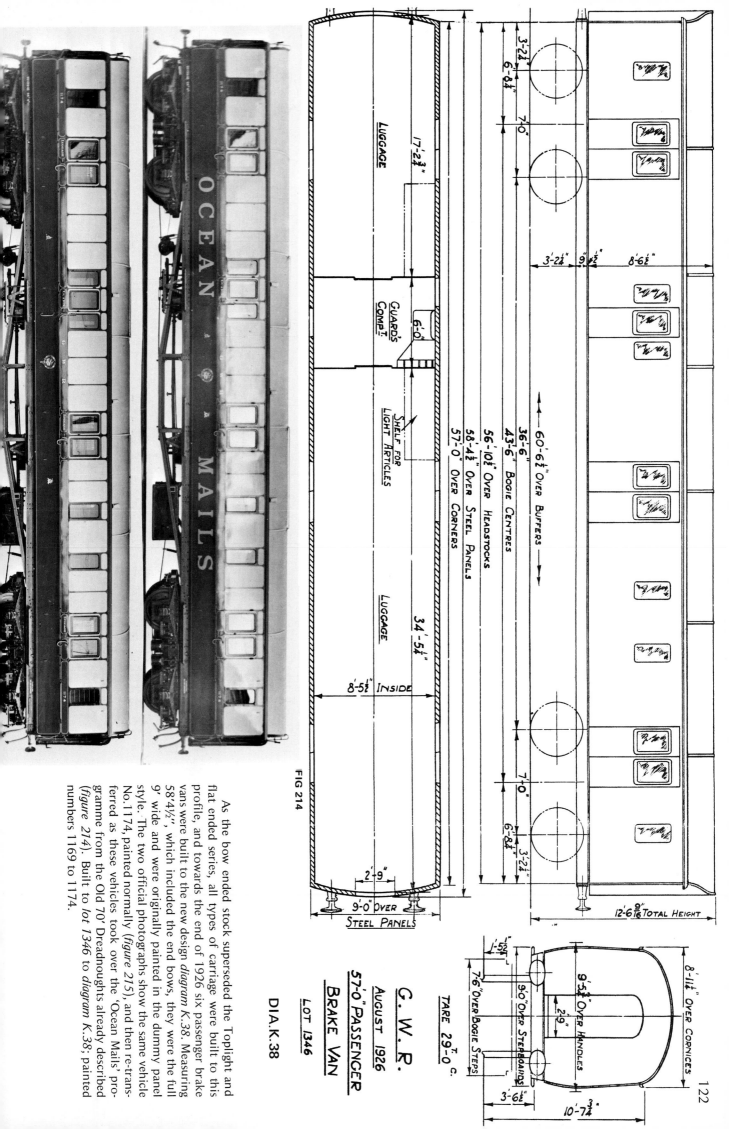

FIG 214

OCEAN MAILS

Diagram labels (plan/elevation):

- LUGGAGE
- GUARDS COMP.T
- SHELF FOR LIGHT ARTICLES
- LUGGAGE
- 17'-2¾"
- 6'-0"
- 34'-5¼"
- 8'-5½" INSIDE
- 60'-6⅝" OVER BUFFERS
- 57'-0" OVER CORNERS
- 58'-4½" OVER STEEL PANELS
- 56'-10½" OVER HEADSTOCKS
- 43'-6" BOGIE CENTRES
- 36'-6"
- 3'-2¼"
- 6'-8¼"
- 7'-0"
- 3'-2¼" 9" 4½" 8'-6½"
- 2'-9"
- 9'-0" OVER STEEL PANELS
- 12'-6⅜" TOTAL HEIGHT
- 5¼"
- 9'-0" OVER STEPBOARDS
- 9'-5¾"
- 2'-9"
- 7'-6" OVER BOGIE STEPS
- 8'-11¼" OVER CORNICES
- 3'-6⅛"
- 10'-7¾"

TARE 29 T.0 c.

DIA. K.38

G.W.R.

AUGUST 1926

57'-0" PASSENGER

BRAKE VAN

LOT 1346

122

As the bow ended stock superseded the Toplight and flat ended series, all types of carriage were built to this profile, and towards the end of 1926 six passenger brake vans were built to the new design *diagram K.38*. Measuring 58'4½", which included the end bows, they were the full 9' wide and were originally painted in the dummy panel style. The two official photographs show the same vehicle No.1174, painted normally (*figure 215*), and then re-transferred as these vehicles took over the 'Ocean Mails' programme from the Old 70' Dreadnoughts already described (*figure 214*). Built to *lot 1346* to *diagram K.38*; painted numbers 1169 to 1174.

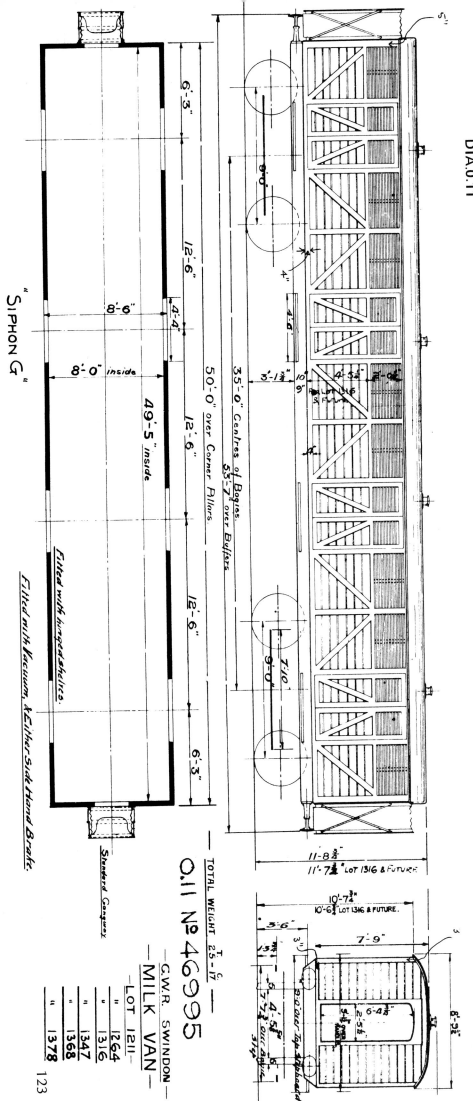

I make no excuse for showing another Siphon G similar to that on *page 73*, as this vehicle, although to the same classification, *diagram O.11*, as previously, was not built until this period of 1925. The drawing shows all the dimensions necessary for a good model, but the diagonals again look suspect, and Jim Whittaker suggests following the photograph rather then the drawing. My picture, *figure 216* taken at Henley in 1949, shows heavy angle iron trussing has replaced the 'Bars 1' and electricity superseded gas for illumination; also roof board brackets have appeared. *Lot 1347* to 1925 was for Nos. 1290 to 1309 inclusive.

LOT.1347

DIA.0.11

FIG 216

"SIPHON G"

Fitted with hinged shelves.

Fitted with Vacuum, & Either Side Hand Brake.

Standard Gangway.

O.11 No 46995

TOTAL WEIGHT 25-17

— G.W.R. SWINDON —

— MILK VAN —

— LOT 1211 —

123

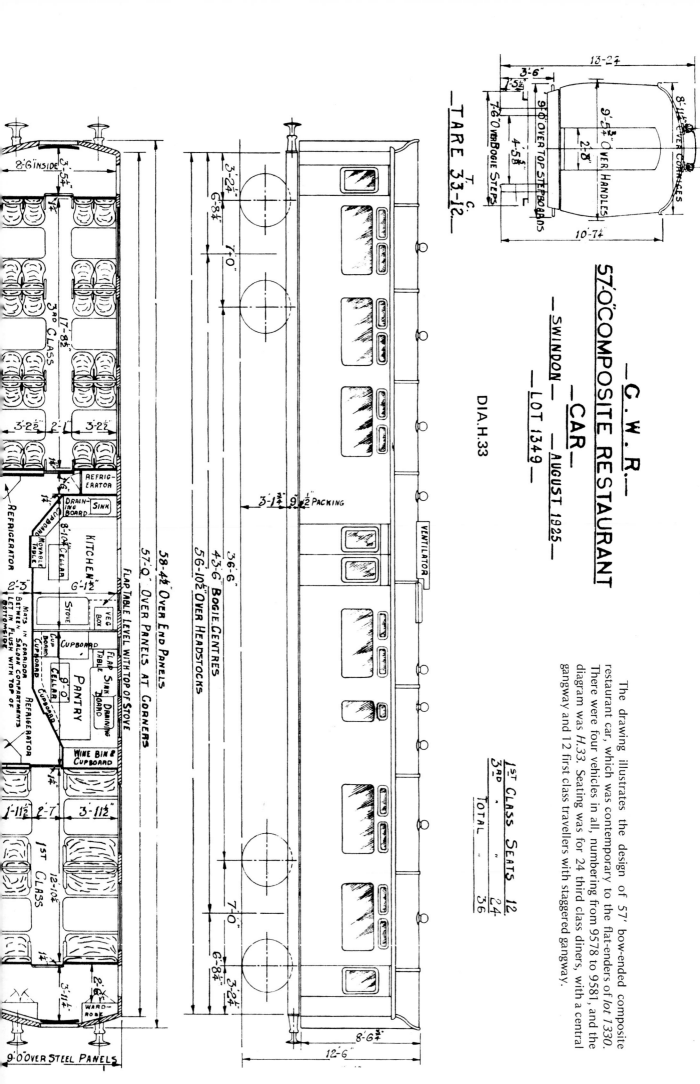

— G.W.R. —
57'0" COMPOSITE RESTAURANT CAR
— SWINDON —
— LOT 1349 — AUGUST 1925 —

DIA. H.33

TARE 33-12.

The drawing illustrates the design of 57' bow-ended composite restaurant car, which was contemporary to the flat-enders of lot 1330. There were four vehicles in all, numbering from 9578 to 9581, and the diagram was *H.33*. Seating was for 24 third class diners, with a central gangway and 12 first class travellers with staggered gangway.

1ST CLASS SEATS	12
3RD	24
TOTAL	36

9-5¾" OVER TOP STEPBOARDS
7-6" OVER BOGIE STEPS
8-11½" OVER CORNICES
13-2¾"
3-6"
5¾"
9-5¾" OVER HANDLES
2-8"
4-5¾"
2-5¾"
10-7¼"

3-5¾"
8-6" INSIDE
3RD CLASS
17-8½"
3-2¾" 2-1" 3-2¾"
REFRIGERATOR
DRAINING BOARD SINK
8-10¾" CELLAR
CUPBOARD
MOVABLE TABLE
KITCHEN
6-1½"
STOVE
VEG BOX
CUP BOARD CUPBOARD
CELLAR
PANTRY 9-0"
FLAP TABLE
SINK DRAINING BOARD
CUPBOARD
WINE BIN & CUPBOARD
REFRIGERATOR
REFRIGERATOR
MATS IN CORRIDOR BETWEEN SALOON COMPARTMENTS LET IN FLUSH WITH TOP OF BOTTOMSIDE
2-3"
1-11½" 2-7" 3-11½"
1ST CLASS
12-10½"
3-11½"
2-2"
WARDROBE
9-0" OVER STEEL PANELS

3-2¾"
6-8¼"
7-0"
3-1¾" 9½" PACKING
36-6"
43-6" BOGIE CENTRES
56-10½" OVER HEADSTOCKS
57-0" OVER PANELS AT CORNERS
58-4½" OVER END PANELS
FLAP TABLE LEVEL WITH TOP OF STOVE

VENTILATOR
7-0"
6-8¼"
3-2¾"
8-6¾"
12-6"

DIA.C.46

The general design of main line stock had now been standardised at 57' with bow-ends making the length 16½' longer. The widths settled at 9' over panels and height from rail head 126"; bogies were now of the new 7' plate design, but the stock was still being painted with pseudo-panels. The picture in *figure 217* shows the livery of the 1925's which has the garter crests and the two motifs separated by two compartments. This full 3rd, 70' carriage was No.4748 of *lot 1337, diagram C.46* and is placed here to show a comparison with the evolving 57' standard length brake 3rd. Of particular interest, also as this series of *diagram C.46,* were the last 70' carriages (apart from trailer cars) to be built for main line expresses.

The drawing depicts the brake 3rd of which eighteen were made under two consecutive *lots, Nos.1353* and *1354.* Diagram was *D.94* and running numbers 4751-62 and 4763-9.

FIG 217

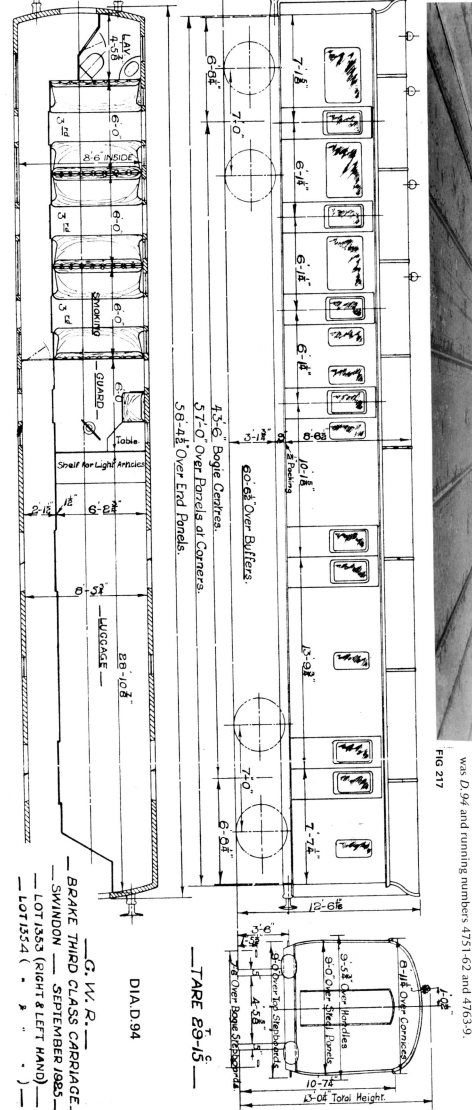

— G.W.R. —
— BRAKE THIRD CLASS CARRIAGE. —
— SWINDON — SEPTEMBER 1925 —
— LOT 1353 (RIGHT & LEFT HAND) —
— LOT 1354 („ „ „) —

DIA.D.94

— TARE 29-15 —

FIG 219

LOT. 1355
DIA. E. 129

FIG 218

We come now to illustrations of the 'B' sets. These formations were of two similar coaches of non-corridor, Brake composite design, and they were built to work branch line and local services in lieu of, and supplementing, the autocar services. They were unusual in that the outward ends were bowed, whilst the inner close-coupled ends were also bowed. I could never see any sense in this, because internally the arc of the bowed ends was straightened out with a false wall!!! It will be seen from the official pictures on this page that when built the pairs were painted in the pseudo-panelled chocolate and cream style. The 'B' set in *figure 218* and the individual brake composite No.6565 (*figure 219*,) were amongst the prototypes of these paired sets and ran on 9' bogies; subsequent lots were fitted with the 7' plate bogie.

Running Nos. of *lot 1355* were 6545/7/51/3/6/60/1/3/6 and the design was *diagram E.129.*

Two detail photographs of the original batch of 'B' set design are shown here. On the left, *figure 220,* the system of close coupling can be seen. Two channel section plates are slotted in their centres through which extends the coupling bar proper. Permanently in contact with each other in compression, the channel plates serve as buffing gear on curves. Vacuum and steam hoses can be seen, vacuum on the left and steam on the right. The small flexible hose is the electricity control of the lighting from panels in the guard's compartment. Of particular interest is the close-up of the pseudo-panel painting; there were no panels but the paint shop still painted them in! The gear at the top of the ends is the butterfly valves for the "Emergency Cord". In the position shown the valves are shut; when the chain is pulled, these butterflies are upright.

FIG 220

FIG 221

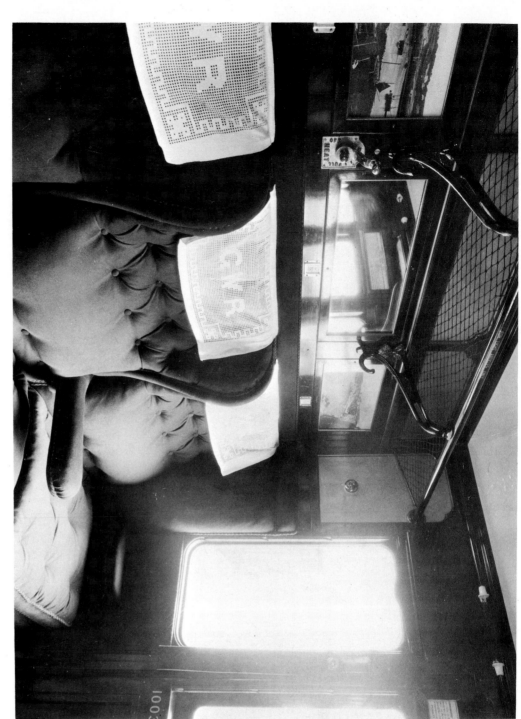

FIG 222

The next five pages are devoted to that interesting experiment, the main line articulation sets. Having tried out the system on the suburban sets already mentioned, plans were formulated to proceed with the express version. As before, the trains were to be in two and three car sets, all coupled together to form an eight coach express rather than one long articulated train. This was, of course, to gain the advantages of articulation by the saving of bogies, but to avoid the whole train being immobilized due to the failure of any one vehicle. To make up the expresses, the stock was compiled thus:— from the engine backward: one brake 3rd and two 3rds as a set of three, followed by a set of two vehicles, a 3rd dining saloon, a kitchen car, and a 1st class diner as a set of three, then a 3rd dining saloon, a 1st class carriage and a brake 1st on three bogies. This first page shows the drawing of the 1st class diner, *diagram H.30* with an official photograph of the 3 car dining set as built (*figure 224*), and below, the 1st class diner as converted to individual stock in the mid-thirties (*figure 223*).

Figure 222 gives a good idea of the interior of a main line 1st class compartment in the 1920's. The upholstery was dark chocolate in colour, with white antimacassars at the back of every seat. The arm-rests were folding, rising upwards to make room for the seating of four passengers instead of three. Soft leather arm slings were affixed to the door styles and there were four electric lamps per compartment, which had individual switches in each corner. The small brass ticket holders were for seat reservation numbers, and one can just see the communication cord in the top right. Note the carriage class on the door plus the number of the vehicle and the letter 'A' denoting it was the first compartment in the carriage. Incidentally, the number 10033 tells that this was one of the articulated first class vehicles of *diagram A.16, lot 1363*.

It is of interest to note that in 1936, when the artics were converted to individual coaches, they were re-trimmed internally, and *figure 230* on page 133 shows the new upholstery of the same vehicle.

DIA.A.16

128

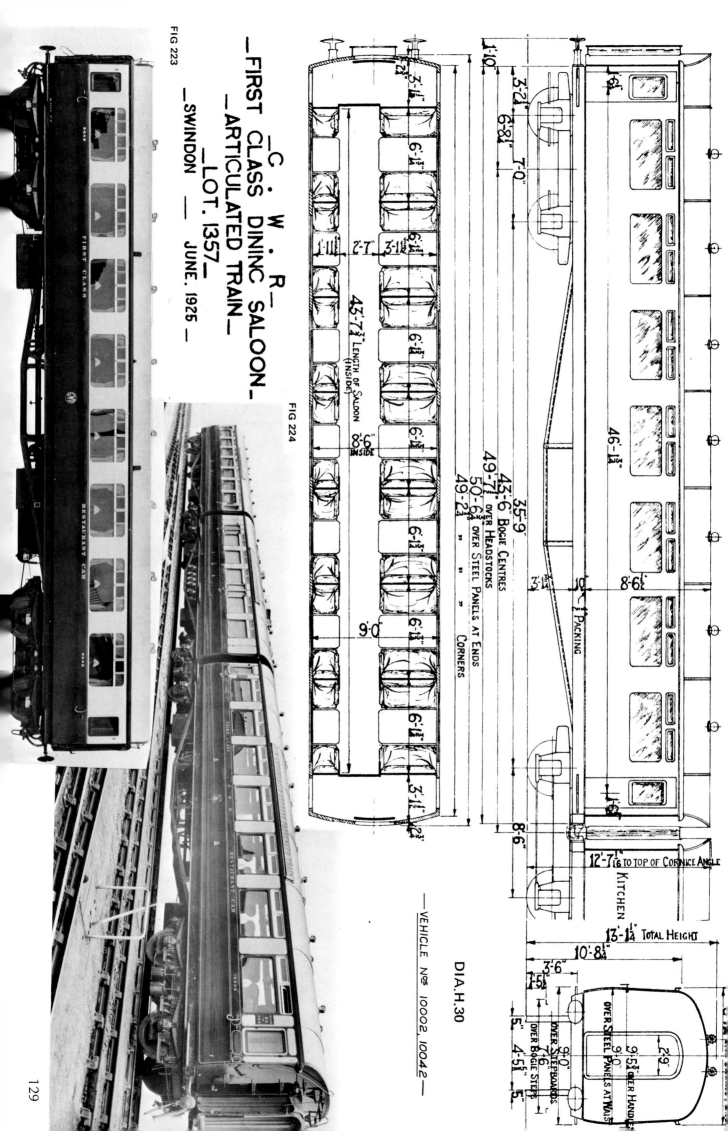

FIG 223

FIG 224

— G · W · R —
— FIRST CLASS DININC SALOON —
— ARTICULATED TRAIN —
— LOT. 1357 —
— SWINDON — JUNE. 1925 —

DIA. H.30

— VEHICLE N⁰S 10002, 10042 —

43'-7¾" LENGTH OF SALOON (INSIDE)

8'-6" INSIDE

9'-0"

35'-9"
43'-6" OVER HEADSTOCKS
49'-7½" BOGIE CENTRES
50'-6¾" OVER STEEL PANELS AT ENDS
49'-2¾" " " " CORNERS

46'-1¾"

8'-6½"

PACKING

12'-7½" IS TO TOP OF CORNICE ANGLE

KITCHEN

13'-1¼" TOTAL HEIGHT

10'-8¼"

9'-5¾" OVER HANDLES
9'-0" OVER STEEL PANELS AT WAIST
9'-0" OVER STEPBOARDS
OVER BOGIE STEPS

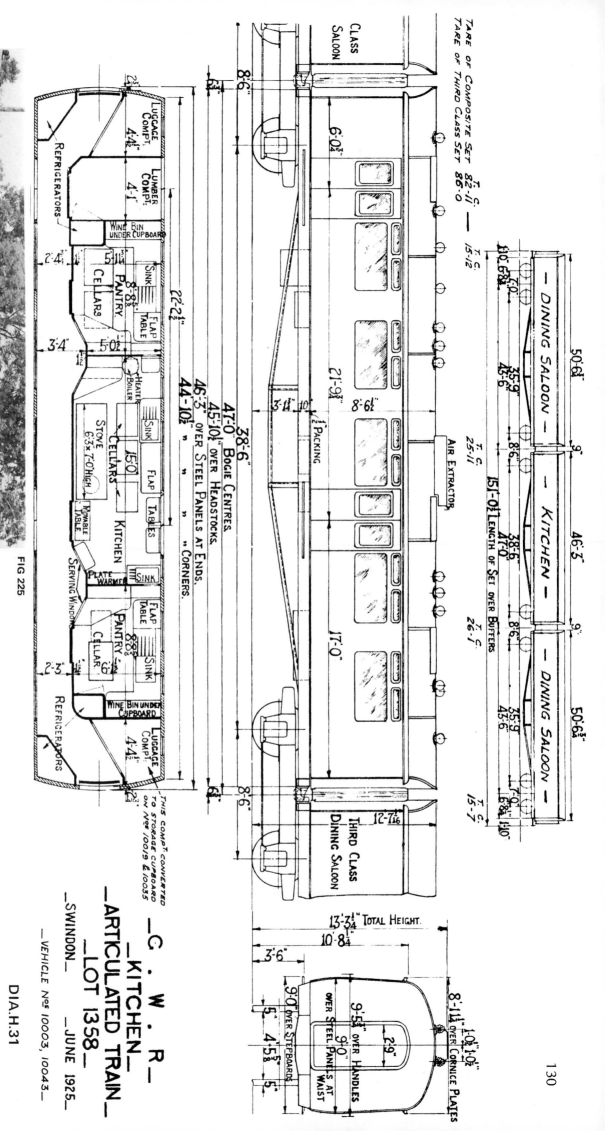

FIG 225

The drawing illustrated the kitchen car and shows the comprehensive interior fittings, whilst the photograph depicts No.9659 (re-numbered) at Henley, when rebuilt as a separate coach, (figure 225). The diagram was *H.31*. Note that the vehicle has been lengthened at each end.

DIA.H.31

— G. W. R —
— KITCHEN —
— ARTICULATED TRAIN —
— LOT 1358 —
— SWINDON —
— JUNE 1925 —
— VEHICLE Nos 10003, 10043 —

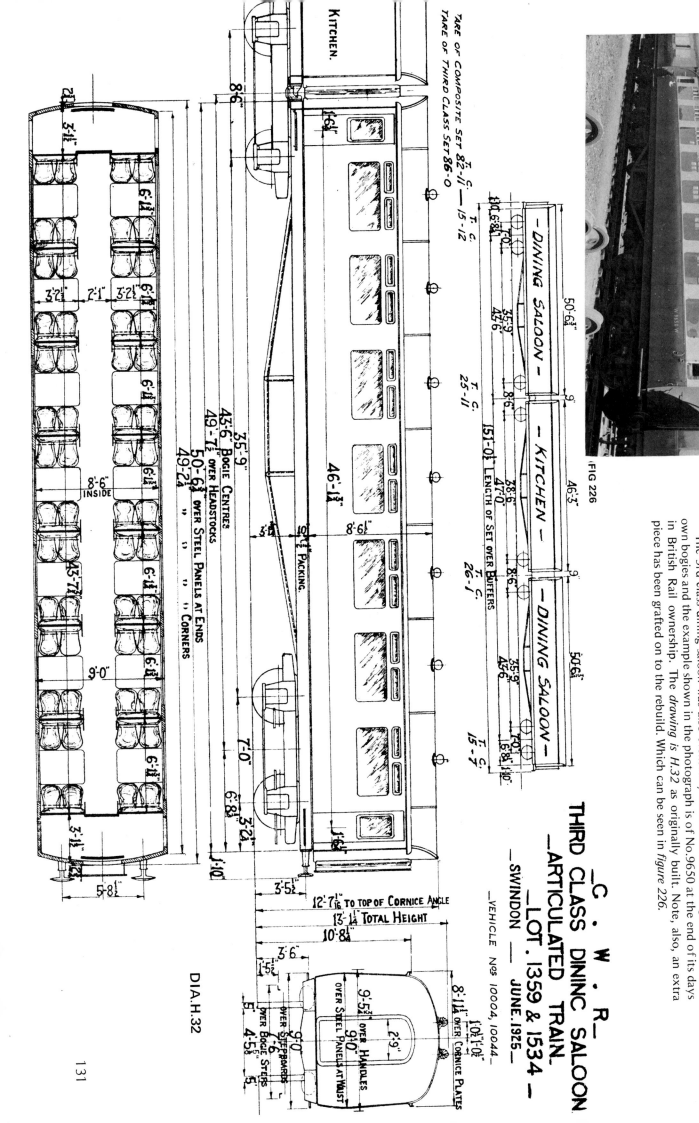

The 3rd class dining saloon was also eventually converted to a carriage running on its own bogies and the example shown in the photograph is of No.9650 at the end of its days in British Rail ownership. The *drawing* is H.32 as originally built. Note, also, an extra piece has been grafted on to the rebuild. Which can be seen in *figure 226.*

(FIG 226)

DINING SALOON.

KITCHEN.

DINING SALOON.

— G · W · R —
THIRD CLASS DINING SALOON
— ARTICULATED TRAIN. —
— LOT . 1359 & 1534 —
— SWINDON —   JUNE. 1925.
— VEHICLE Nos 10004, 10044 —

DIA. H.32

KITCHEN.

TARE OF COMPOSITE SET 82-11
TARE OF THIRD CLASS SET 86-0

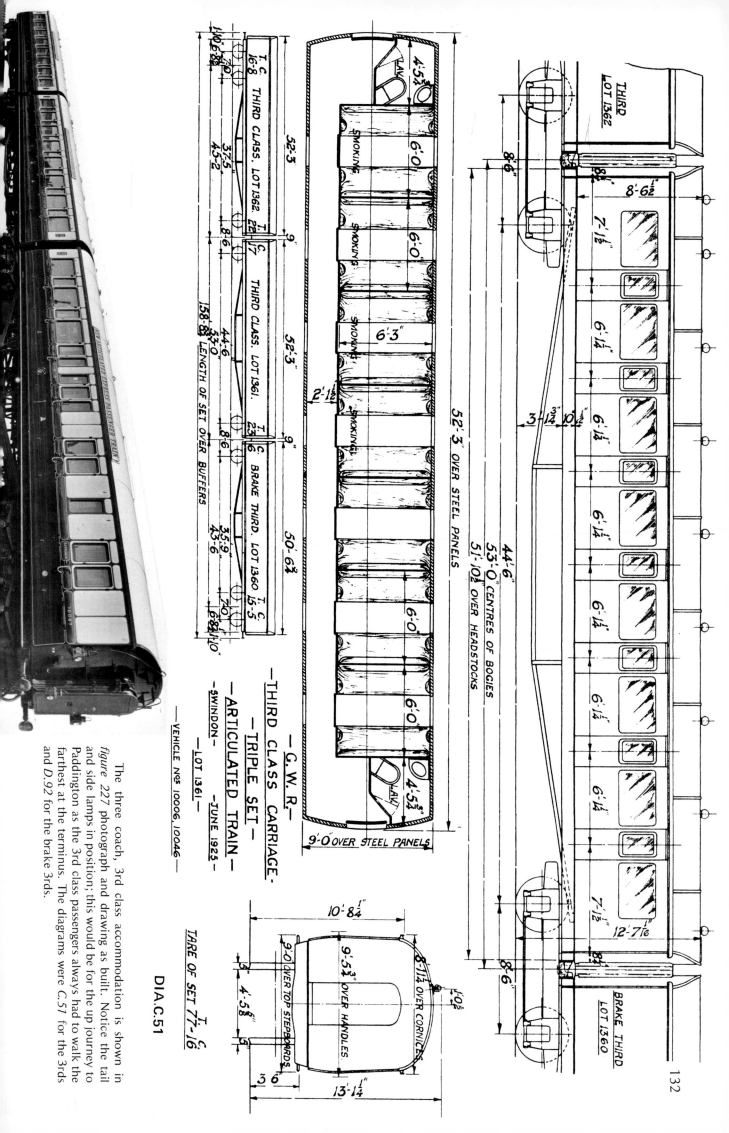

— G.W.R. —
— THIRD CLASS CARRIAGE —
— TRIPLE SET —
— ARTICULATED TRAIN —
— SWINDON —
— JUNE 1925 —
— LOT 1361 —

— VEHICLE Nos 10006, 10046 —

TARE OF SET 77-16 T.C.

DIA.C.51

THIRD LOT 1362

BRAKE THIRD LOT 1360

THIRD CLASS. LOT 1362.

THIRD CLASS. LOT 1361.

BRAKE THIRD. LOT 1360.

9'-0" OVER STEEL PANELS

52'-3" OVER STEEL PANELS

53'-0" CENTRES OF BOGIES

51'-10½" OVER HEADSTOCKS

158'-8½" LENGTH OF SET OVER BUFFERS

The three coach, 3rd class accommodation is shown in figure 227 photograph and drawing as built. Notice the tail and side lamps in position; this would be for the up journey to Paddington as the 3rd class passengers always had to walk the farthest at the terminus. The diagrams were C.51 for the 3rds and D.92 for the brake 3rds.

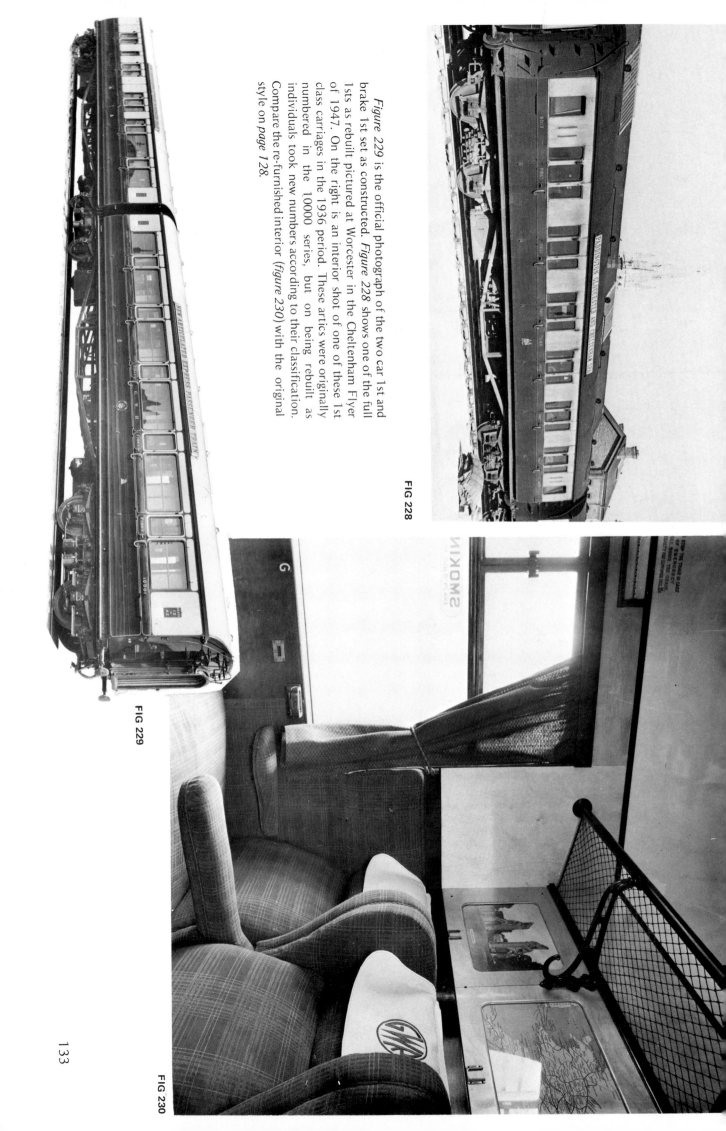

FIG 228

FIG 229

FIG 230

Figure 229 is the official photograph of the two car 1st and brake 1st set as constructed. Figure 228 shows one of the full 1sts as rebuilt pictured at Worcester in the Cheltenham Flyer of 1947. On the right is an interior shot of one of these 1st class carriages in the 1936 period. These artics were originally numbered in the 10000 series, but on being rebuilt as individuals took new numbers according to their classification. Compare the re-furnished interior (*figure 230*) with the original style on *page 128*.

FIG 231

DIA.W.7

Another Beetle C is shown on the top left of this page, built to *diagram W.7*. This brown vehicle's number was 219.

At the top right is one of the ventilated Fruit Ds. This example is an official picture of the type which was dual fitted with both patterns of brake, vacuum and Westinghouse. The diagram was Y.3. When fitted with just vacuum brakes, vehicles were coded "Fruit C".

The *diagram O.22* referred to a Siphon G design of 1926 in which the frames have gone inside instead of being outside as previously, and the sides are horizontally planked right up to the louvres. Made under three lots Nos. were *lot 1370* No. 1270 of 1926; *lot 1385* No. 1227-1237 of 1929; *lot 1396* No. 1186-1200 of 1929.

This photograph is of another model built by Jim Whittaker, and is included not only to show the excellence of the work, but to show the differences between the O.11 design and the O.22's. Note particularly the superb model 9' volute bogies on this miniature (*figure 233*).

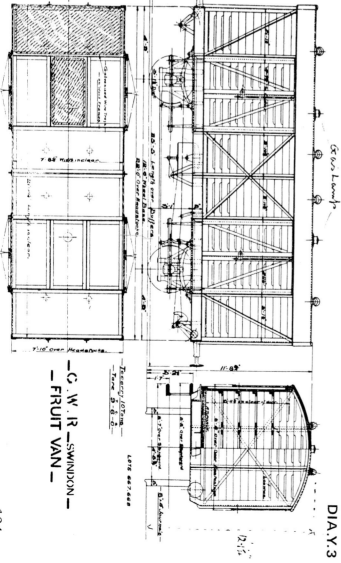

FIG 232

DIA.Y.3

— G. W. R —SWINDON—
— FRUIT VAN —

134

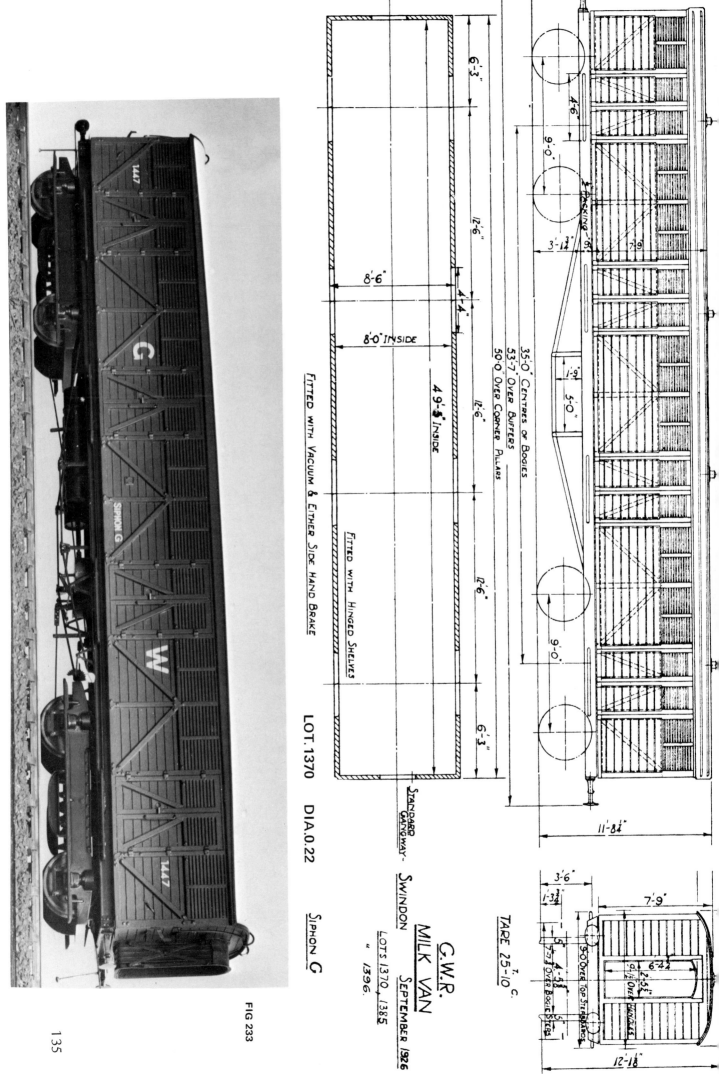

FIG 233

FITTED WITH VACUUM & EITHER SIDE HAND BRAKE

LOT.1370   DIA.0.22   SIPHON G

FITTED WITH HINGED SHELVES

STANDARD GANGWAY

35'-0" CENTRES OF BOGIES
53'-7" OVER BUFFERS
50'-0" OVER CORNER PILLARS

G.W.R.
MILK VAN
SWINDON   SEPTEMBER 1926
LOTS 1370, 1385
" 1396.

TARE 25-10 T. C.

6'-3"   12'-6"   12'-6"   6'-3"

8'-6"

8'-0" INSIDE

4'-9⅝" INSIDE

4'-4"

9'-0"   9'-0"

4'-6"

3'-1¼"   PACKING

1'-9"   5'-0"   7'-9"

11'-8¼"

3'-6"   7'-9"
1'-3¾"
9'-0" OVER TOP STEP BOARDS
4'-5⅝"
2'-5⅝"
9½" OVER HANDLES
6'-4¼"
7'-3" OVER BOGIE STEPS
12'-1⅛"

FIG 234

FIG 236

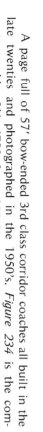

FIG 238

A page full of 57' bow-ended 3rd class corridor coaches all built in the late twenties and photographed in the 1950's. Figure 234 is the compartment side of No.4789, figure 235 the same side of No. 4800. Figure 236 is the corridor side of No.4859, and figure 237 ditto of 4796 and bottom

FIG 237

FIG 235

left, figure 238 is No.5150 in Swindon station. All these carriages were built to diagram C.54 to seven lots from 1926 to 1929.

Some running numbers were 4557-62, 477-4854, 4857-80, 4881-4912, 5001-5086, 5145-54, 5156-80.

LOT. 1369

DIA.C.54

136

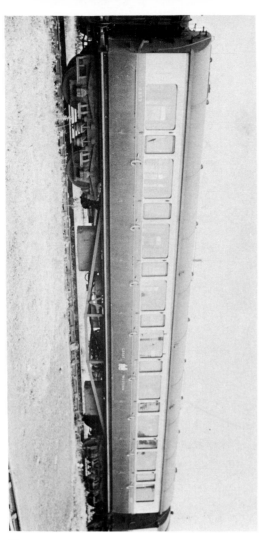

FIG 239

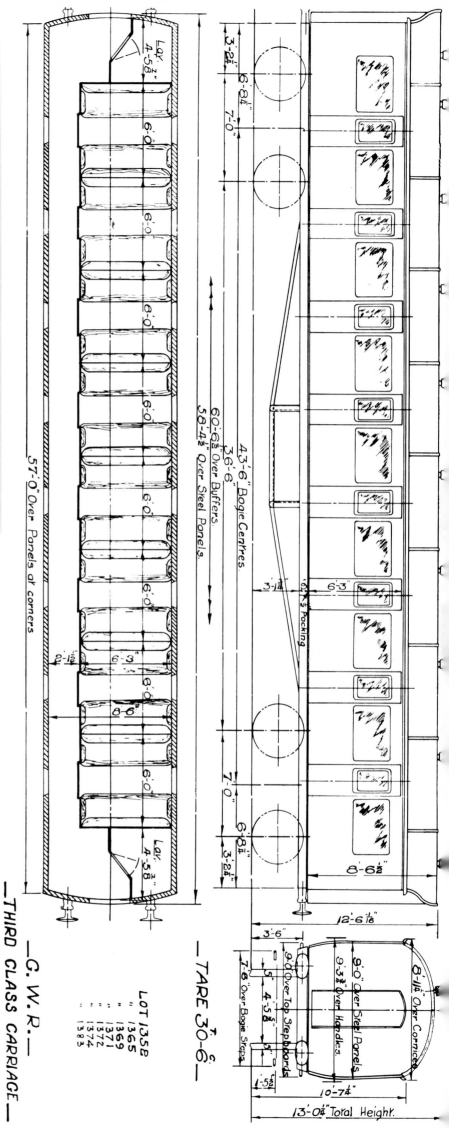

Lay:
4-5⅛"

6'-0"

6'-0"

6'-0"

6'-0"

6'-0"

6'-0"

6'-3"

6'-0"

8'-6"

2-1½"

6'-0"

Lay:
4-5⅛"

57'-0" Over Panels at corners

58-4½" Over Steel Panels.

60-6⅝" Over Buffers

36'-6"

43'-6" Bogie Centres.

3-2¼"

6-8¼"

7'-0"

3-1¼"

6'-3"

6"⅜ Packing

7'-0"

6-8¼"

3-2¼"

8'-6½"

12'-6⅞"

8'-11¼" Over Cornices

3'-6"

7'-6" Over Bogie Steps

9'-0" Over Top Stepboards

9'-0" Over Steel Panels

9'-3¾" Over Handles

5'-4⅝"

5"

1-5⅜"

10'-7¼"

13'-0¾" Total Height.

— G. W. R. —

— TARE 30-6 —

LOT 1358
,, 1365
,, 1369
,, 1371
,, 1372
,, 1374
,, 1383

— THIRD CLASS CARRIAGE —

— SWINDON — JANUARY 1923 —

LOT.1374
DIA.C.54

This is the offical drawing of the C.54, showing the 8 compartments all 6'3" in width for the 3rd class passengers and 60" long. The corridor is 21½" wide. The photograph illustrates No.4889 of lot 1374 of 1927 (figure 239).

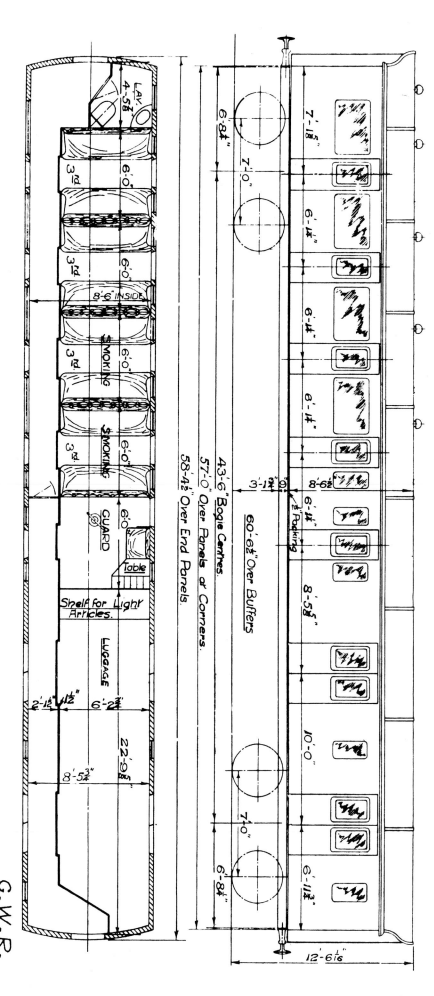

FIG 240

G.W.R.
BRAKE THIRD CLASS CARRIAGE

LOTS 1375.1384.

DIA.D.95

In the same series as the previously mentioned stock, is the brake 3rds, *diagram D.95*, exactly the same size in outline. The accommodation consisted of four passenger compartments which occupied half the vehicle, and the other half being for luggage and the guard. Still with the false panel painting, the vehicle in the photograph is No.4932, (*figure 240*). Other numbers were 4913-44 and 5087-5132.

FIG 241

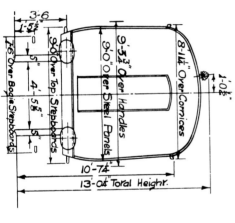

− *TARE* 30ᵀ·4ᶜ −

3-6
1-5½
9-5⅜ Over Handles
9'-0" Over Steel Panels
8-1¼" Over Cornices
1-0½"
7-6 Over Bogie Stepboards
3-0 Over Top Stepboards
5"
4-5½"
5"
10-7¼
13-0¾ Total Height.

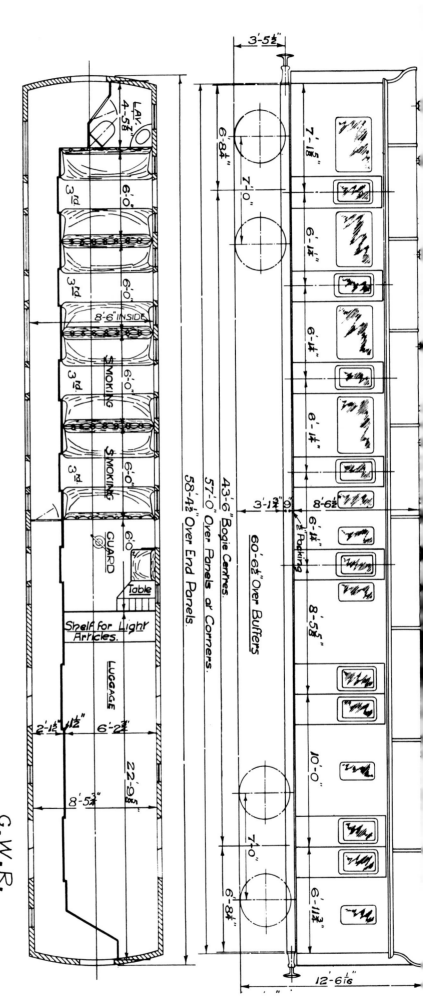

G.W.R.
BRAKE THIRD CLASS CARRIAGE

DIA.D.95
LOT.1375

LAV.
4-5⅞"

3ʳᵈ   6'-0"

3ʳᵈ   6'-0"

8'-6" INSIDE

3ʳᵈ   6'-0"   SMOKING

3ʳᵈ   6'-0"   SMOKING

3ʳᵈ   6'-0"

GUARD

6'-0"

Table

Shelf for Light Articles.

LUGGAGE

2-1½   1½"   6-2½"

22-9½"

8-5¾"

3-5½"
6-8¼"
7'-0"
7-1⅛"
6-1¼"
6-1¼"
6-1¼"
8-1¼"
8-6½"
3-1¼" 9"
⅛" Packing
6-1¼"
8-5⅝"
10-0"
7-0"
6-8¼"
6-11¾"
43-6" Bogie Centres.
57-0" Over Panels at Corners.
58-4½" Over End Panels.
60-6½" Over Buffers
12-6⅛"

Bow-ended main line stock of the twenties, represented here with the official drawing of the brake 3rd to *diagram D.95* described on the previous page. This official plan is of the right-handed pattern, whereas the picture on *page 138* is the left-handed variety. *Figure 241* illustrates No.5098 of *lot 1384*.

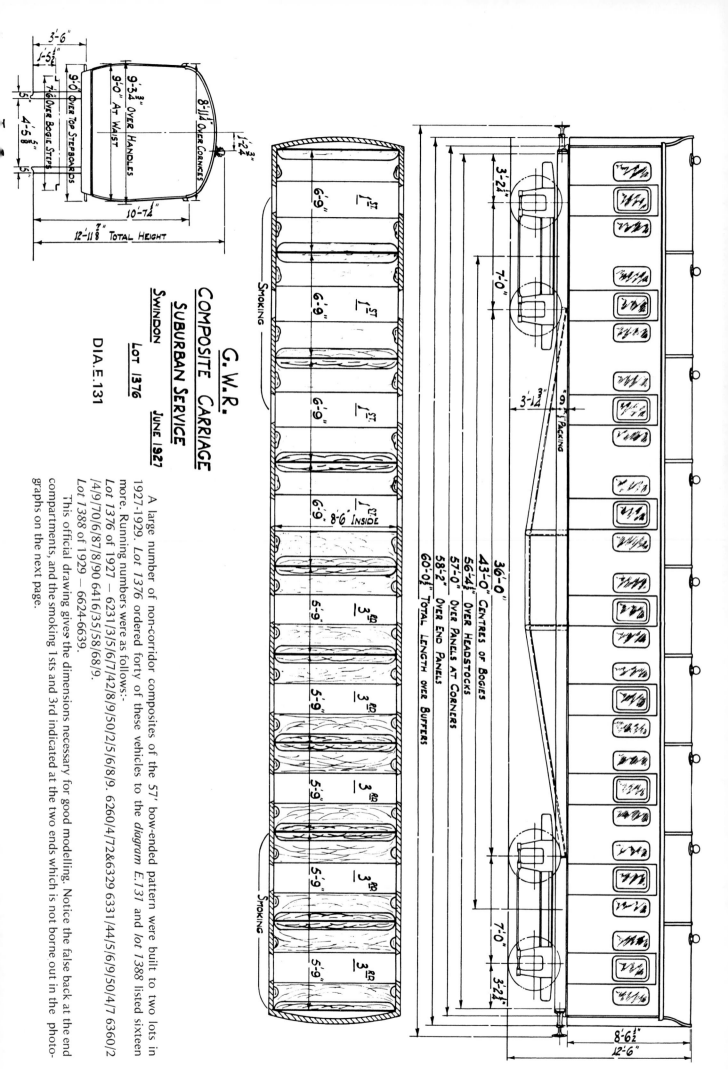

G.W.R.
COMPOSITE CARRIAGE
SUBURBAN SERVICE

SWINDON

LOT 1376   JUNE 1927

DIA.E.131

A large number of non-corridor composites of the 57' bow-ended pattern were built to two lots in 1927-1929. *Lot 1376* ordered forty of these vehicles to the *diagram E.131* and *lot 1388* listed sixteen more. Running numbers were as follows:-

Lot 1376 of 1927 — 6231/3/5/6/7/42/8/9/50/2/5/6/8/9. 6260/4/72&6329 6331/44/5/6/9/50/4/7 6360/2 /4/9/70/6/87/8/90 6416/35/58/68/9.

Lot 1388 of 1929 — 6624-6639.

This official drawing gives the dimensions necessary for good modelling. Notice the false back at the end compartments, and the smoking 1sts and 3rd indicated at the two ends which is not borne out in the photographs on the next page.

Dimensions on carriage diagram:

- 6'-9" 1ST
- 6'-9" 1ST
- 6'-9" 1ST
- 6'-9" 1ST 8'-6" INSIDE
- 5'-9" 3RD
- 5'-9" 3RD
- 5'-9" 3RD
- 5'-9" 3RD
- 5'-9" 3RD
- SMOKING

End elevation dimensions:
- 3'-6"
- 1'-5¼"
- 9'-0"
- 9'-3¾" OVER HANDLES
- 9'-0" AT WAIST
- 8'-11¼" OVER CORNICES
- 7'-6" OVER TOP STEPBOARDS
- 7'-6" OVER BOGIE STEPS
- 5"
- 5"
- 4'-5⅝"
- 10'-7¼"
- 12'-11⅞" TOTAL HEIGHT
- 1'-2¾"

Side/plan elevation dimensions:
- 3'-2¼"
- 7'-0"
- 3'-1¼"
- 9" PACKING
- 36'-0"
- 43'-0" CENTRES OF BOGIES
- 56'-4½" OVER HEADSTOCKS
- 57'-0" OVER PANELS AT CORNERS
- 58'-2" OVER END PANELS
- 60'-0¼" TOTAL LENGTH OVER BUFFERS
- 7'-0"
- 3'-2¼"
- 8'-6½"
- 12'-6"

Two pictures of the *diagram E.131* composites figure on this page. *Figure 242* at the top shows No.6345 in the late twenties livery, having the coat of arms crest, whereas in the lower photograph the same class of carriage, No.6237, has the mid twenties garter arms as the insignia with the heraldic devices on either side. Note that the smoking compartments are in the centre of the vehicles, and not at the ends as shown in the drawing on *page 140.*

FIG 243

LOT.1376

DIA.E.131

141

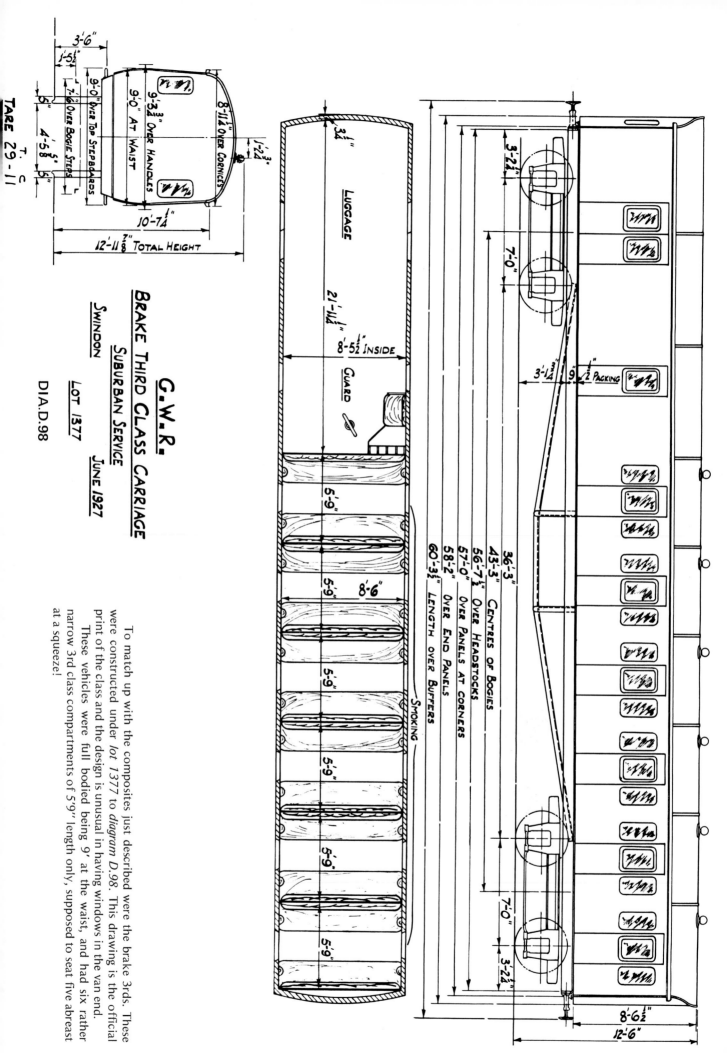

TARE 29-11

T.C

BRAKE THIRD CLASS CARRIAGE

G.W.R.

SUBURBAN SERVICE

SWINDON

LOT 1377   JUNE 1927

DIA. D.98

LUGGAGE

GUARD

SMOKING

To match up with the composites just described were the brake 3rds. These were constructed under *lot 1377* to *diagram D.98*. This drawing is the official print of the class and the design is unusual in having windows in the van end. These vehicles were full bodied being 9' at the waist, and had six rather narrow 3rd class compartments of 5'9" length only, supposed to seat five abreast at a squeeze!

142

FIG 244

FIG 245

Three interesting pictures from Roye England's camera are shown here, all of No.4979. One of the *diagram D.98* suburban brake 3rds top, *figure 244*, shows the outside of the carriage, in British Rail days. The *figure 245* illustrates the inside of the guard's compartment looking towards the centre of the carriage. From the left to the right is the first aid cabinet and tools on top of the electric control gear, next is the coach lighting switches, with the guard's steam heater underneath. Steam gauge and vacuum gauge are shown above the hand brake. Next is the letter rack and the guard's seat and cupboard. Notice the pocket for the guard's flag on the partition. The lower photo, *figure 246*, shows the van end looking towards the coupling. Note the side drop-lights have a grill of upright bars, whereas the end fixed lights have horizontal grills. There are hooks around the cantrail for hanging mail bags etc., and the rings in the side boards at 18" high are for tying up dogs and other animals in transit. Running numbers of the *diagram D.98* were 4945-84.

LOT.1377

143

FIG 246

FIG 247 FIG 248

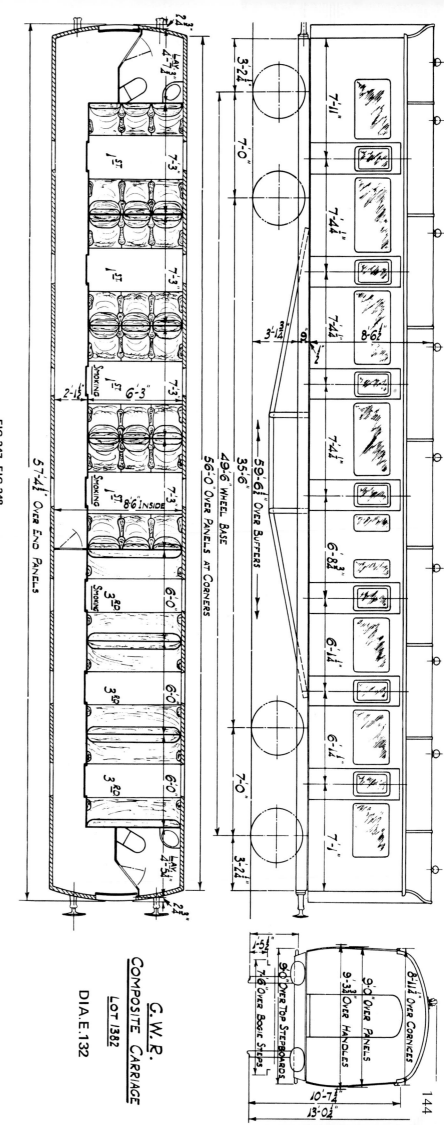

G. W. R.
COMPOSITE CARRIAGE
LOT 1382

DIA. E.132

Corridor stock for main line included the 56' composites built to *diagram E.132* in 1928, and they are shown here in photograph and drawing. The layout was four 1st's and three 3rds, 7'3" and 6'0" long respectively.

Running numbers were many and varied: 6 0 1 1 - 6 / 8 - 2 3 / 5 / 7 / 3 1 / 2 6035/8-45/6051/4/5/65/6/7/70/2-4/6-83/5/ 6089-94/6

In *figure 247* is No.6085, compartment side, and *figure 248* shows the corridor side of the same vehicle.

144

In 1929 another series of auto-trailers were made, under *lot 1394*, twelve vehicles in all, to a new design having flush sides, with one large smoking compartment and a small non-smoking saloon at the rear, separated by a large guard's vestibule. The pictures show No.170 when almost new in 1929 (*figure 249*) and also in 1948 when painted in the all-brown livery of the war years (*figure 250*). The other official picture, *figure 250*, shows another in the same series, No.163, giving a full broadside view useful for modelling. Notice the bogies are of the 7' pattern.

LOT.1394
DIA.A.27

FIG 249

FIG 250

FIG 251

145

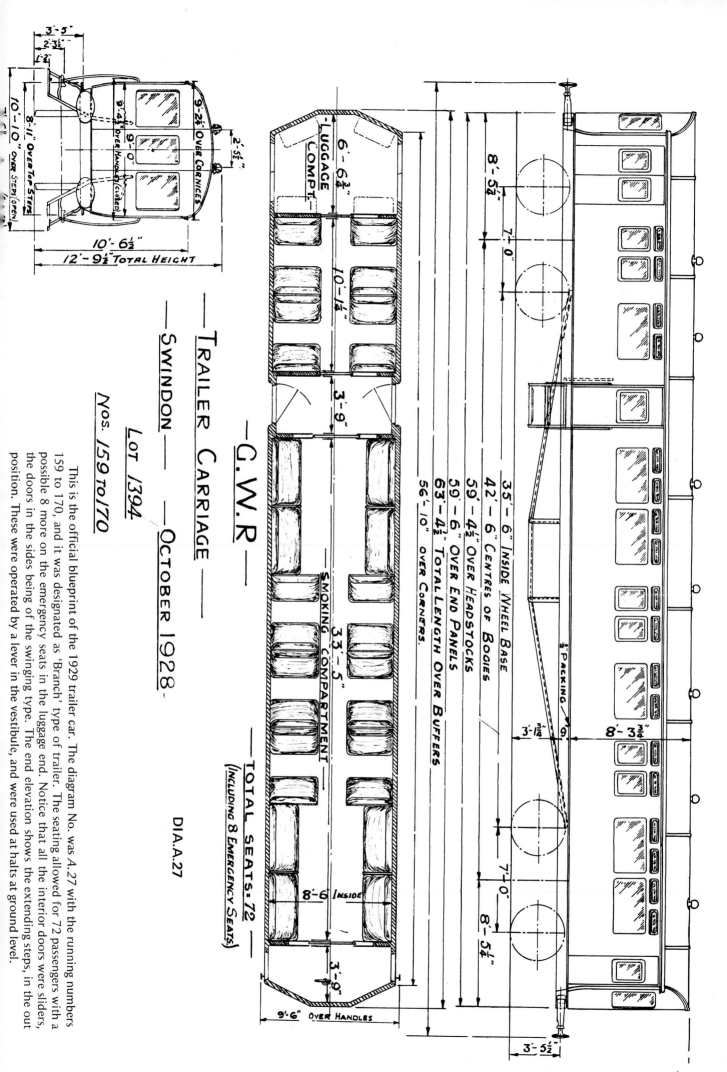

— G.W.R —

— TRAILER CARRIAGE —

— SWINDON — OCTOBER 1928 —

LOT 1394

NOS. 159 TO 170

DIA. A.27

10'-6½"

12'-9½" TOTAL HEIGHT

9'-2¼" OVER CORNICES

9'-0"

9'-4½" OVER HANDLES (CLOSED)

2'-5¼"

3'-5"

2'-3½"

1'-2"

10'-10" OVER TOP STEPS (OPEN)

8'-11" OVER STEPS

7'-0"

LUGGAGE COMPT.

6'-6¾"

10'-1¼"

3'-9"

SMOKING COMPARTMENT

33'-5"

3'-9"

8'-6" INSIDE

9'-6" OVER HANDLES

TOTAL SEATS=72
(INCLUDING 8 EMERGENCY SEATS)

35'-6" INSIDE WHEEL BASE

42'-6" CENTRES OF BOGIES

59'-4½" OVER HEADSTOCKS

59'-6" OVER END PANELS

63'-4½" TOTAL LENGTH OVER BUFFERS

56'-10" OVER CORNERS.

8'-5¼"

7'-0"

½" PACKING

3'-1¾"

9"

8'-3¾"

7'-0"

8'-5¼"

3'-5½"

This is the official blueprint of the 1929 trailer car. The diagram No. was A.27 with the running numbers 159 to 170, and it was designated as 'Branch' type of trailer. The seating allowed for 72 passengers with a possible 8 more on the emergency seats in the luggage end. Notice that all the interior doors were sliders, the doors in the sides being of the swinging type. The end elevation shows the extending steps, in the out position. These were operated by a lever in the vestibule, and were used at halts at ground level.

146

FIG 253

LOT.1395
DIA.C.54

FIG 254

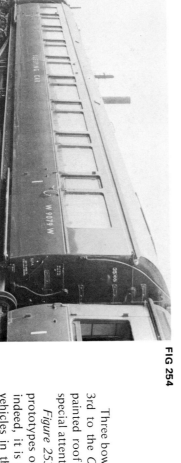

DIA.J.15

Three bow-ended vehicles feature on this page. At the top, *figure 252*, is another example of the corridor 3rd to the *C.54 diagram*, No.5177, which was made on the mixed *lot of 1395* of 1929. Note the white painted roof of the period and the blue tops to the axle boxes which indicated those bearings needing special attention and oiling.

Figure 253, the middle picture, is of the 3rd class sleeper constructed to *diagram J.11*. These were the prototypes of the full-sided vehicles with recessed doors which set the pattern for future coach prototypes indeed, it is possible to see the 'Centenary' stock outline in these sleepers of *lot 1419*. There were three vehicles in the order, No's. 9094 to 9096, and being very wide they were restricted to the Red Triangle diagram.

The other sleeper at bottom left is a rebuild one of the *J.10* series of three, which were first built on order *lot 1395* originally No's. 5140—42 compo sleepers. They were the first sleepers on the Great Western to provide all third class accommodation, albeit some was of the couchette type. Starting on the Neyland run two were eventually changed into eight compartment 3rds like that above, and one was converted to a composite, and renumbered 9079. The picture shows this condition. (*Figure 254*)

147

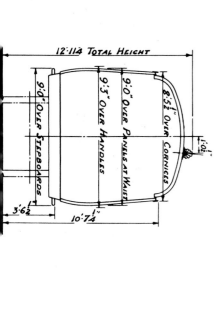

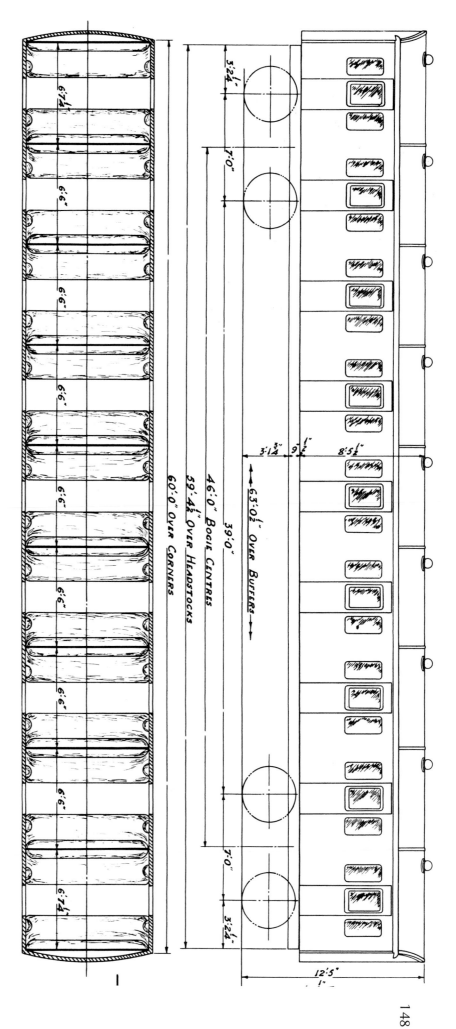

— G . W . R —
— THIRD CLASS CARRIAGE —
— CROSS COUNTRY SERVICE —
— SWINDON — AUGUST 1930 —

LOT.1403

DIA.C.61

This drawing shows one of the extra wide non-corridor stock of the 60' length, which were formed into set trains for London, Birmingham and South Wales cross country services. Notice that the 3rd compartments are 6'6'' in length and still have the false backs at the ends, and are running on 7' bogies. The lot number was 1403, the *diagram* C.61, and the running numbers were 5565 to 5576.

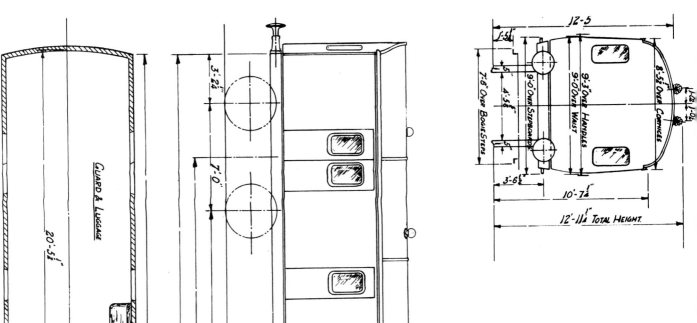

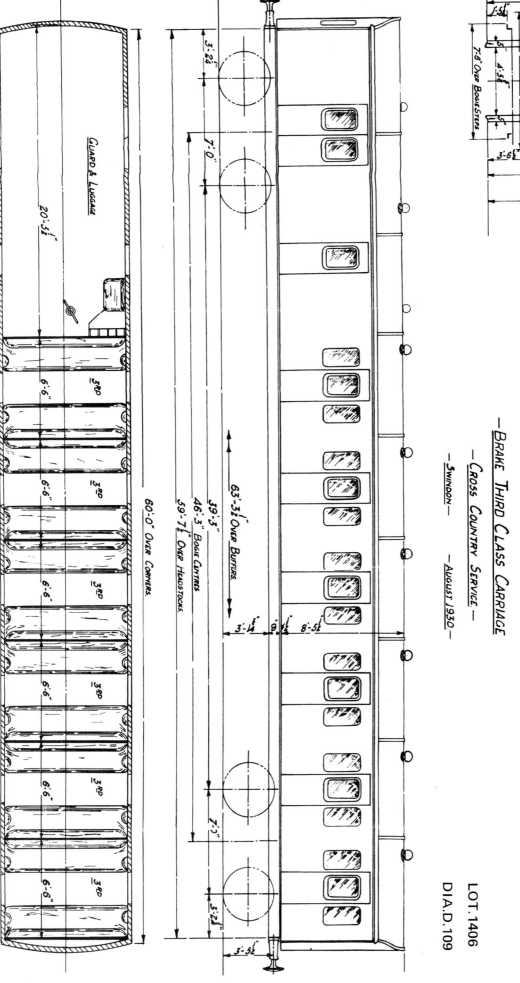

This is the brake 3rd outline of the same series as previously described, built to *lot 1406*. The diagram was D.109 and numbers 5589 to 5600.
The composites to the same design were *diagrams E.141 and E.142* numbered 6644-9, 6431-4, 6436-43.

— G. W. R. —

— BRAKE THIRD CLASS CARRIAGE —

— CROSS COUNTRY SERVICE. —

— SWINDON —   — AUGUST 1930 —

LOT. 1406

DIA. D.109

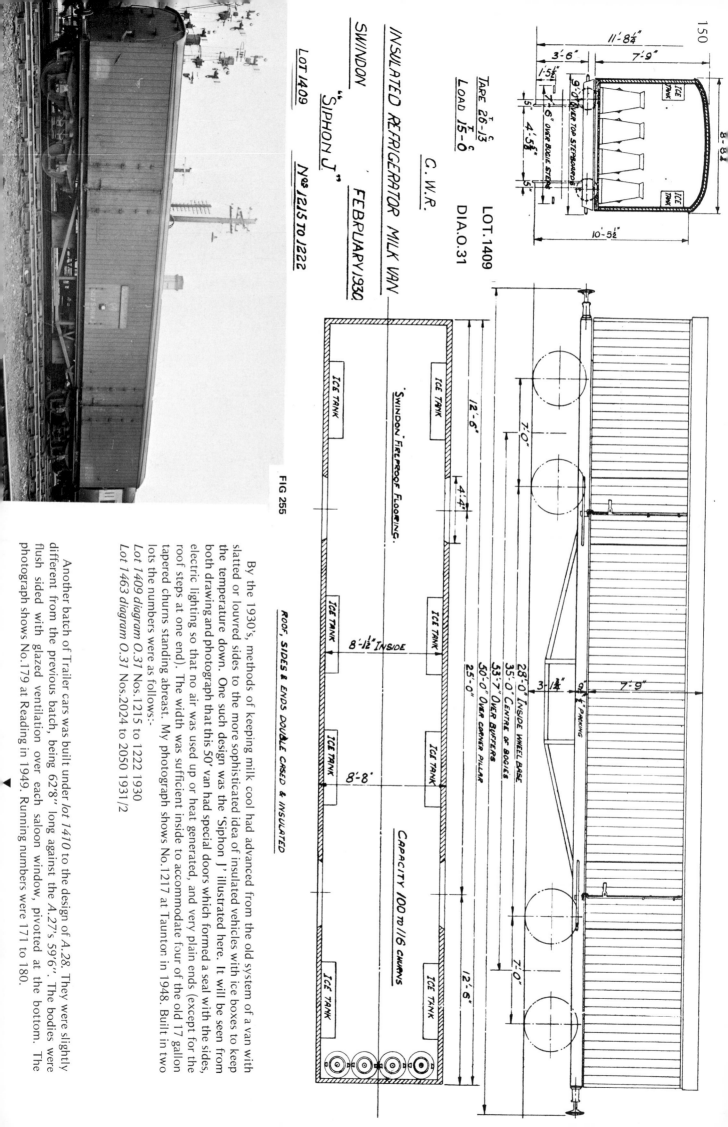

INSULATED REFRIGERATOR MILK VAN

SWINDON   FEBRUARY 1930

"SIPHON J"   Nos 1215 TO 1222

LOT 1409

C.W.R.

TARE 26-3

LOAD 15-0

LOT.1409   DIA.O.31

FIG 255

ROOF, SIDES & ENDS DOUBLE CASED & INSULATED

'SWINDON' FIREPROOF FLOORING.

CAPACITY 100 TO 116 CHURNS

By the 1930's, methods of keeping milk cool had advanced from the old system of a van with slatted or louvred sides to the more sophisticated idea of insulated vehicles with ice boxes to keep the temperature down. One such design was the 'Siphon J' illustrated here. It will be seen from both drawing and photograph that this 50' van had special doors which formed a seal with the sides, electric lighting so that no air was used up or heat generated, and very plain ends (except for the roof steps at one end). The width was sufficient inside to accommodate four of the old 17 gallon tapered churns standing abreast. My photograph shows No.1217 at Taunton in 1948. Built in two lots the numbers were as follows:-

Lot 1409 diagram O.31 Nos.1215 to 1222 1930
Lot 1463 diagram O.31 Nos.2024 to 2050 1931/2

Another batch of Trailer cars was built under lot 1410 to the design of A.28. They were slightly different from the previous batch, being 62'8" long against the A.27's 59'6". The bodies were flush sided with glazed ventilation over each saloon window, pivoted at the bottom. The photograph shows No.179 at Reading in 1949. Running numbers were 171 to 180.

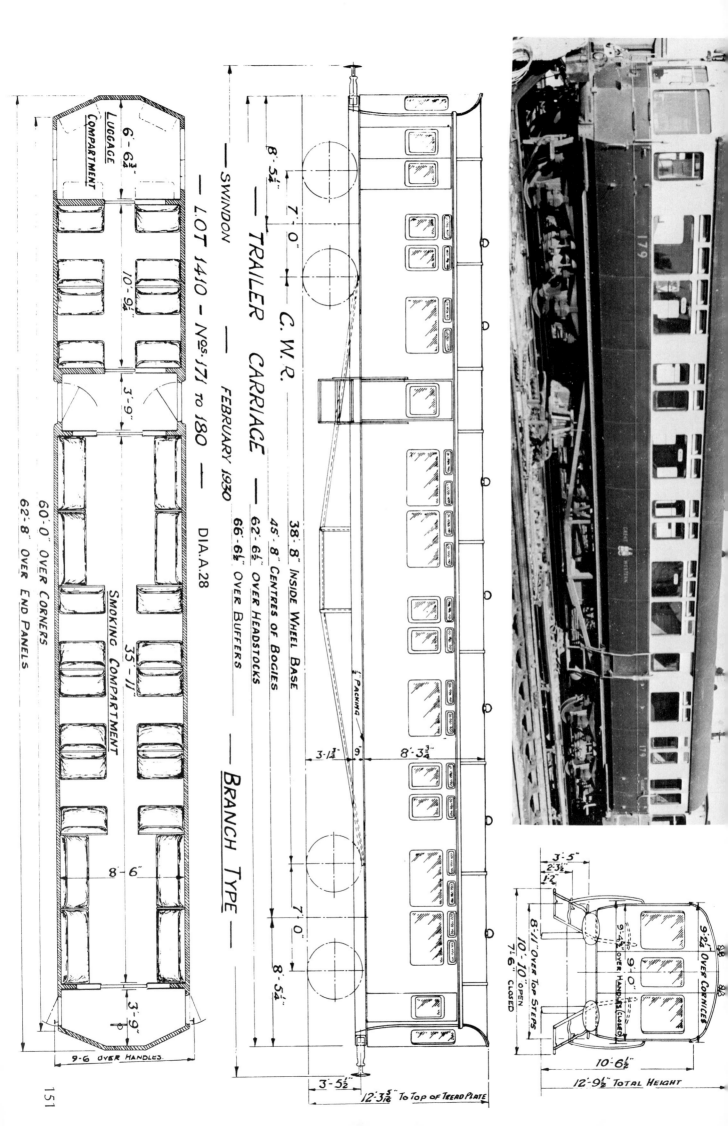

TRAILER CARRIAGE — C.W.R.

SWINDON — FEBRUARY 1930

LOT 1410 — Nos. 171 to 180 — DIA.A.28

BRANCH TYPE

LUGGAGE COMPARTMENT

6'-6¾"

10'-9¼"

3'-9"

SMOKING COMPARTMENT

35'-11"

8'-6"

3'-9"

60'-0" OVER CORNERS

62'-8" OVER END PANELS

9'-6 OVER HANDLES.

38'-8" INSIDE WHEEL BASE

45'-8" CENTRES OF BOGIES

62'-6½" OVER HEADSTOCKS

66'-6½" OVER BUFFERS

8'-5¼"

7'-0"

7'-0"

8'-5¼"

½" PACKING

3'-1¾"   9"

8'-3¾"

3'-5½"

12'-3 5/16" TO TOP OF TREAD PLATE

179

GREAT WESTERN

179

3'-5"

2'-3½"

1'-2"

8'-11" OVER TOP STEPS

10'-10" OPEN

7'-6" CLOSED

9'-4½" OVER HANDLES (CLOSED)

9'-0" OPEN

9'-2¼" OVER CORNICES

10'-6½"

12'-9½" TOTAL HEIGHT

DIA.A.28

Still with the Trailer cars to *diagram A.28* this page shows many details of the interior of No.174 of this series. The Great Western 4mm circle held a meeting at Didcot in 1959 and Jim Arnold took these pictures which should be of great help to modellers. *Figure 258* shows a general view of inside the smoking saloon looking towards the driving compartment. Note that hanging straps are only fitted between the long seats and not between the transverse. Standing passengers here could hang on to the seat backs! *Figure 259*, middle right, looks out through the vestibule to the non-smoking saloon. Notice the large framed pictures and notice boards. The paintwork inside was — white ceiling, cream upper panels and mahogany lower. Upholstery when photographed was green rep. Interior doors on these vehicles were double sliding type. The interesting upright picture, *figure 257*, illustrates the lever by which the guard could operate the swing steps. The pigeon holes above were for letters as the Great Western had their own station-to-station mail service and this rack was for sorting and storage of these letters and notices. In the top left can be seen the electric bell by which the crew exchanged orders Codes used were — 1 ring "go ahead", 2 rings "set back", 3 rings "stop" 4 rings "blow of brakes", 5 rings "ease up on couplings". The small picture, *figure 260*, shows the comparison between the *diagram A.28* design and the converted SRM No.204 taken at Plymouth.

FIG 257

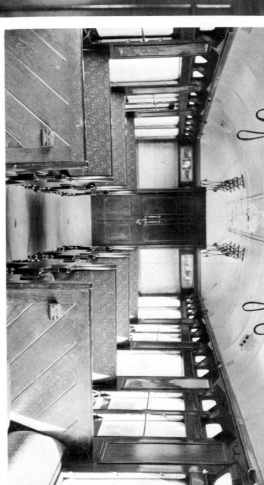

FIG 258

FIG 260

FIG 259

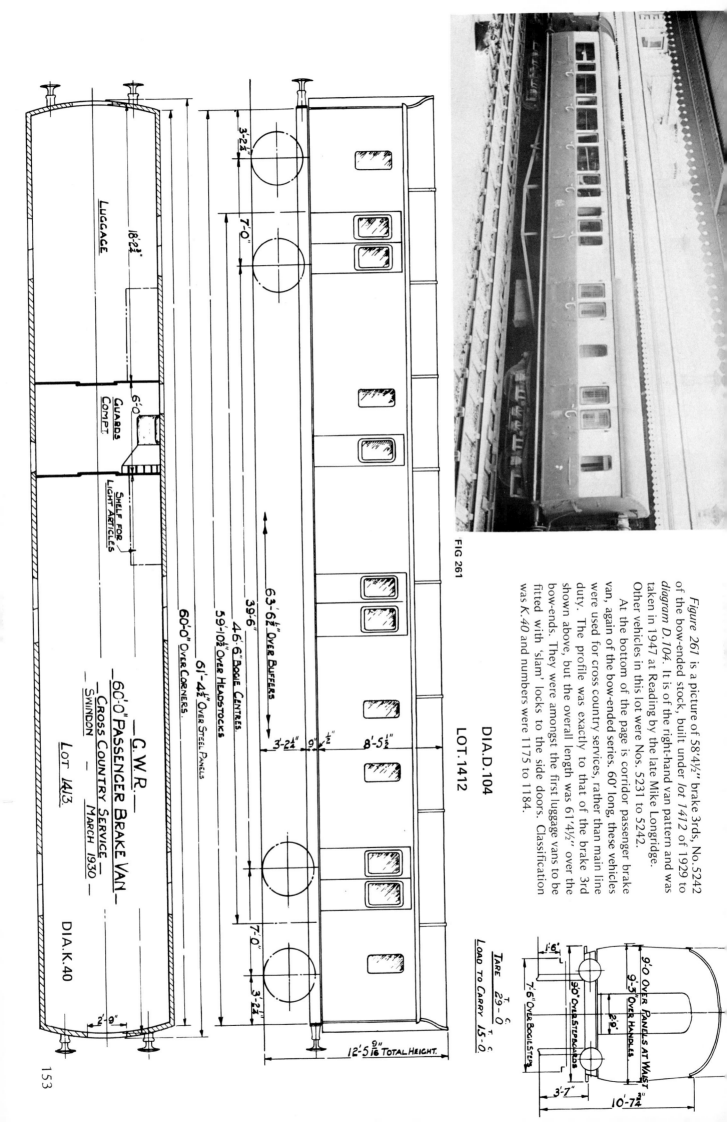

FIG 261

Figure 261 is a picture of 58'4½" brake 3rds, No. 5242 of the bow-ended stock, built under lot 1412 of 1929 to diagram D.104. It is of the right-hand van pattern and was taken in 1947 at Reading by the late Mike Longridge. Other vehicles in this lot were Nos. 5231 to 5242.

At the bottom of the page is corridor passenger brake van, again of the bow-ended series. 60' long, these vehicles were used for cross country services, rather than main line duty. The profile was exactly to that of the brake 3rd shown above, but the overall length was 61'4½" over the bow-ends. They were amongst the first luggage vans to be fitted with 'slam' locks to the side doors. Classification was K.40 and numbers were 1175 to 1184.

DIA.D.104

LOT.1412

— G.W.R. —
— 60'-0" PASSENGER BRAKE VAN —
— CROSS COUNTRY SERVICE —
— SWINDON — MARCH 1930 —

LOT 1413

DIA.K.40

153

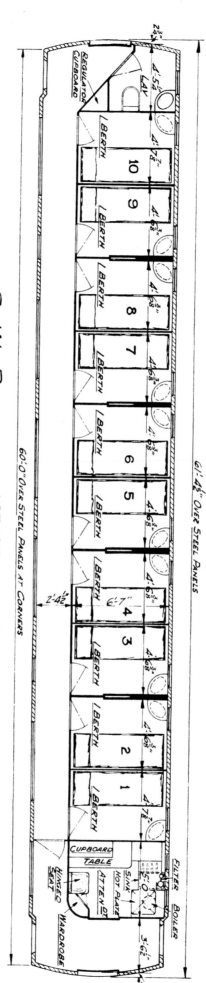

G.W.R.
FIRST CLASS SLEEPING

LOT.1418
DIA.J.12

The official drawing illustrates one of the spacious 1st class sleeping cars of 1930. These were the first sleepers of the premier class to be designed at Swindon since the grouping in 1923, and large vehicles they were, when one considers that only 10 passengers were carried! The vehicles had the full 9'7" bulging sides and each single compartment measured approx. 4'7" x 6'7". There was a fully fitted attendant's compartment at one end, similar to that on the continental wagonslit. Notice the end profile to the doors, another leader towards the 'Centenaries'. Six wheeled bogies were fitted, and double floors were fitted to ensure some medium of sound insulation. Lot Nos. were 1418 to diagram J.12, painted number 9080-81-87-88, and No.1439 to J.12, painted numbers 9065 to 9068. See page 148 for photograph.

Following on from the rather abortive articulated design of dining facilities for the West Country Expresses, the drawing office set to and planned a series of stock, which although separated vehicles in themselves, usually ran in sets of three. A composite dining saloon and a 3rd class saloon, with the kitchen car sandwiched in between, was designed. All to the 9'7" width, they were, of course, restricted to the 'Red Triangle' routes and were mainly intended for the 'Cornish Riviera' and Torbay expresses. It is interesting to note that this period, 1930 to 1935, was perhaps the peak of prosperity for the Great Western and it showed in the passenger facilities provided. 3rd class passengers were in the majority now and this can be seen in the ratio of accommodation provided. These dining cars, for instance, on the 'Cornish Riviera' consisted of one full 3rd saloon and one composite saloon providing seating for only sixteen 1st class diners but for forty-eight 3rd class munchers!

The drawing on page 155 gives the layout of the kitchen car; note that the serving windows are now in a vestibule which avoided congestion in the corridors.

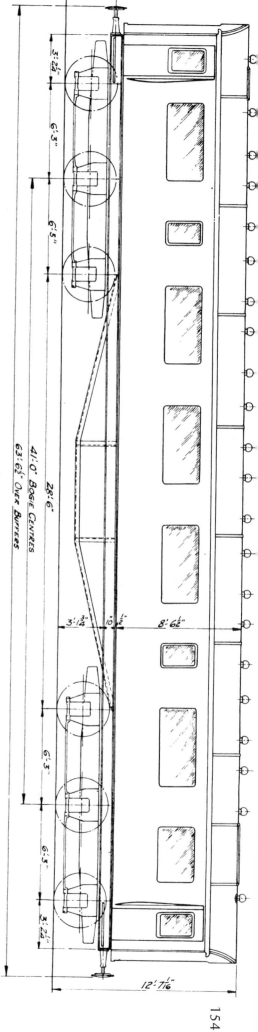

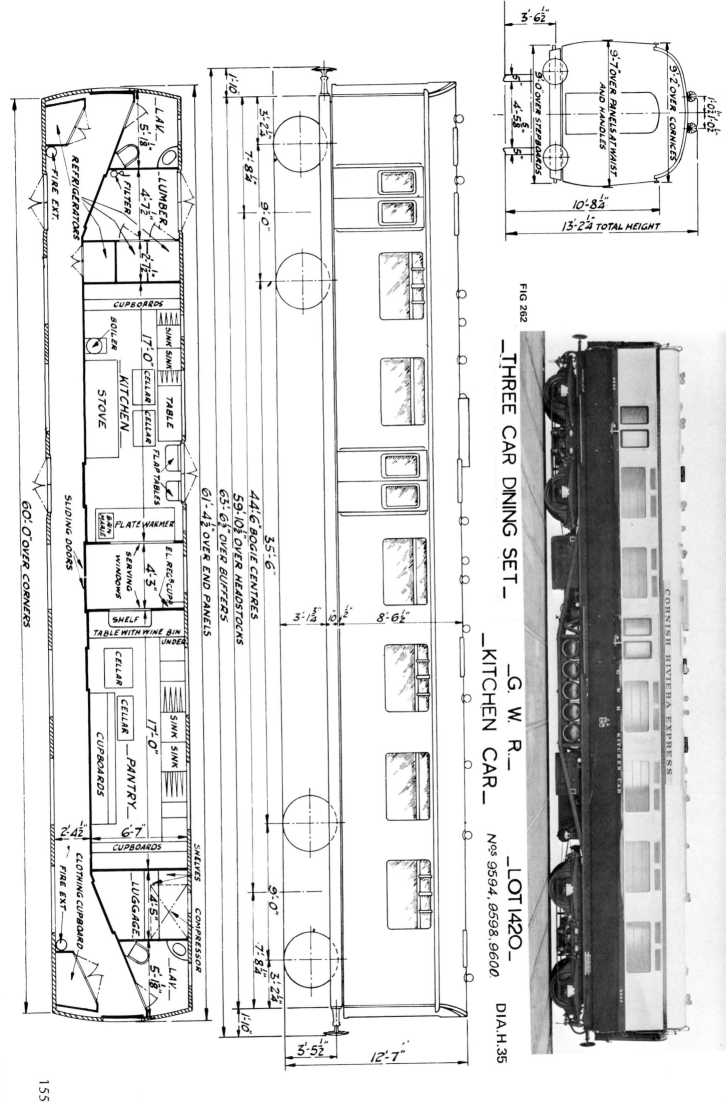

—THREE CAR DINING SET—

—G.W.R.—
—KITCHEN CAR—

FIG 262

Nᵒˢ 9594, 9598, 9600

—LOT 1420—

DIA.H.35

CORNISH RIVIERA EXPRESS

G.W.R. KITCHEN CAR

Side elevation dimensions:

3'-6½"
9'-7" OVER PANELS ATHWART AND HANDLES
9'-2" OVER CORNICES
5"
9'-0" OVER STEPBOARDS
4'-5⅝"
5"
1'-0½"·1'-0½"
10'-8¼"
13'-2¼" TOTAL HEIGHT

1'-10"
3'-2¼"
7'-8¼"
9'-0"

3'-1¼" 10'-½" 8'-6½"

9'-0"
7'-8¼"
3'-2¼"
1'-10"

3'-5½"
12'-7"

Plan dimensions:

LAV.
5'-1⅛"
LUMBER
4'-7½"
2'-1¼"
FILTER
REFRIGERATORS
FIRE EXT.

CUPBOARDS
BOILER
SINK SINK
CELLAR
TABLE
CELLAR
STOVE
KITCHEN
17'-0"
FLAP TABLES
B-N WARE
PLATE WARMER
SERVING WINDOWS
SHELF
EL.REC.CUPD.
TABLE WITH WINE BIN UNDER
4'-3"

SLIDING DOORS
60'-0" OVER CORNERS

35'-6"
44'-6" BOGIE CENTRES
59'-10½" OVER HEADSTOCKS
63'-6½" OVER BUFFERS
61'-4½" OVER END PANELS

CELLAR
CELLAR
CUPBOARDS
PANTRY
SINK SINK
17'-0"
CUPBOARDS
SHELVES
2'-4½"
6'-7"

LUGGAGE
4'-5"
CLOTHING CUPBOARD
FIRE EXT.
COMPRESSOR
LAV.
5'-1⅛"

Official photographs of the 'Cornish Riviera' stock since 1929 are shown here. At the top, *figure 263*, is No.9582, one of the composite dining saloons just referred to, seating 32 passengers, 16 for each class. The 1st class eaters were provided with a table lamp with a red shade, and antimacassars on the seat backs. *Figure 264*, is the large full 3rd dining saloon, this one being No.9588, and in the large picture, *figure 265* is the interior decor of vehicle No.9586. Note the 'modern' style of the period. One final point to modellers, the door handles on these vehicles were chromiumplated, not brass. Lot and running numbers of all eighteen carriages were as follows:-

Lot 1420   Kitchen car
           Diagram H.35
           Painted numbers 9594 to 9600
Lot 1421   Composite Diner *Diagram H.36*
           Painted numbers 9582 to 9587
Lot 1422   3rd Diner   *Diagram H.37*
           Painted numbers 9588 to 9593

FIG 263

FIG 265

FIG 264

Lot 1426 diagram C.59 Nos. 5258 to 5280

Having dealt with the restaurant facilities on the new 'Cornish Riviera' stock, other vehicles used on the expresses will be described briefly and illustrated. Firstly, a full 3rd class 60' carriage of the same extreme width design. The official drawing gives most of the relevant details, and one should note that although the diners had the recessed door profiles of the impending 'Centenary' design this was only for vehicles with doors at the ends of coaches, the doors on the ordinary stock following the line of the 'bulging' sides. The eight compartments on this 'Riviera' stock were very spacious, being 6'4" long by

G.W.R.

THIRD CLASS CARRIAGE – – **SWINDON** – **JUNE 1929** –

– **MAIN LINE SERVICE** –

LOT 1426

DIA. C.59

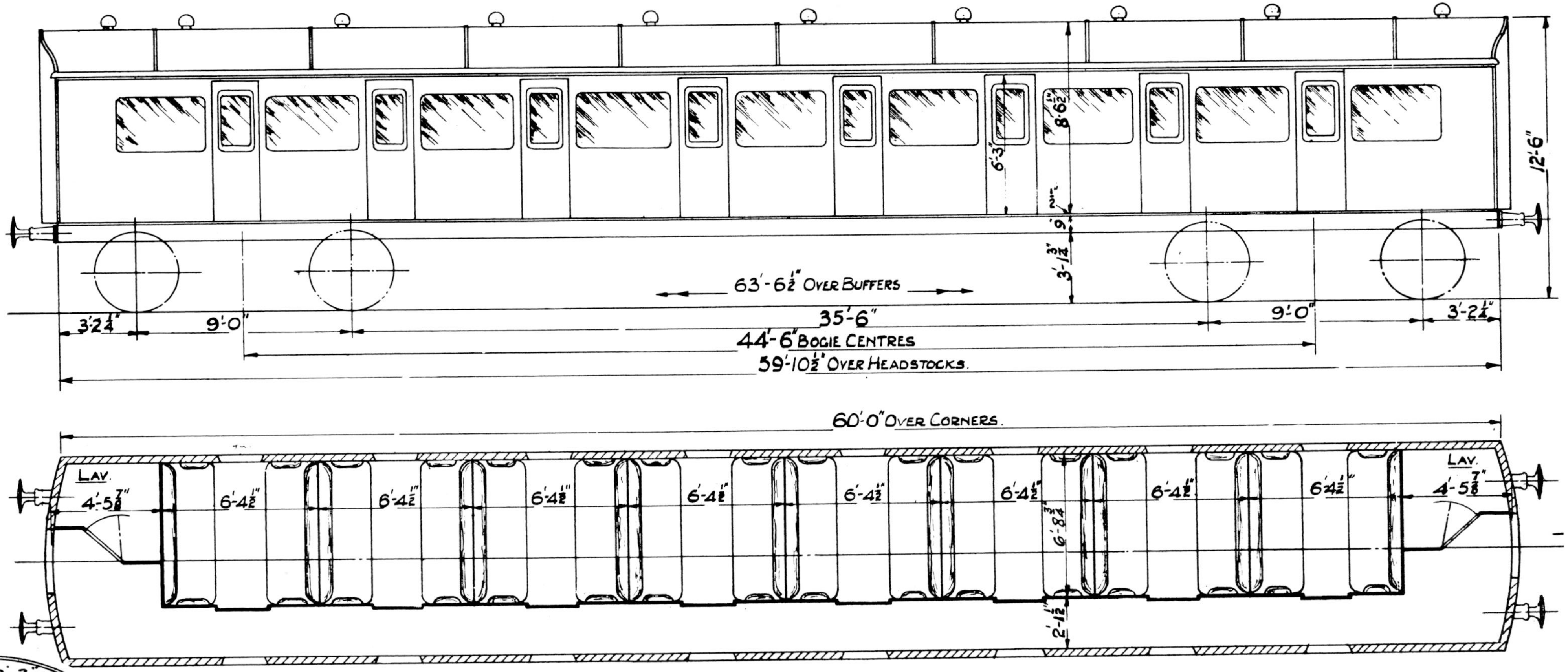

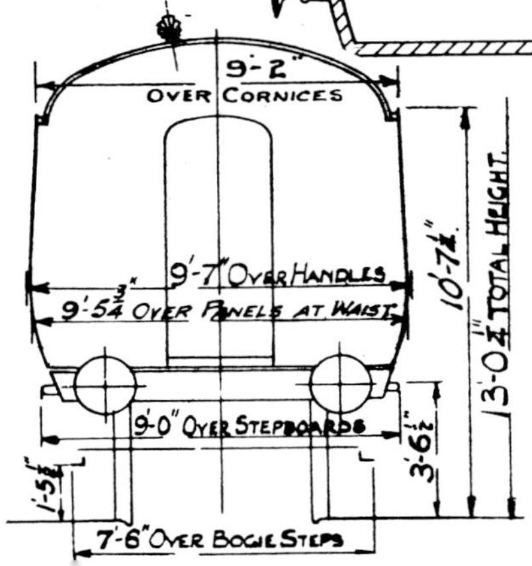

FIG 266

CORNISH RIVIERA EXPRESS

1'-5½"
7'-6" OVER BOGIE STEPS
9'-0" OVER STEPBOARDS
9'-5¾" OVER PANELS AT WAIST
9'-7" OVER HANDLES
9'-2" OVER CORNICES
3'-6½"
10'-7¼"
13'-0¼" TOTAL HEIGHT.

LAV. 4'-5⅞"
6'-4½"
6'-4½"
6'-4½"
6'-4½"
6'-4½"
6'-4½"
6'-8¾"
6'-4½"
6'-4½"
LAV. 4'-5⅞"
2'-1½"
60'-0" OVER CORNERS.

3'-2¼"
9'-0"
63'-6½" OVER BUFFERS
35'-6"
44'-6" BOGIE CENTRES
59'-10¾" OVER HEADSTOCKS.
9'-0"
3'-2¼"
6'-3"
3'-1¾"
9"
2'-4½"
8'-6½"
12'-6"

side. The photograph of No.5258 show the contemporary livery of the 1930's which still had the white roof. The small chocolate panels on the coach end panels gave the seating numbers so that passengers holding reserved tickets could find their seats easily.

FIG 267

FIG 269

LOT.1425
DIA.E.138

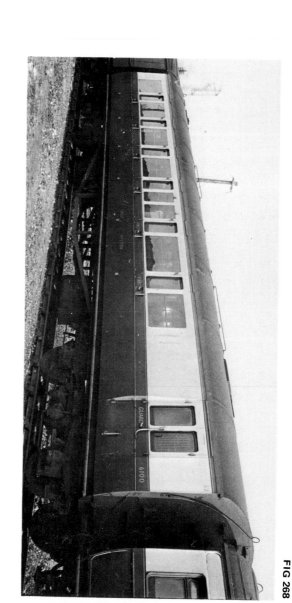

FIG 268

These three photographs show examples of the 'Riviera' stock in later days. Top, *figure 268*, is No.6100 one of the brake composites of *lot 1425* which was at Banbury in 1947 when pictured. Note again the profile and recessed doors at the end only. The other two pictures illustrate both sides of the C.59 full 3rds, to the drawing on the previous page. Note the recessed door handles, which had to be thus because the coach side was already out to the limit of the loading gauge. Running numbers of the brake composites were *lot 1425 diagram 138*, Nos. 6087-8/95/97/98/6100/7/8/18/20/21/24/34/47 6148/51-3.

158

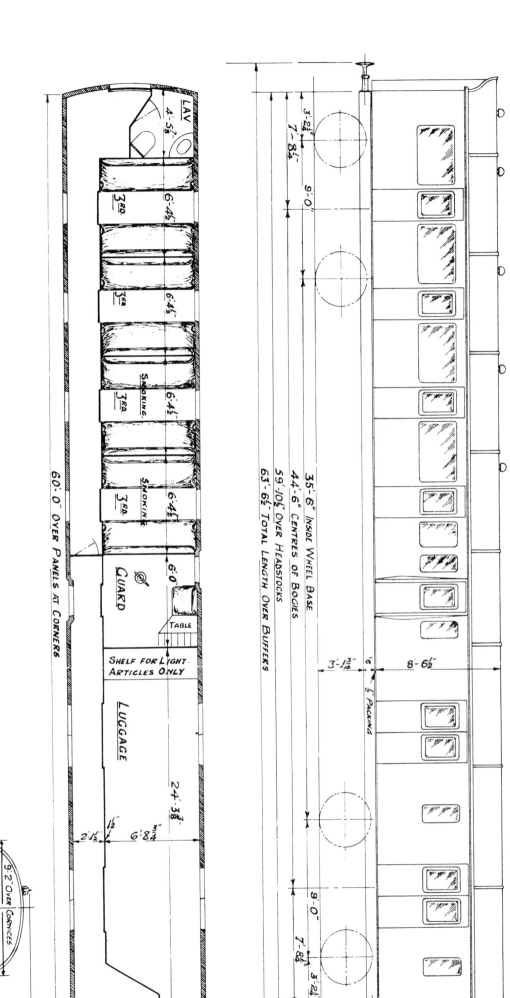

— G. W. R. —

— BRAKE THIRD CLASS CARRIAGE. —

— MAIN LINE SERVICE. —

— SWINDON. —

LOT 1427   — JUNE 1929. —

DIA.D.105

The brake 3rd of the 'Riviera' stock is drawn on this page and again one can see the single recessed door, but this time in the centre, for the use of the guard. All other doors followed the profile. The drawing is of a right-hand van design.

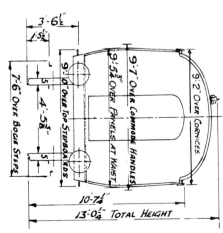

FIG 270

FIG 271

Both sides of No.5284 are shown on this page, the vehicle being a brake 3rd of *diagram D.105* built to the drawing on the previous page, but with one subtle difference — this coach has the left-handed van as compared with the right-handed version in the drawing. Note that one end has no steps or roof handrail and all the corridor gangways are of the suspended type.

Details of these brake 3rds are:-

Lot 1427 of 1930 to *diagram D.105*, Painted numbers 5281 to 5292

Finally in the Cornish Riviera stock sequence, we have an example of the 60' double ended slips. Built to *diagram F.23* there were only three vehicles, Nos.7898, 7899, and 7900. Their outline followed the same design as the previous express stock, and the recessed doors were this time at each end, serving the luggage/guard compartments. Note that, as with all slip coaches, there was no access from the corridor to the slip compartment, and that a swing door in the corridor separated the 1st and 3rd class travellers.

Roye England's pictures of No.7898 standing at Didcot in 1959, *figures 272 and 273*, show the British Rail strawberry and cream painting, and some good detail on the slip end, including the slip hook itself. Notice one feature which is not shown on the original drawing, — one of the end windows is much smaller than the other!

◄

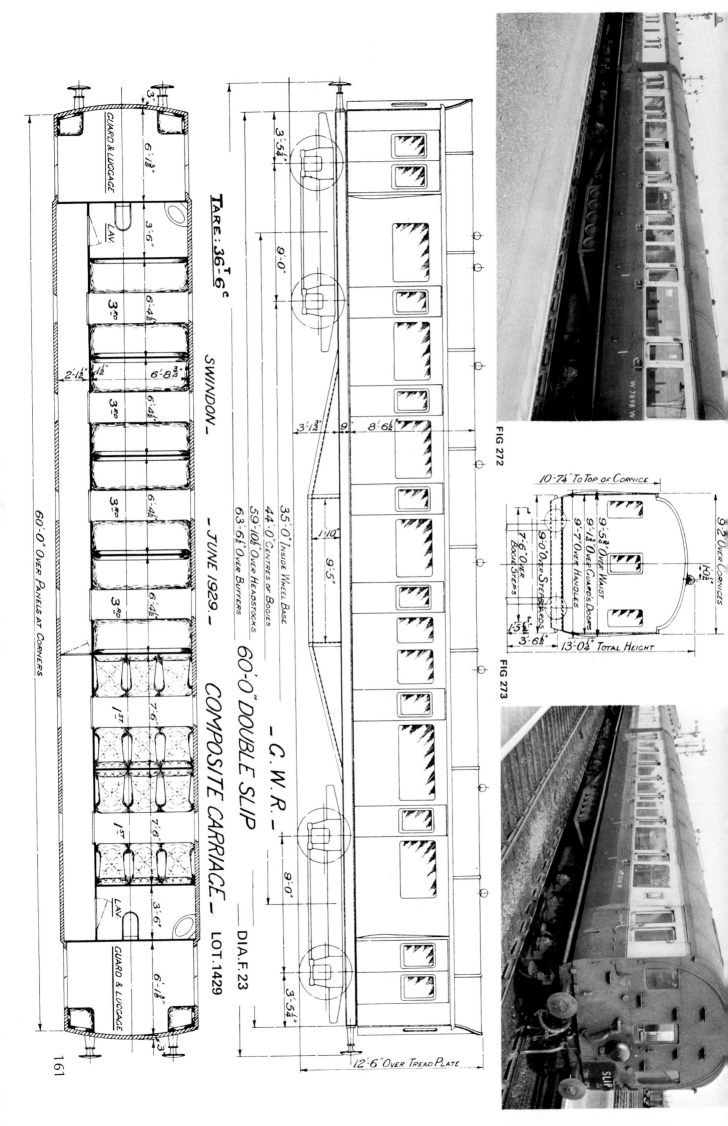

FIG 272

FIG 273

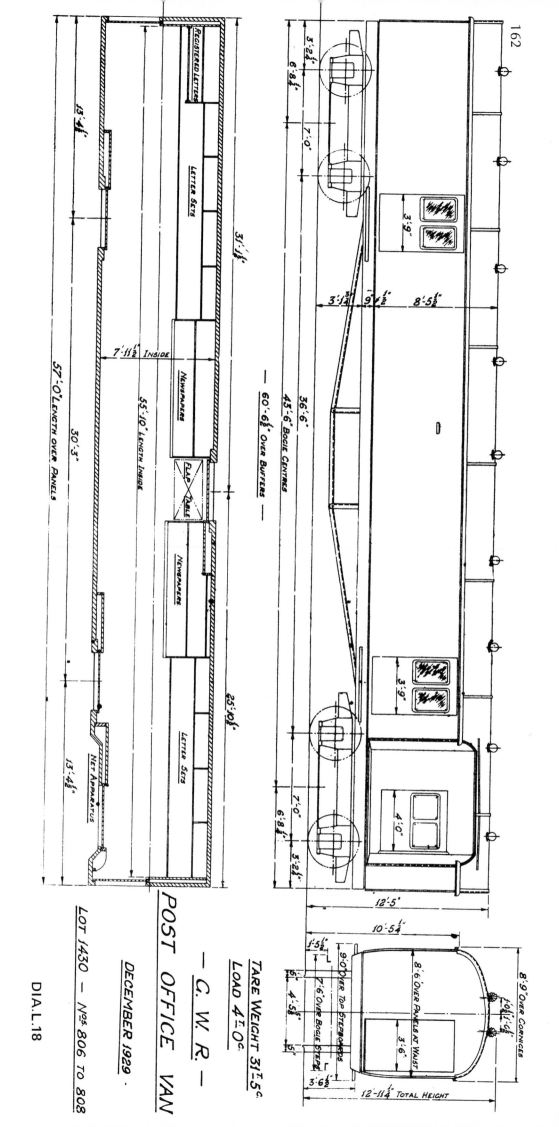

POST OFFICE VAN

— G.W.R. —

DECEMBER 1929.

LOT 1430 — Nos. 806 TO 808

TARE WEIGHT 31T.5c.

LOAD 4T.0c.

DIA. L.18

The postal trains of the Great Western have already been mentioned and in 1929 three new sorting vans were ordered under lot 1430. They were complete with tractator arms and nets on the near side only. The running numbers were 806 to 808 and the drawing here shows the side elevation, which had the T.P.O. gear fitted, and also the plan giving the internal layout. On the off side the completely blank panels were only relieved by one double windowed sliding door in the centre but this was seldom used in service. The inland 'Postal' running from Paddington to Penzance started from the capital at 10.10 p.m. and arrived at Penzance approx. 6.30 a.m.

The up journey began at 6.40p.m. and arrived in London at 3.55a.m. The train was usually composed of six of the special T.P.O. vans all of which had the large side gangways. The first three vehicles were fitted with tractator arms for setting down mail at various points in the Duchy and for picking up. Two vans out of the six were equipped with the extending nets. The question has been asked, did these trains always remain facing in the one direction, or were they turned around at each end on triangles, like those on the old LMSR, or turntables, as was once done at Aberdeen? The answer to this question is that as on the 'UP' (or Eastward) journey, mail was only picked up latterly at

FIG 274

FIG 275

Liskeard, so there was no need to turn the train, and one van was equipped with a net on the 'offside' specially to pick up at this one station.

As regards the actual operation of picking up and setting down, these two obviously-posed pictures show the modus operandi. The mail that is to be picked up is set up on a high rotating arm by the side the the track by a special post office official who has to know the time and running conditions of the mail train. The arm of this standard is bent over at the top so that it can be swung out towards the line. The mail bag itself is enclosed in a stiff leather pouch and suspended from the end of the rotating staff. On the coach is a large collapsible net which is operated by a lever in the carriage by a responsible person who has to know exactly where the train is, in order to extend the net at the right place. A strong rope in the shape of a letter 'V' is stretched across the mouth of the net and as the train passes the picking up post the rope catches the pouch, detaches it from the extended arm, and throws it into the net from where it tumbles down the incline through the 4' square aperture into the carriage. Whilst the net is out, a warning bell rings in the van, and all the sorting staff stand well clear as the pouch really comes in with a bang! For the outgoing mail, a similar operation takes place, but at a lower level, so that the two systems do not foul each other. A static oblong net is fixed by the side of the track, and small traductor arms extended from the coach from a doorway in advance of the pick-up net. These ends are duplicated, so that one swings one way and the other in the opposite direction; they are swung out by an operator in the car moving a lever.

The pictures explain the technique well, and the vehicle shown is No.806, which is one of *lot 1430*. The other carriages in the picture are a Post Office storage van No.1201 of *diagram M.15 lot 1185*, and trailing, a 'Toplight' brake 3rd *diagram D.36*, No.2360. Note the cabin in the picture fitted with lineside telephone by means of which the postman could ascertain the running of the 'Postal'. As well as the West Country T.P.O, other trains ran to South Wales and cross country from Cardiff to Crewe, but without apparatus.

FIG 276

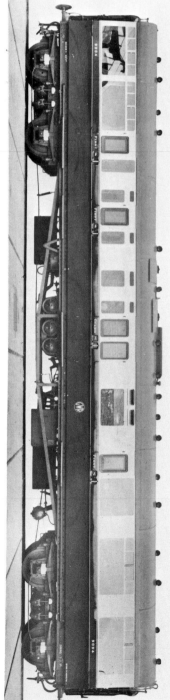

FIG 277

LOT.1431
DIA.G.59

FIG 278

To the same dimensions as the 'Cornish Riviera' stock of 1930 were two 1st class brake saloons, Nos. 9004 and 9005, constructed on *lot 1431*. They were designed for private hire, being completely self contained units of top quality, containing a dining saloon and a separate 1st compartment with a large kitchen and pantry in the central vestibule which was supplied with gas and electric apparatus. There was a small guard's cabin and end windows in the bow ends, notwithstanding the corridor gangways.

The photographs show the vehicles in three different liveries. The original condition is as shown in the centre picture, *figure 277*, with the white roof. At the top, *figure 276*, the circular totem device has replaced the coat of arms, and the large windows have sliding ventilators in place of the hinged toplights, whilst in the lower photograph (*figure 278*) coach 9005 is seen at Paddington in 1950, still in the last Great Western livery. Note that the single compartment has been knocked out to make a larger saloon.

The photograph from Paddington archives shows the old and the new style of trailer conversions. Leading is No.182, a 70' rebuilt vehicle which was originally S.R.M. No.56. There were six such ones, numbering from 181 to 186 and the new lot number was *1432* to *diagram A.26*. The small conversion table from the official drawing on page 166 is added under *figure 279* and indicates which cars were which. Running as per *figure 279*, the driver could operate from either end of the unit, as shown in the end of No.182, or, in the reverse direction, in the driving end of the slab-sided trailer. Note that in the drawing of A.26 the bogies have been changed for the 7' plate variety. Altogether there were 19 trailers converted to *Dia.A.26 from S.R.Ms.*

FIG 279

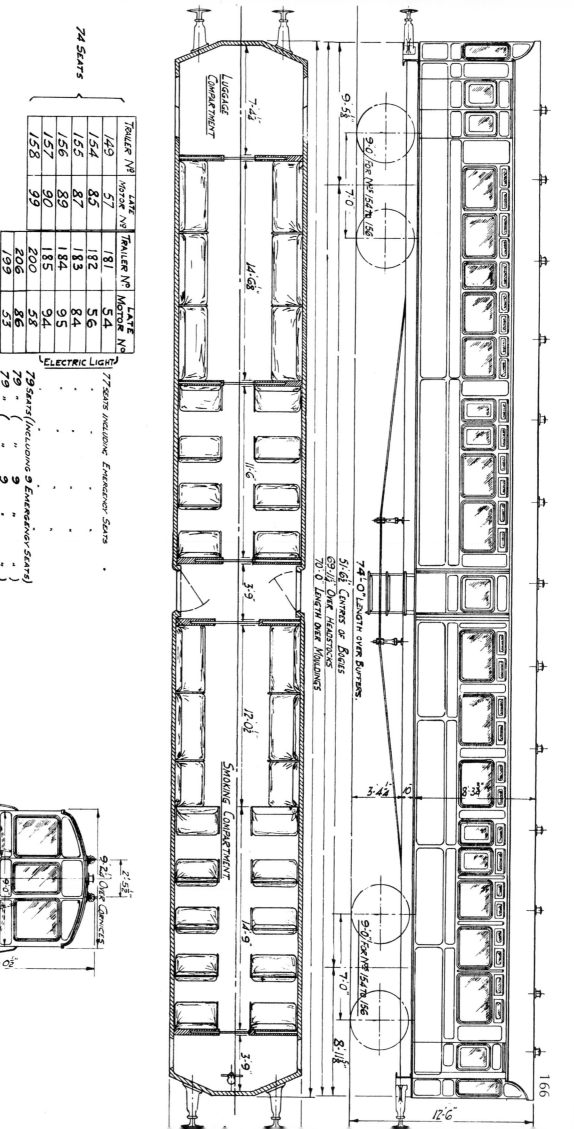

LOT. 1432

G.W.R.
TRAILER CARRIAGE
SWINDON
FEB. 1928

TARE. 32 - 0

74 SEATS

TRAILER Nº	LATE MOTOR Nº	TRAILER Nº	LATE MOTOR Nº
149	57	181	54
154	85	182	56
155	87	183	84
156	89	184	95
157	90	185	94
158	99	199	53
		200	58
		206	86

"ELECTRIC LIGHT"

77 SEATS INCLUDING EMERGENCY SEATS

79 SEATS (INCLUDING 9 EMERGENCY SEATS)
79 " (" 9 " ")
79 " (" 9 " ")

LUGGAGE COMPARTMENT

SMOKING COMPARTMENT

7·4½"
14·6⅛"
11·6"
3·9"
12·0½"
14·9"
3·9"

74·0" LENGTH OVER BUFFERS.
51·6½" CENTRES OF BOGIES.
69·11½" OVER HEADSTOCKS
70·0" LENGTH OVER MOULDINGS

9·5⅝"
9·0" FOR Nº⁵ 154 TO 156
7·0"
9·0" FOR Nº⁵ 154 TO 156
7·0"
8·11½"

3·4½"
10
8·3¾"

9·2½" OVER CORNICES
9·0"
2·5½"
10·10"

13·0½"

12·6"

166

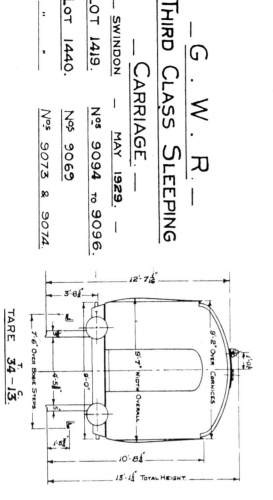

— G. W. R. —

THIRD CLASS SLEEPING

— CARRIAGE. —

— SWINDON — MAY 1929. —

LOT 1419. Nos 9094 to 9096.

LOT 1440. Nos 9069

" " Nos 9073 & 9074.

TARE 34 - 13. T. C.

DIA. J.11

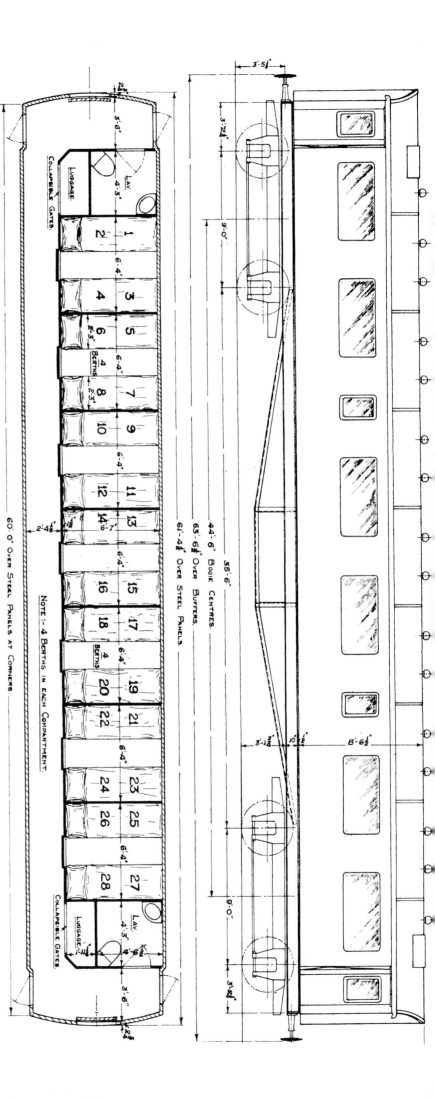

Having described the 1st class main line sleeper on *page 154* this drawing is of the 3rd class version of the stock, and it is apparent from the drawing that the main difference is that where the first class vehicles catered for one person per compartment, this carriage was planned to accommodate four travellers to each compartment, by means of top bunks hinged over the lower berths. Also, the 3rd class passengers had to fend for themselves for there was no attendant, although a small cupboard was provided at each end for luggage.

Lot 1419, diagram J.11 Nos.9094 to 9096

Lot 1440, diagram J.11 Nos.9069 9072 to 9094

FIG 280

FIG 281

To show the subtle differences between the 3rd class 'Riviera' stock sleeper and the 1st class sleeper, these four pictures are reproduced and although years apart the outline is the same. The lower official photo, *figure 282*, shows No.9067 of the 1st class category as originally built. *Figure 283* illustrates 3rd class No.9069 at Old Oak Common in 1948, just before Nationalization. The two smaller pictures, *figures 280 and 281*, show No.9072 in B.R. days with both corridor and berth sides.

DIA.J.12

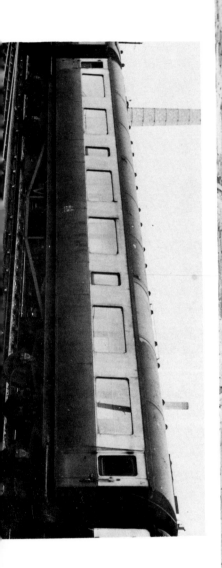

FIG 282

LOT.1442
DIA.J.13

No.9075 was the only composite sleeper built new under the aegis of the Great Western Railway. In the same series as the *J.11 and J.12* this vehicle was given the *diagram J.13*. The longer half of the vehicle was given over to 1st class accommodation and three compartments were assigned to the 3rd class travellers. There was no provision for an attendant, and the lavatory was at one end only. *Figure 284* shows the berth side of 9075 in 1947 on the West Wales run and *figure 285* the corridor side in 1931 when outshopped. Notice the Great Western transfer has been staggered off the top of the coat of arms.

FIG 285

LOT.1442
DIA.J.13

No.9075 was the only composite sleeper built new under the aegis of the Great Western Railway. In the same series as the *J.11 and J.12* this vehicle was given the *diagram J.13*. The longer half of the vehicle was given over to 1st class accommodation and three compartments were assigned to the 3rd class travellers. There was no provision for an attendant, and the lavatory was at one end only. *Figure 284* shows the berth side of 9075 in 1947 on the West Wales run and *figure 285* the corridor side in 1931 when outshopped. Notice the Great Western transfer has been staggered off the top of the coat of arms.

FIG 285

169

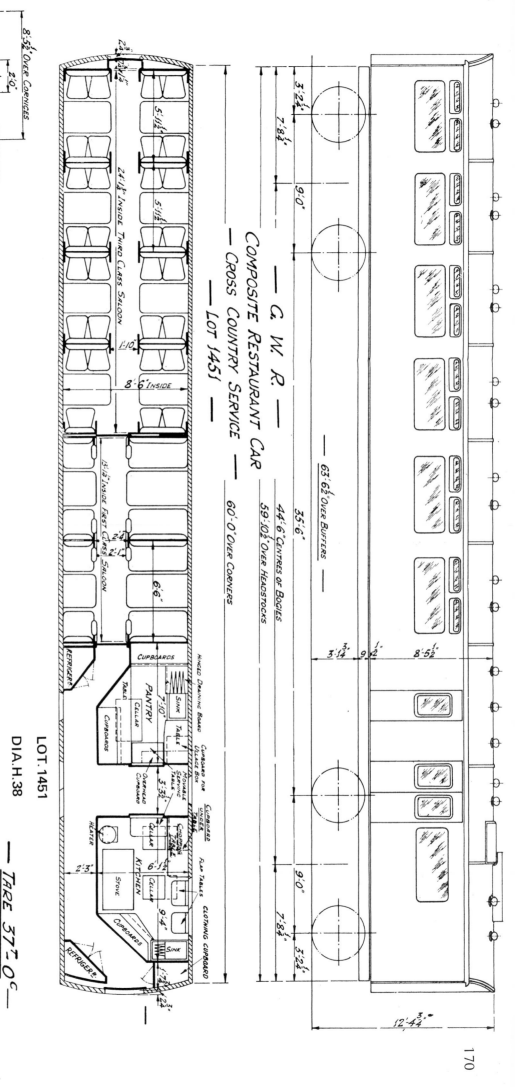

G. W. R.

COMPOSITE RESTAURANT CAR

— CROSS COUNTRY SERVICE —

— LOT 1451 —

CROSS COUNTRY SERVICE

24'-1½" INSIDE THIRD CLASS SALOON

8'-6" INSIDE

13'-3½" INSIDE FIRST CLASS SALOON

60'-0" OVER CORNERS

44'-6" CENTRES OF BOGIES

59'-10½" OVER HEADSTOCKS

63'-6½" OVER BUFFERS

35'-6"

9'-0"

7'-8½"

3'-2½"

12'-4¾"

REFRIGER:

CUPBOARDS

PANTRY

CELLAR

SINK

TABLE

CUPBOARDS

HINGED DRAINING BOARD

CUPBOARD FOR ULLAGE BOX

OVERHEAD CUPBOARD

MOVABLE SERVING TABLE

CUPBOARD UNDER TABLE

FLAP TABLES

CLOTHING CUPBOARD

HEATER

STOVE

KITCHEN

CELLAR

CELLAR

CUPBOARDS

SINK

REFRIGER:

LOT. 1451

DIA. H.38

— TARE 37T-0C —

9'-0" Over Top Steps Boards
9'-0" Over Handles
9'-3" Over Panels
8'-5½" Over Cornices
2'-0"
3'-6½"
10'-7¼"
13'-0" Total Height

Ten compact dining cars of the same outline as the 'Riviera' stock, but only 9' wide instead of 97", were built in 1931 for cross country services. They were of the end kitchen pattern, with a small 1st class saloon seating 12 diners in the centre of the car, and a larger, but rather cramped, dining compartment seating 31 passengers at the other end, separated by a sliding door partition. As built they were to the drawing on this page, but when rebuilt after the war the large windows were fitted with sliding vents, in place of the hinged toplights originally in place, as shown in the photograph, figure 286. Numbers were as follows:-

Lot 1451 to diagram H.38, Nos. 9601 to 9610

FIG 286

170

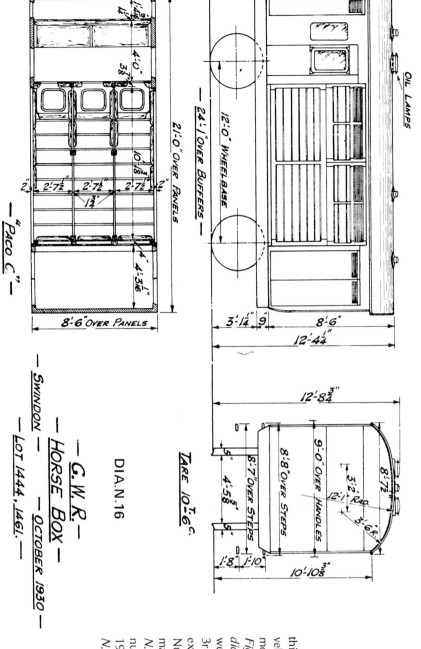

— OIL LAMPS —

24'-1" OVER BUFFERS

12'-0" WHEELBASE

3'-1¼" 9   8'-6"
12'-4¼"

12'-8¾"

8'-7½"
8'-7" OVER STEPS
8'-8" OVER STEPS
9'-0" OVER HANDLES
3'-2
12'-1 RAD.
3'-6" R.
4'-5⅝"
5"   5"
1'-8" 1'-10"
10'-10⅜"

TARE 10T. 6C.

— "PACO C" —

2" 2'-7½" 2'-7½" 2'-7½" 2"
1⅜"
21'-0" OVER PANELS
1'-8¾" 4'-0" 3⅜"
4¼" 10⅛"
14 4" 4'-3⅜"

8'-6" OVER PANELS

DIA.N.16

— G.W.R. —
— HORSE BOX —
— SWINDON —
— OCTOBER 1930 —
— LOT 1444, 1461. —

FIG 287

FIG 288

Two vehicles of the later stage of bow-ended design are illustrated on this page. Although standard length of 61'4½", the width of these vehicles was kept down to 9'3", which meant that they could traverse most of the system and not suffer the restrictions of the wider vehicles. Figure 287, shows No.5691, one of lot 1466, which were built to diagram C.60 in 1932. They were numbered from 5689 to 5708 and were still fitted with the 7' plate bogie. Figure 288 is one of the brake 3rds of the same design standing at Reading Station in the 1950's; this example is No.5380. Note the recessed door for the guard only. Numbering details were lot 1454 to diagram D.111, Nos. 5373-5380 making eight vehicles in all. Also on this page is a 4mm drawing of the N.15 Horse Box, made in two lots. In the first lot 1444 of 1930, the numbers were various between 489 and 514; in the second lot 1461 of 1931, the numbers were 515 to 599, but some of these were of diagram N.16.

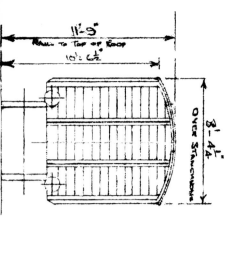

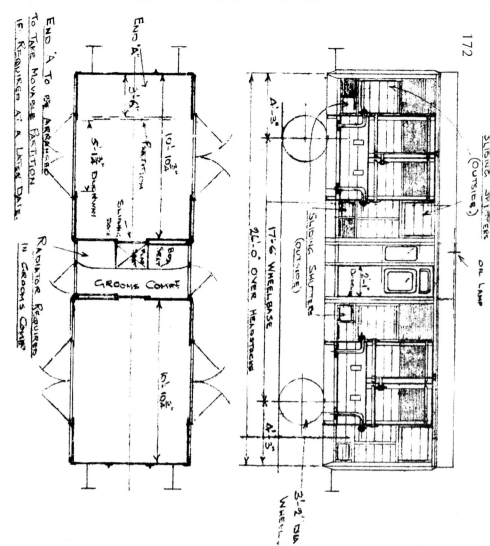

DIAGRAM OF
SPECIAL CATTLE WAGON

LOT.1467
DIA.W.13

FIG 289

The design of cattle box for passenger trains altered slightly in 1931 as this drawing of *diagram W.13* shows. The wheelbase was 17'6" and the side doors were made wider, to take moveable partitions across the vehicle. I have no evidence that this was ever so, but the idea was to enclose a beast in a small area, thus enabling it to ride the swaying vehicle better than an open space. Comparison with the photograph of No.722 will show the differences in the construction of the doors. The official original drawing is rather blurred but has been included to help modellers.

Two of these three pictures show the 'Torquay' Pullman passing Twyford. One train has five Pullmans and one Great Western vehicle; the larger picture shows six Pullmans, and the train at the top has seven.

The Great Western Super Saloons, eight vehicles which were undoubtedly the finest carriages the Great Western ever built, follow on the next five pages. They were constructed for the lucrative Ocean traffic, which was increasing as many Transatlantic liners called at Plymouth.

The years 1929 and 1930 saw the 'boat trains' running up to Paddington from Plymouth Millbay with some genuine Pullman cars in their make-up.

Although the vehicles were privately owned, the Pullman experiment on the Great Western is worthy of note, as it led indirectly to the building at Swindon of some high quality carriages to act as the Company's own 'Pullmans'. The Great Western had used several Pullman cars on the Ocean specials in the early months of 1929 and furthered this arrangement by putting on a regular Pullman service on July 8th of that year, called the 'Torquay Pullman Limited'. Some details would perhaps be of interest as little has been written about this train.

The schedule was for Mondays and Fridays and it left Paddington at 11.00a.m., arriving at Torquay at 2.40p.m. and finally at Paignton at 2.50p.m. The return up journey left Paignton at 4.30p.m. from Torquay at 4.50, and arrived in London at 8.30p.m.

The seating capacity of the train was 260, made up as follows: Car A, 3rd class - 30; B, 3rd class - 36; C, 3rd class - 42; D, 1st class - 20; E, 1st class - 24; F, 3rd class - 42; G, 3rd class - 36; H, 3rd class - 30. Of the eight vehicles composing the train the leading and trailing brake 3rds had 6 wheeled bogies, whilst all the other cars were equipped with the 4-wheeled Pullman type. Buck eye couplings and Pullman gangways were fitted and each car had its own interior decor. Amongst the names of the carriages were 'Zena' and 'Ione'. The exterior was the usual amber and cream, decorated with gold lines and scrolls. However, this experiment did not have success. The hire of the vehicles with attendants was found to be too costly, so plans were made to construct eight coaches to the very finest specification to take the place of the Pullmans on the Boat trains.

173

FIG 290

FIG 291

FIG 291A

FIG 292

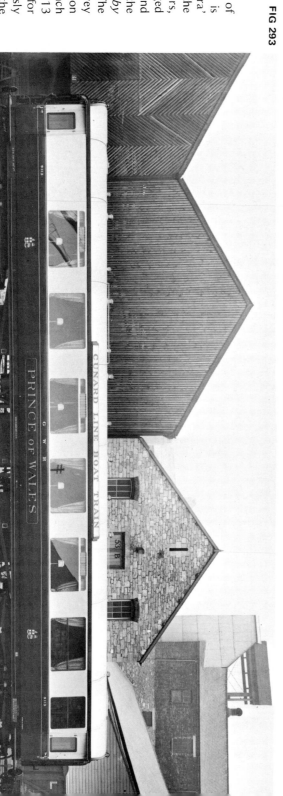

FIG 293

The 'Supers' were made to the standard length of 61'4½", but their width was to the limit, 9'7". It is obvious from their outline that the 1929 'Riviera' dining cars had a lot to do with their design, as the Supers had the same full waists and recessed doors, but with the difference that all the doors were hinged on the door stile nearest the centre of the vehicle, and set at an angle of 30° to the side. Full details of the interiors are described in *Great Western Coaches by M. Harris* published by *David & Charles Ltd.* The maiden run of the first three vehicles was to convey distinguished guests from Plymouth to London, on the occasion of the maiden voyage of the French Lines 'Colombie', (*figure 292, on this page*) No.9113 is shown at Swindon with the roof boards used for this special journey. Below, *figure 293*, and obviously taken at the same time, is the same vehicle with the 'Cunarder' roof boards. Note that the side shown is that away from the toilets.

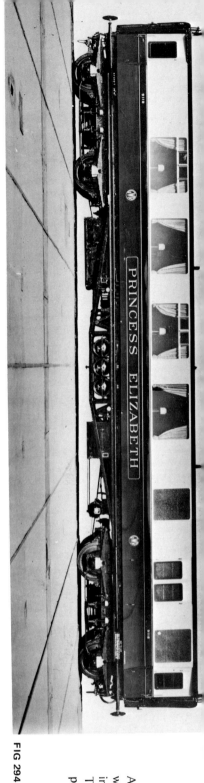

FIG 294

Three more official photographs are shown here. At the top is No.9118 which, with 9117, was rebuilt with a small kitchen, to avoid the necessity of including a separate kitchen car in the special train. This also enabled the car to be used on its own for a private party.

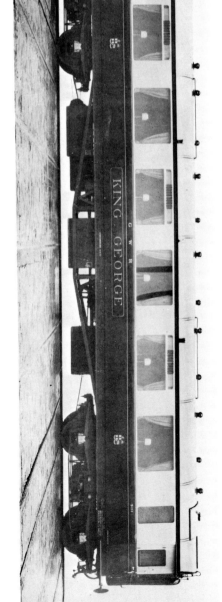

FIG 295

The central picture is of No.9111, which was the first coach to be made, and shows the lavatory side of the carriage, (figure 295). Finally, at the bottom is 'Prince of Wales' again, but this time the lavatory side. Note that when rebuilt, No.9118 had the circular totem transfers in place of the coat of arms. (figure 296).

Details of classification—

Lot no. 147, Nos. 9111 and 9112 to diagram G. 60

Lot no. 147, Nos. 9113 to 9118 to diagram G.61

FIG 296

175

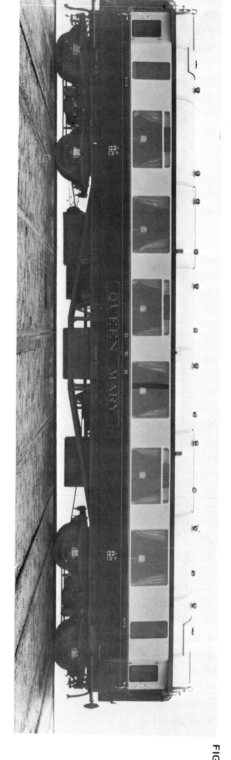

FIG 297

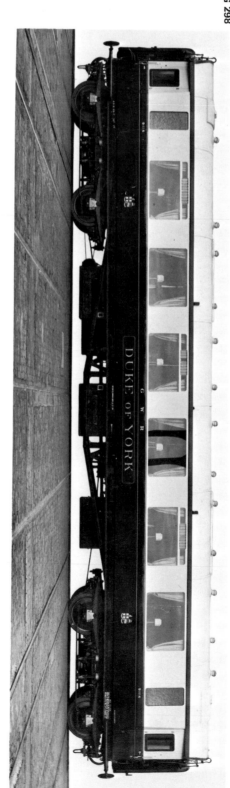

FIG 298

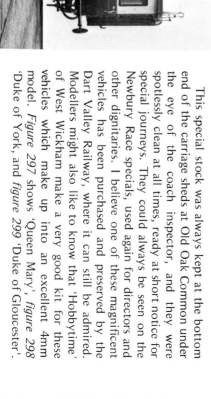

FIG 299

This special stock was always kept at the bottom end of the carriage sheds at Old Oak Common under the eye of the carriage inspector, and they were spotlessly clean at all times, ready at short notice for special journeys. They could always be seen on the Newbury Race specials, used again for directors and other dignitaries. I believe one of these magnificent vehicles has been purchased and preserved by the Dart Valley Railway, where it can still be admired. Modellers might also like to know that 'Hobbytime' of West Wickham make a very good kit for these vehicles which make up into an excellent 4mm model. *Figure 297* shows 'Queen Mary', *figure 298* 'Duke of York, and *figure 299* 'Duke of Gloucester'.

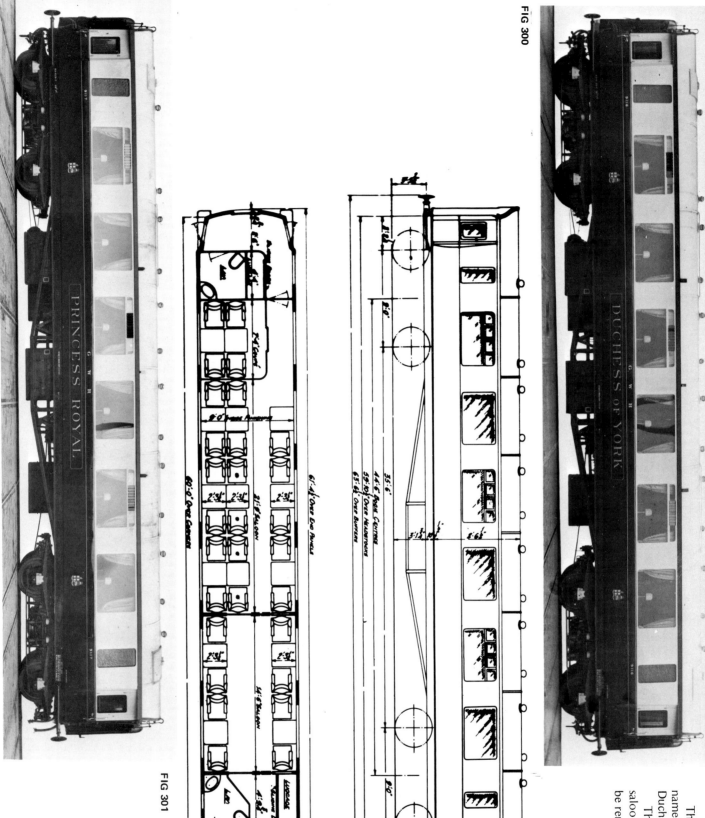

FIG 300

This page illustrates the last two Super Saloons, namely Princess Royal, No.9117, (*figure 300*), and Duchess of York, No.9116 (*figure 301*).

The drawing shows the internal layout of the saloons and the seats marked with an asterisk could be removed. (Not to 4mm scale).

FIG 301

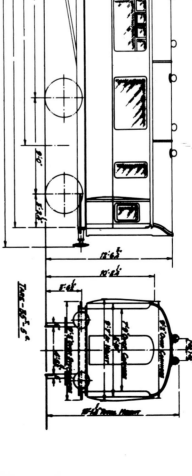

DIA.G.60

- G. W. R. -
- SALOON -
- MAIN LINE SERVICE -
- SWINDON - JANUARY - 1863 -

FIG 302

The interior shot in *figure 302* shows the main saloon in one of the 'Supers'. Notice here that there are single chairs on one side and two on the other side of the aisle. On *page 94 of Great Western Coaches by M. Harris* the small saloon is shown which has a wide passageway and only single chairs and tables, each side.

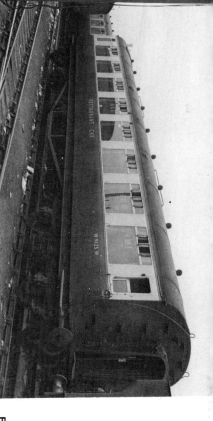

FIG 303

FIG 304

FIG 305

On this page are three types of bow-ended 3rd class carriages. In *figure 303* is one of the 60' 3rd class dining saloons made under *lot 1469* to *diagram H.40*. These vehicles used to run as one of a pair in the principal expresses, the other vehicle being a kitchen-first saloon of the *H.39 diagram*. Numbers were 9621-30 and the *H.39's* were 9611-20.

The photo shows No.9625 in the B.R. days with the windows changed to sliding ventilator tops. *Figure 305* bottom left, is one of the brake 3rd sixty-footers made under *lot 1478*, standing at Didcot station and showing the compartment side. This example has a left-hand van. The other two photographs illustrate both sides of a *C.62 diagram* full-corridor 3rd of the 60' bow-end series; note that both vehicles are fitted with the 7' plate bogie. The middle picture, *figure 304* is of No. 5393, and the lower right is No. 5445. The complete *lot was 1477* with painted numbers 5393 to 5446.

LOT.1477
DIA.C.62

FIG 306

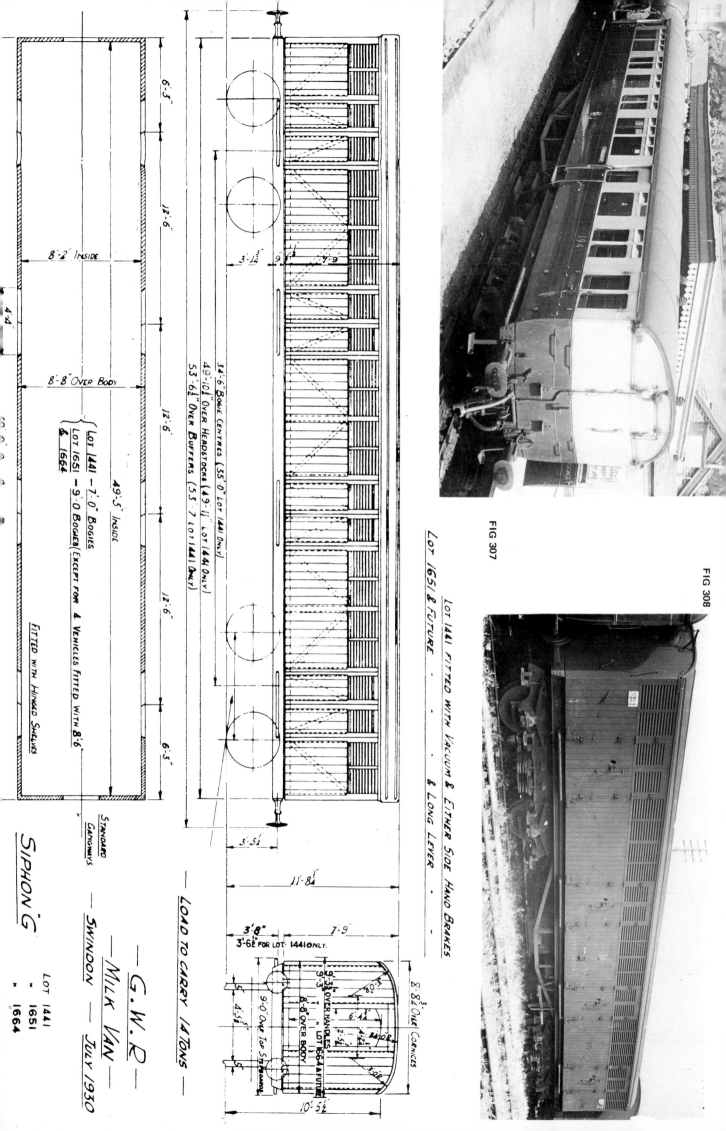

SIPHON 'G'

— G.W.R —
— MILK VAN —
— SWINDON — JULY 1930 —

LOT 1441
" 1651
" 1664

LOAD TO CARRY 14 TONS

LOT 1441 FITTED WITH VACUUM & EITHER SIDE HAND BRAKES

LOT 1651 & FUTURE — — — — & LONG LEVER — —

FITTED WITH HINGED SHELVES

STANDARD GANGWAYS

LOT 1441 – 7'-0" BOGIES
LOT 1651 – 9'-0 BOGIES (EXCEPT FOR 4 VEHICLES FITTED WITH 8'-6"
& 1664

34'-6" BOGIE CENTRES (35'-0 LOT 1441 ONLY)
49'-10½" OVER HEADSTOCKS (49'-11 LOT 1441 ONLY)
53'-6½" OVER BUFFERS (53'-7 LOT 1441 ONLY)

49'-5" INSIDE

8'-2" INSIDE
8'-8" OVER BODY

6'-3"   12'-6"   12'-6"   12'-6"   6'-3"

4'-4"

9'-1"   7'-9"   3'-1½"

11'-8½"

3'-8"
3'-6½" FOR LOT 1441 ONLY.

7'-9"   3'-5½"

8'-8¾" OVER CORNICES
9'-3½" OVER HANDLES
9'-0 OVER TOP STRAPPING
8'-8" OVER BODY
LOT 1664 & FUTURE
9'-3½" OVER HANDLES
9'-0" OVER TOP STRAPPING

10'-5½"

FIG 307

FIG 308

Two vehicles feature above. On the left is one of the short 'Branch' trailer cars, of *diagram A.30*, being No. 194 standing in Wallingford station in 1947. It is of particular interest as it shows the blank 'luggage' end with its peculiar arrangement of handles and steps. Note the vacuum pipe passed over the coupling hook before going under the buffer beam. This was to avoid the regulator gear. On the right is shown No. 2992, one of the later Siphon G's built to *digram O.33*. The difference in *lot.1441, 1651 and 1664* was in the hand brake, explained on the drawing. These Siphons were ventilated milk vans, which usually carried more parcel traffic than milk. Being fitted with gangways and electric light, they were often marshalled at the head of express trains, conveying parcels and luggage. I have also seen them used as pigeon specials transporting racing pigeons to their point of departure in baskets, for release by station staff.

FIG 310

LOT.1480
DIA.A.30

FIG 309

Ancient and Modern! Two pictures showing two totally different forms of Auto-car working. In the top picture, *figure 309*, car no. 110, which was originally steam rail car no. 12 of 1904, is seen being shunted in Woodstock yard by '517' class *No. 1159* on the 7th of July 1947, just before the branch was closed. A diagram of this trailer can be found on *page 30*. The lower photograph, *figure 310*, illustrates British Railways carrying on the tradition of working trailer cars in tandem with a 0—6—0T as the motive unit. These two cars were of *lot 1480* to *diagram A.30* and are shown in the Plymouth area where the practice of tandem trailers lasted for fifty years and more.

Of three separate lots, K.40 vans had slight differences in the wheelbase. Lot 1413 has already been illustrated on page 137 where it will be seen that the distance over the bogie pins was 46'6". In lot 1481 shown here in drawing and picture, (figure 311) the measurement has been reduced by 2', bringing it down to 44'6". The bogies were the same in both instances, being the 7' plate type.

The photograph illustrates No. 75 in the 1930 livery with white roof and double waist lining. Other numbers were 71 to 74, 76 to 85.

FIG 311

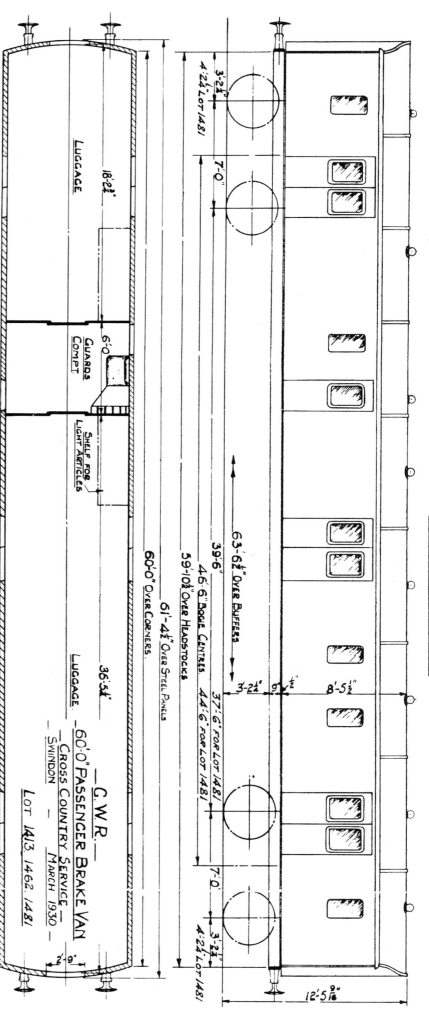

LOT.1481
DIA.K.40

The 1932, two T.P.O. vans were constructed for and ran on the South Wales mail service connecting Bristol with Carmarthen. No nets or arms were fitted to one van, as picking up or setting down mails was not operated on this route. The drawing shows the layout of the vans, and it can be seen that, although the gear is not fitted, the special doors and alcoves are present in the vehicles so that they could be equipped at a later date if necessary. It had flat ends, of course, and large side gangways. A 'late fee' letter box was fitted into both sides. *Lot no. 1484* had two vans only, Nos. 848 and 849 to *diagram L.19*. No. 848 had mail apparatus.

— G.W.R. —
— POST OFFICE VAN —
— SWINDON — SEPT. 1932 —
LOT 1484 — Nos 848 & 849

DIA. L.19

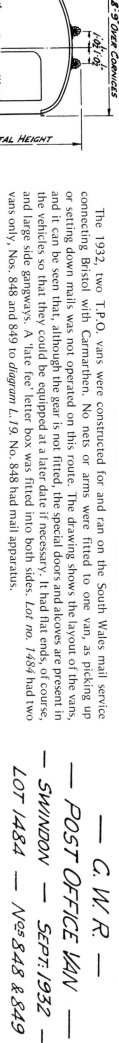

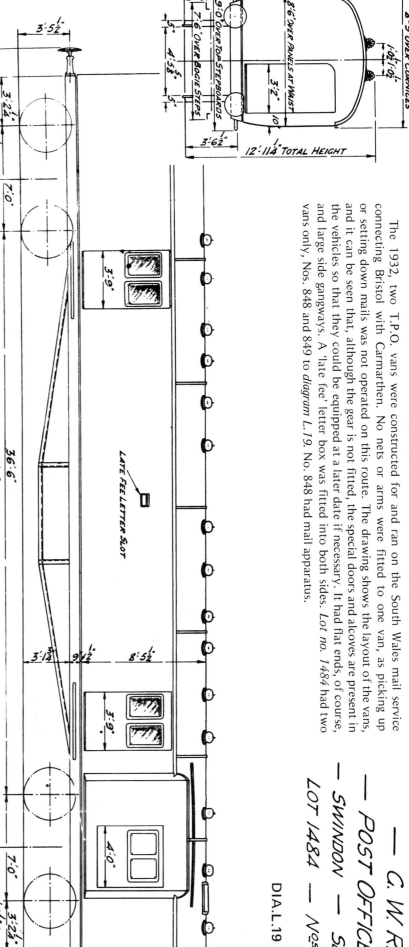

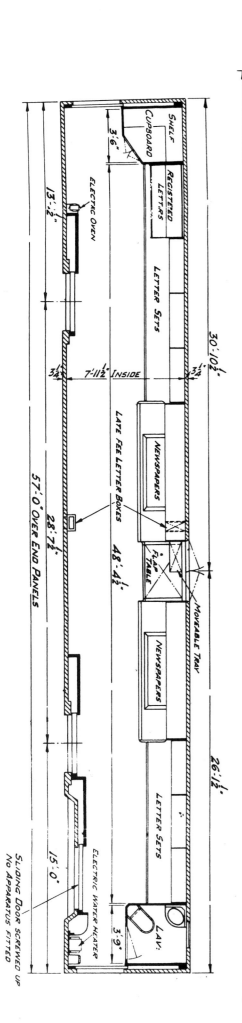

FIG 312

FIG 313

No. 849 in its original condition is shown at the top of the page with the off-side facing the camera. At the bottom is No. 796, a one-off of *lot 1500*, another sorting van which was used as a spare for the two on the South Wales run. This van, however, was not identical to the two on *lot 1484* as the doors and underframe details are slightly different; *diagram was L.20*. Note the transfers in different placing.

LOT.1500
DIA.L.20

Lot 1489 consisted of two batches of corridor 3rds. The first series built to *diagram C.64* numbered from 5709 to 5743, and the second order was for C.65's having flat-ends and numbered from 5744 to 5778. So this drawing and photograph illustrate the last batch of bow-ended corridor coaches to be made.

The/ were 9'3" wide over the waist, to the standard length of 61'4½" of the end panels and fitted with the 9' steel plate bogies. The photographs shows No. 5743, the last bow-ended vehicle built, in the strawberry and cream livery of B.R. standing at Didcot in 1959.

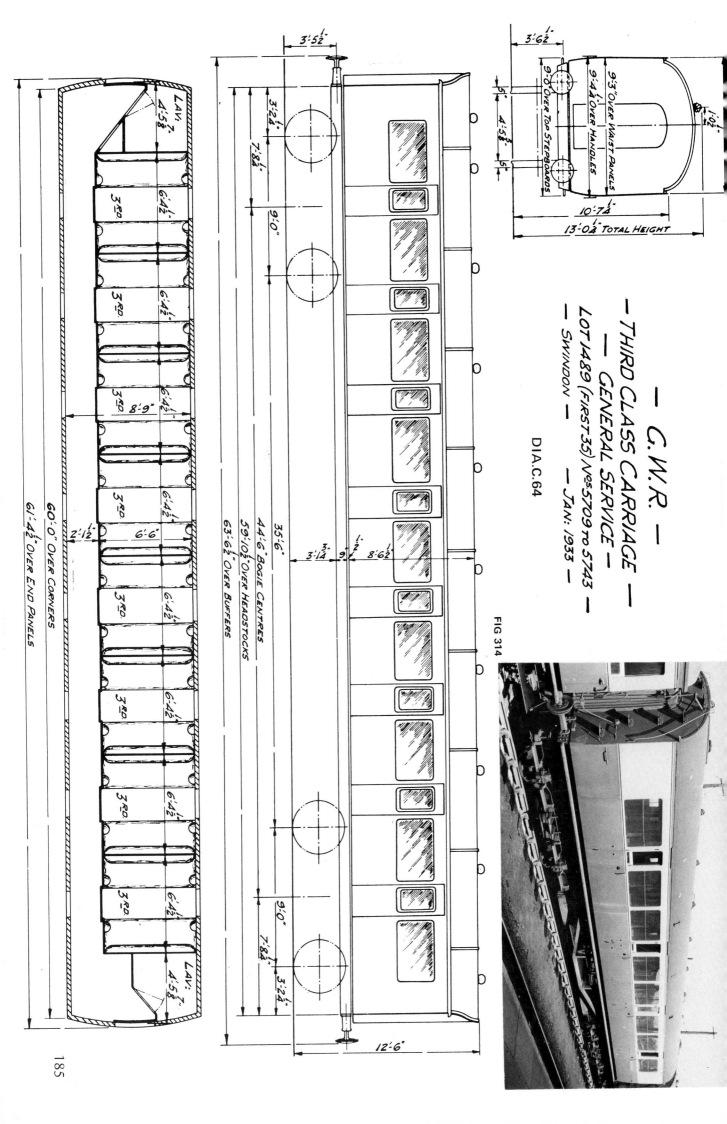

— G.W.R. —

— THIRD CLASS CARRIAGE —

— GENERAL SERVICE —

LOT 1489 (FIRST 35) Nos 5709 TO 5743 —

— SWINDON —   — JAN: 1933 —

DIA.C.64

FIG 314

FIG 315

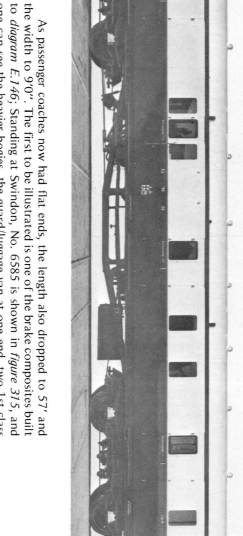

DIA.K.41

FIG 317

FIG 316

As passenger coaches now had flat ends, the length also dropped to 57' and the width to 9'0". The first to be illustrated is one of the brake composites built to *diagram E.146*; Standing at Swindon, No. 6585 is shown in *figure 315*, and one can see the heavier bogies, the guard/luggage van at one end, two 1st class compartments, and four 3rds.

The other two photographs show examples of the passenger brake van to the *diagram K.41*. Again flat-ended and to the same length width and outline as the coach top left, they were the first vans to use the new type of lighter 9' bogies, which had a single transverse bolster, with coil springs.

Figure 316 shows No. 103 at Oxford in 1948 branded 'PARCELS TRAIN BRAKE VAN' 'RETURN TO PADDINGTON'. Note the gas cylinder. Painted numbers were 101 to 110.

186

FIG 318

FIG 319

FIG 320

DIA.P.21

In the 1933 to 1934 period the four large open scenery trucks, code-named 'GOLIATH', were considered redundant in that condition, and two were rebuilt as 'MONSTERS'. The photographs on this page show the conversion. Top left is No. 489, fitted with the American bogies, at Thingley Jet. At the bottom, *figure 320*, is the official photo of No. 486 fitted with 7' plate bogies, and showing the 16" lettering of the thirties. The large picture of the interior, *figure 319*, shows not only the construction of the vehicle, but also the wheel beams for restraining vehicles conveyed inside. Note that the racks upon which the beams slide can stretch across the doors. The original lot was 1192. Re-built vehicles were to *diagram P.21* and numbers were 486 and 489.

187

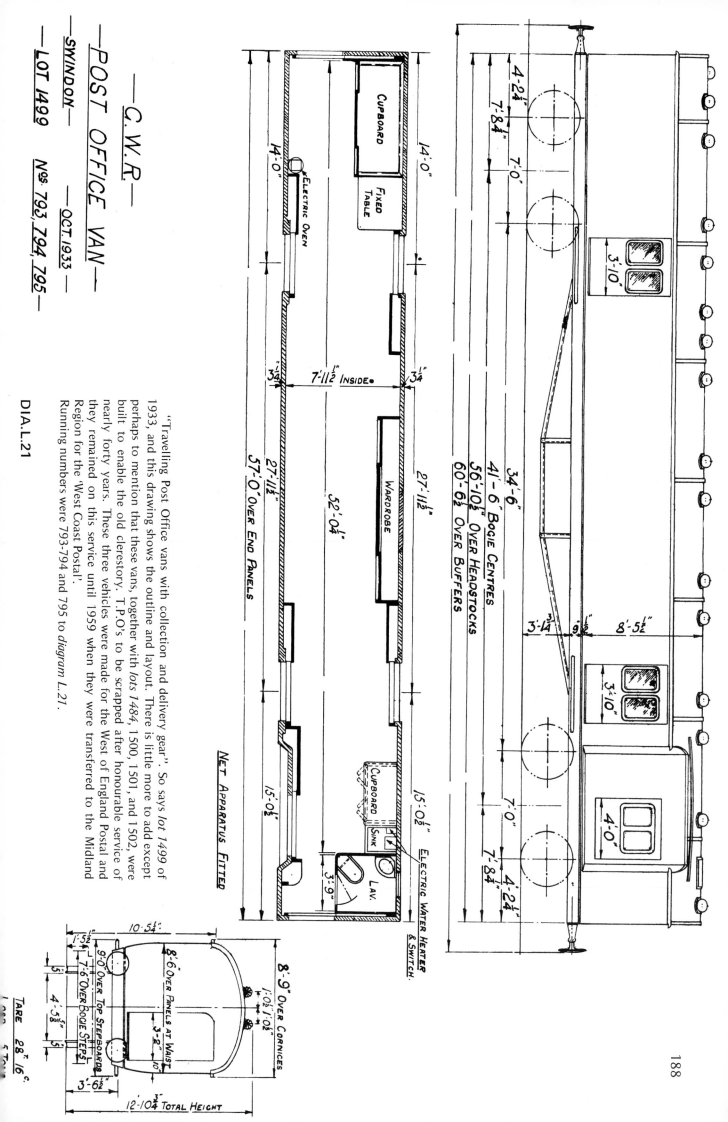

C.W.R.

POST OFFICE VAN

SWINDON

LOT 1499

Nos. 793, 794, 795

OCT. 1933

DIA. L.21

"Travelling Post Office vans with collection and delivery gear". So says *lot 1499* of 1933, and this drawing shows the outline and layout. There is little more to add except perhaps to mention that these vans, together with *lots 1484, 1500, 1501,* and *1502,* were built to enable the old clerestory. T.P.O's to be scrapped after honourable service of nearly forty years. These three vehicles were made for the West of England Postal and they remained on this service until 1959 when they were transferred to the Midland Region for the 'West Coast Postal'.
Running numbers were 793-794 and 795 to *diagram L.21*.

NET APPARATUS FITTED

CUPBOARD

FIXED TABLE

ELECTRIC OVEN

14'-0"

14'-0"

3/4"

7'-11½" INSIDE

3/4"

57'-0" OVER END PANELS

52'-0¼"

27'-11½"

27'-11½"

15'-0½"

WARDROBE

CUPBOARD

SINK

LAV.

3'-9"

15'-0½"

ELECTRIC WATER HEATER & SWITCH.

4'-2½"

7'-8¼"

7'-0"

34'-6"

41'-6" BOGIE CENTRES

56'-10½" OVER HEADSTOCKS

60'-6½" OVER BUFFERS

3'-10"

3'-10"

4'-0"

3'-1¾"

9½"

8'-5¼"

7'-0"

7'-8¼"

4'-2½"

8'-9" OVER CORNICES

8'-6" OVER PANELS AT WAIST

9'-0" OVER TOP STEPBOARDS

7'-6" OVER BOGIE STEPS

3'-2"

3'-6½"

4'-5⅝"

10'-5¼"

1'-5¾"

1'-0¼"

1'-0"

1'-0"

12'-10¾" TOTAL HEIGHT

TARE 28T. 16C.

188

FIG 321

FIG 322

These photographs show the operating side of both Nos. 794 and 795. In the top two pictures taken by Roye England, one can see close-up details of the pick-up and set down gear on coach 794. In the lower offical photograph, *figure 323*, No. 795 is seen in the white roof livery. Note the small electric lamps on the side, set in line with the set-down gear. It was the practice of the postal train to letter each coach from the engine, A, B, C, etc. Note this one has plate B affixed.

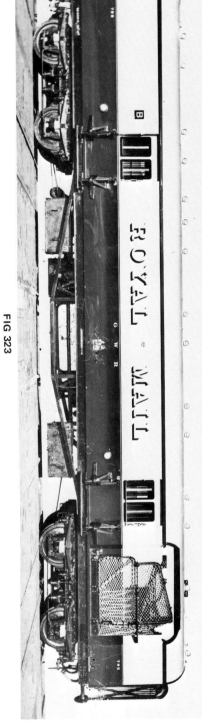

FIG 323

DIA. L.21

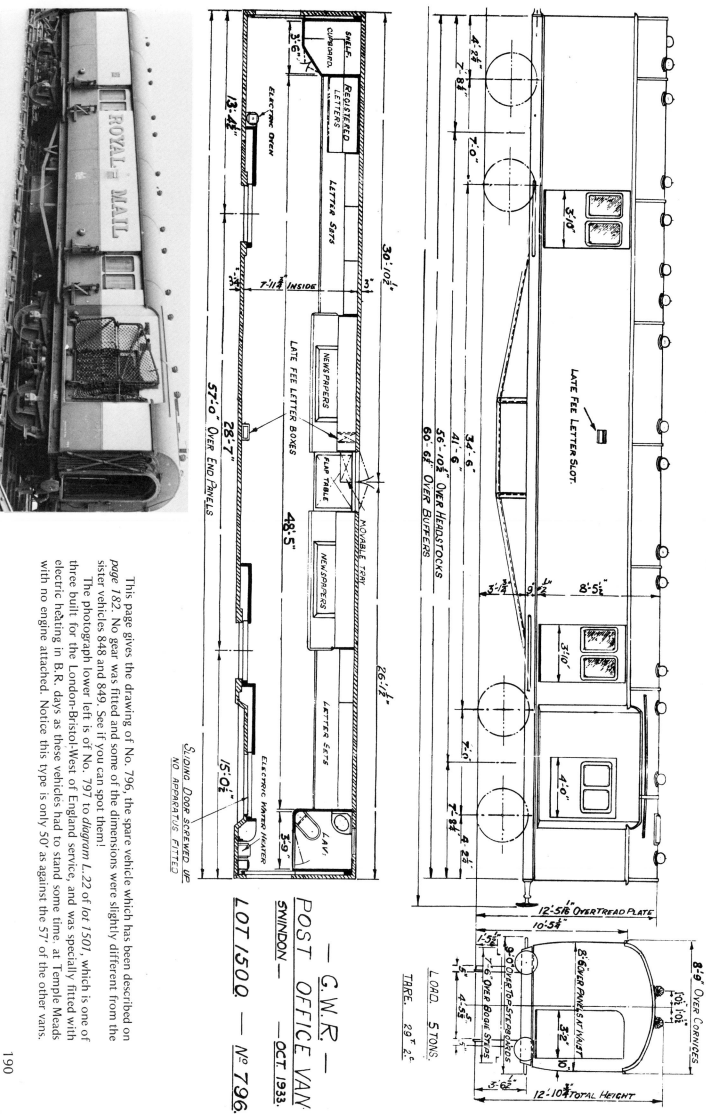

This page gives the drawing of No. 796, the spare vehicle which has been described on *page 182*. No gear was fitted and some of the dimensions were slightly different from the sister vehicles 848 and 849. See if you can spot them!

The photograph lower left is of No. 797 to *diagram L.22 of lot 1501*, which is one of three built for the London-Bristol-West of England service, and was specially fitted with electric heating in B.R. days as these vehicles had to stand some time, at Temple Meads with no engine attached. Notice this type is only 50' as against the 57' of the other vans.

GWR

POST OFFICE VAN

— SWINDON — — OCT. 1933.

LOT 1500. — No 796.

LOAD. 5 TONS. TARE. 29 T. 2 c.

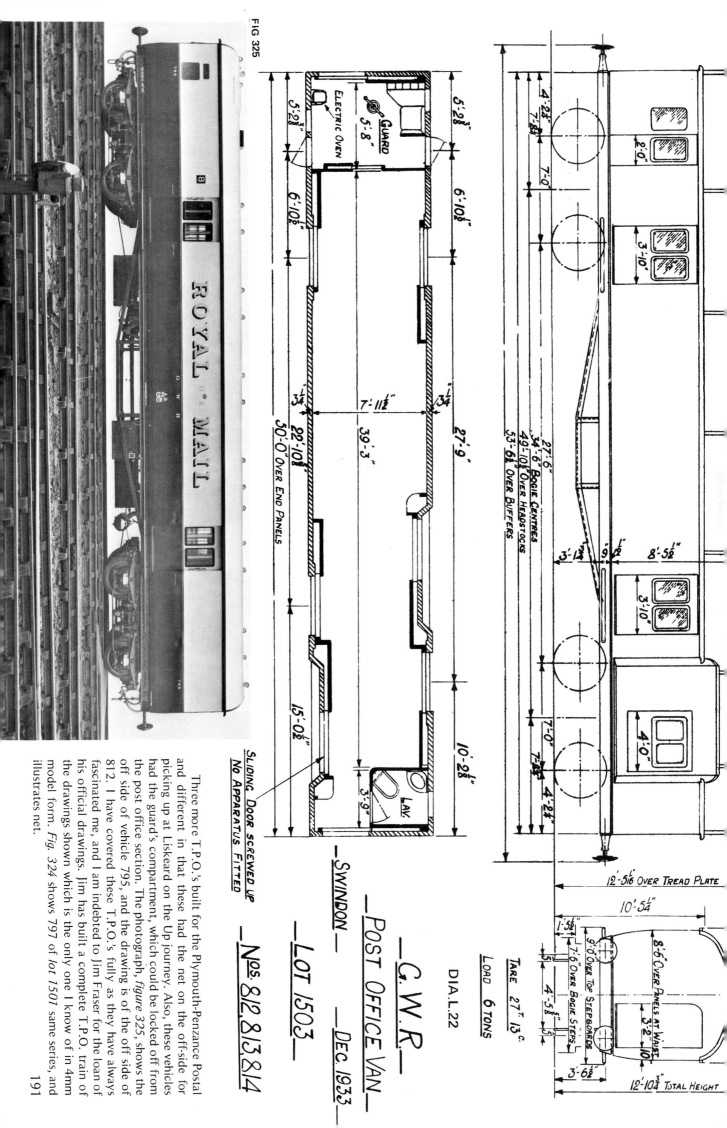

FIG 325

SLIDING DOOR SCREWED UP
NO APPARATUS FITTED

ELECTRIC OVEN

GUARD

LAV.

ROYAL MAIL

G W R

B

G.W.R.
— POST OFFICE VAN —
— SWINDON —
— LOT 1503 —
— DEC. 1933 —
Nos 812.813.814

DIA.L.22

LOAD 6 TONS

TARE 27T. 13c.

5'-2⅞"
5'-2⅛"
5'-8"
6'-10½"
27'-9"
10'-2⅞"
7'-11½"
39'-3"
22'-10⅞"
15'-0½"
30'-0" OVER END PANELS
3'-9"
3⅛"
3⅛"

53'-6½" OVER BUFFERS
49'-10¾" OVER HEADSTOCKS
34'-6" BOGIE CENTRES
27'-6"
4'-2⅜"
7'-8½"
7'-0"
2'-0"
3'-10"
3'-1⅛"
9'-½"
8'-5½"
3'-10"
4'-0"
7'-0"
7'-8½"
4'-2⅜"

12'-5⁵⁄₁₆" OVER TREAD PLATE
10'-5¼"
1'-5½"
4'-5⅝"
9'-0" OVER TOP STEPBOARDS
7'-6" OVER BOGIE STEPS
8'-6" OVER PANELS AT WAIST
3'-2"
3'-6½"
12'-10¾" TOTAL HEIGHT

Three more T.P.O.'s built for the Plymouth-Penzance Postal and different in that these had the net on the off-side for picking up at Liskeard on the Up journey. Also, these vehicles had the guard's compartment, which could be locked off from the post office section. The photograph, *figure 325*, shows the off side of vehicle 795, and the drawing is of the off side of 812. I have covered these T.P.O.'s fully as they have always fascinated me, and I am indebted to Jim Fraser for the loan of his official drawings. Jim has built a complete T.P.O. train of the drawings shown which is the only one I know of in 4mm model form. *Fig. 324* shows 797 of *lot 1501* same series, and illustrates net.

191

FIG 326

DIA.D.117

LOT.1507

FIG 327

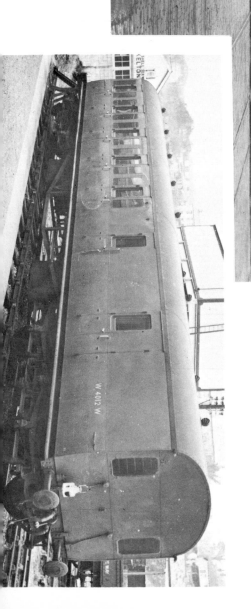

FIG 328

DIA.L.24

LOT.1504

DIA.E.140

LOT.1445

FIG 330

The final picture of T.P.O. vans is one of the *L.24 diagram* type, only 46'6" long and having no pick up or delivery gear. In fact they were just mail bag tenders, although No. 816 was fitted with a "late fee" posting box, and can be seen in *figure 326*. There were three in *lot 1504*; No's. 815, 816 and 817, and their programme was for the London-South Wales service. When photographed at Old Oak Common this vehicle appeared to be the wrong way around! Note the gangways. The picture, *figure 327* is one of a 'B' set seen standing at Kingham station in 1948. This set used to work between Cheltenham and Kingham via Andoversford, usually with a 45XX tank engine. Built under *lot 1445* to *diagram E.140*, these two coaches were numbered 6895 and 6894. As bow-ended stock, they have been placed out of order on this page to compare with the newer 1934 flat ended stock, seen in the official photograph of No. 5877, (*figure 328*). A brake 3rd non-corridor of *lot 1507* to *diagram D.117*. Points of comparison are: longer bogies, no recessed doors, width being 9' instead of 9'3", slam locks, (but not recessed into the coach sides), and only one drop light on the luggage compartment instead of the more usual two. No. 4012 is shown in B.R. days.

LOTS.1507
DIA.D.117

This end view of No. 5871 taken from the compartment end shows the profile of the flat ended coaches well, and it can be seen how flatter the sides are in comparison with the fuller-bodied bow-enders. Note also that the side lamp brackets are no longer fitted, and there are no end steps or hand rails to the roof. The small eyelet in the centre of the end was for fastening the chain which held up the coupling if used next to a slip coach.
Other numbers in this lot were 5868 to 6877.

193

FIG 331

The next two *lots nos. 1508 and 1509*, were of the same size in length and width, even though the vehicles were general purpose corridor stock. The *figure 331*, taken at Didcot in 1959, shows one of the brake composites No. 6916, which was built to *diagram E.148*. Notice that only one door is provided to each pair of compartments, so that in the brake composite there are two doors in the side for four 3rd class compartments, one door for two 1st class compartments, and a double door with only one droplight for guard and luggage. Also note the high position of the large windows, much closer to the cantrail than previously.

The lower picture, *figure 332*, shows this much clearer in No. 5861, in B.R. maroon with yellow and black lining. The diagram for this 3rd corridor coach was C.67 and *lot 1509* was an order of sixty such vehicles numbering 5808 to 5867.

LOT.1508
DIA.E.148

FIG 332

LOT.1509
DIA.C.67

Many of the steam rail cars were eventually converted to trailer cars simply by dispensing with the steam unit, fitting a normal bogie in its place, and making the engine compartment over to extra seating and a luggage vestibule. Two such conversions are shown on this page. At the bottom, *figure 334*, is No. 204, which was originally S.R.M. No. 82 of the *Q diagram*. In the upper official picture, *figure 333*, is seen No. 200, which started life as Steam Rail Motor No. 58 of the *'O' diagram* (see *page 165*). Ten cars were dealt with in this way under *lot 1511* of 1934 and, as they were of 4 different designs, they had four new diagrams as follows—

Nos. 197 and 198, were S.R.M's 39 and 40 of *K diagram* New *diagram A.23*

Nos. 199, 200 and 206 were S.R.M's 53, 58 and 86 of *O and R diagrams* New *diagram A.26.*

Nos. 201 was S.R.M. 199 of *O diagram* New *diagram A.29*

Nos. 202-5 were S.R.M's 73, 74, 82 and 83 of *Q and Q' diagram* New *diagram A.31*

It will be noticed that No. 204 is a shorter vehicle than No. 200 but is running on the American 8' bogies, whereas the long 70' trailer has the short 7' plate bogies. Gas lighting is common to both designs, but an interesting point is that the central doors are hung in different ways, one L.H. and one R.H.

FIG 334

LOT.1511
DIA.A.26

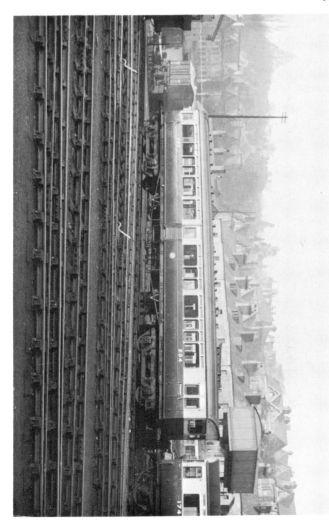

DIA.A.31

FIG 335

196

LOT.1513
DIA.C.67

Two more examples of the 57' corridor stock with flat ends are shown here, both contemporary of one another although the top example is a full 3rd of *C.67 design*, (*figure 335*) and the other coach is a brake composite of the *diagram E.148* already described on *page 171. Figures 336 and 336a* show both ends of No. 6916 in the strawberry and cream livery of B.R., compartment side, whereas No. 5901 (*figure 335*) shows the corridor side of the 3rd and illustrates the four door pattern well. All the pictures were taken at Didcot in 1959.

FIG 336

DIA.E148

The Diesel Rail car No. 1 was first put into service on the Great Western on 4th December 1933. The engine and chassis were built at Slough by A.E.C. Ltd., and the bodywork was by Park Royal Coachworks Ltd. The drawing shows the outline and plan from which it can be seen that seating was provided for 69 passengers. The unit was powered by one engine of 121 B.H.P. driving a bogie at one end, and the driver's controls were duplicated at both ends of the vehicle so that the car could be driven in either direction. No provision was made for a trailer, as the power unit was of insufficient strength to cope with another vehicle. A towing hook was fitted, but was hidden under the streamlined panelling. The buffing gear was also of emergency pattern, consisting of protruding shafts with no heads. This first car was put into local service at Reading. The photograph shows the next development in the streamlined diesel car design, *figure 337*. The vehicle No. 2, was ordered under *lot 1522* to Railcar *diagram V* and had two other sisters, Nos. 3 and 4.

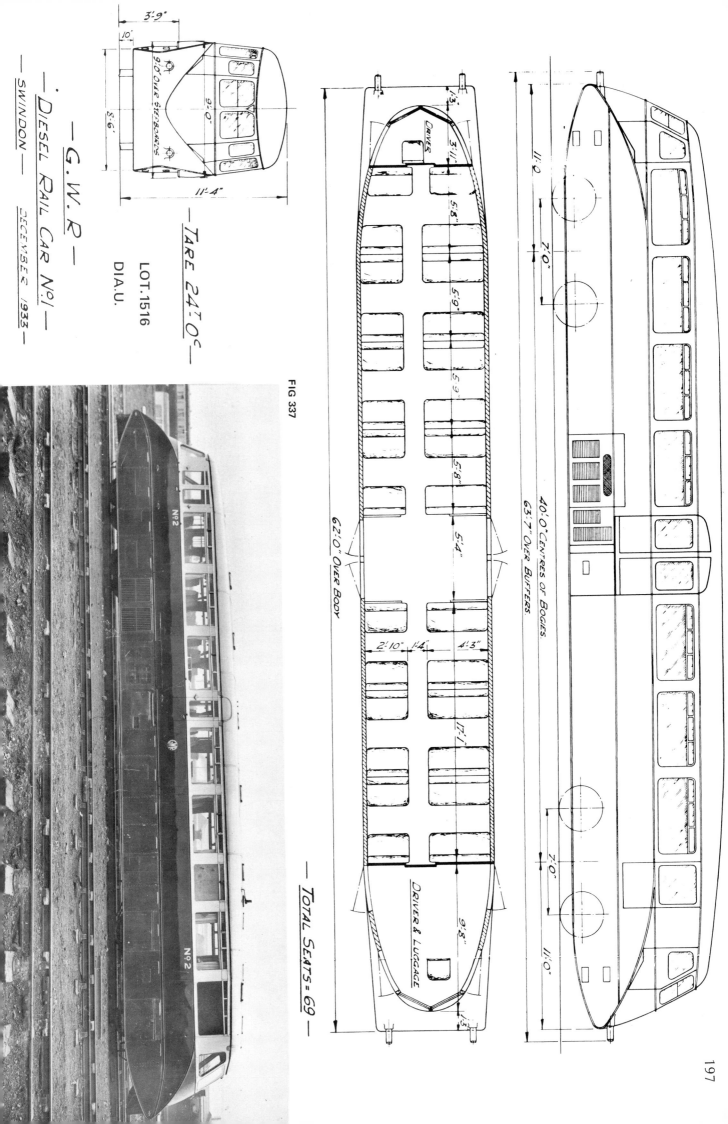

— G.W.R. —
— DIESEL RAIL CAR No. 1 —
— SWINDON —
— DECEMBER 1933 —

— TARE 24T·0c —

LOT. 1516
DIA. U.

3'-9"
10'
9'-0" OVER STEPBOARDS
9'-0"
8'-6"
11'-4"

FIG 337

DRIVER

5'-8"
5'-9"
5'-9"
5'-8"
5'-4"
3'-11"
9'-8"
1'-3"
1'-3"

2'-10"   1'-4"   1'-3"
17'-1"

62'-0" OVER BODY

DRIVER & LUGGAGE

— TOTAL SEATS = 69 —

11'-0"
7'-0"
40'-0" CENTRES OF BOGIES.
63'-7" OVER BUFFERS
7'-0"
11'-0"

No 2

No 2

The cars differed from No. 1 in that two engines were employed, one to each bogie. They were capable of speeds 75 to 80 miles an hour, compared with the 60 maximum of No. 1. These cars were designed for express services and seating was for only 44 passengers, due to the fitting of longer seats with tables between them, and two small lavatory cubicles. Note that with this early design of railcar the side panelling came right down to within 12" of the rail level. *Figure 338 shows No. 4 (with A.E.C. driver!)* This car had a small buffet arrangement.

FIG 338

LOT.1522

DIA.V

198

At the top of this page is another example of the *diagram C.67*. *Figure 339* shows a full corridor 3rd built under *lot 1527* in 1935, in the maroon livery of B.R. Running number is 5946. *Figure 340* shows another from the same *lot no. 5966*, but in the chocolate and cream livery. This picture shows the suspended gangways well. More than fifty vehicles were built to this lot, numbering from 5928 to 5982.

Figure 341 shows one of the kitchen cars of the 'Excursion' stock. They were called 'Excursion' because this new design of carriage was the first main line stock to be built with the open saloon centre gangway type since the 'clerestory' days, and it marked another step forward in the progression of coach construction. The reason for this

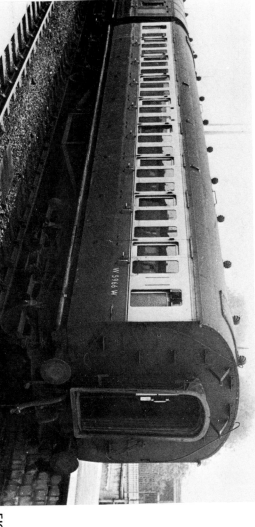

FIG 340

LOT.1527   DIA.C.67

departure was to cater for special parties such as football specials and Sunday trips to the sea, and indeed the first use of these trains was for a Wembley Cup Final in 1935. To serve the customers with refreshments two special kitchen cars were built in Nos. 9633 and 9634, As the 'Excursion' stock was provided with tables, the dining staff were supposed to deliver food to them, but this did not quite work out according to plan. Imagine carrying a hot dinner through five or six open cars of trippers in holiday mood! The two kitchen cars were to *diagram H.42* of *lot 1529*.

LOT.1529   DIA.H.42

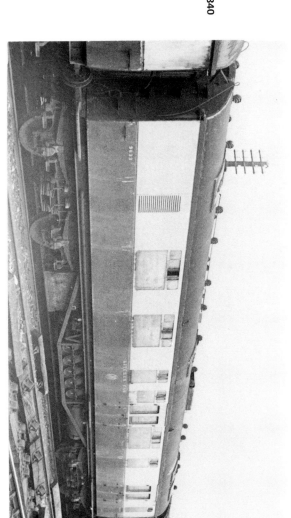

FIG 341

FIG 342

LOT.1530

DIA.C.68

200

These two pictures illustrate the design of 'Excursion' stock in fair detail. The upper picture of No. 4563, *figure 342*, shows the large windows with sliding ventilators. Originally they had the 'Beclawet' drop type which can be seen in the lower official photo. Two doors only were fitted in the side, one at one end and one in the centre. The length was 60' and the width 9', which enabled them to be used on practically all Great Western routes. It will be noticed from the interior shot, *figure 343*, that the decor was of the square modernity style, typical of the mid-thirties. Internal partitions divided the full 3rds into four semi-saloons, but there were no doors on these partitions so that the open plan was retained whilst the divisions did cut down noise somewhat and led to a cosier atmosphere than would be obtained with a completely open car. Diagram was C.68. Nos. 4563 to 4570.

LOT.1531
DIA.D.119

There were four brake 3rds built under *lot 1531* which were designed to run with the 'Excursion' sets. They were unusual in that not only did they have an open type saloon for the passengers but also had an extremely large luggage van with no separate corridor. Just what was the reason for this commodious van? *Harris* suggests in his book, that it was to carry the beer and pop for Sunday excursionists! However, this official photograph shows the capacity of these brake 3rd vans, the example shown being the interior of No. 4571, (*figure 344*). The diagram was D.119 and painted numbers were 4571 to 4574. Note that the guard's compartment could be shut off by sliding doors.

FIG 344

FIG 345

LOT.1533
DIA.H.48

LOT.1335

Still in the same 'Excursion' phase, the restaurant car No. 9639 shown in the top left and top right was the solution to the eating facilities of the open design. The interior shot shows the same rectangular decor, and the leather seats with fluted glass partitions mounted on top give a stark impression of utility, with little or nothing given to comfort or taste. There were two of these vehicles built under lot 1533; the one shown plus its sister, No. 9640, *diagram H.48* ran in pairs and were air conditioned. This 1st class equivalent was *diagram H.47*, Nos. 9641 and 9642. The passenger brake van in *figure 347* was one of the twenty built to *lot 1535* of *K.41 design*. 57' x 9'. It followed contemporary design, except that it had a side corridor separated from the luggage space, making for more security of parcel traffic when marshalled in corridor trains. Running numbers were — Nos. 181 to 200. Date – 1935.

FIG 347

In 1935 the Great Western Railway was 100 years old and to mark this occasion a series of brand new coaching stock was designed and built for the top link expresses to the West. Appropriately named the 'Centenary' stock these superb vehicles were formed in what was then known as the 'Cornish Riviera Limited'. Following very closely on the design of the Supers already referred to, these coaches were built out to the full width of the loading gauge, namely 9'7'', and so were restricted to what were known as the 'Red Triangle' routes. They differed from the Super Saloons in having compartments in the usual manner, entered from the corridors, but they broke new ground in having large 'Beclawet' windows to the compartments, with no access from that side. Later these large drop windows were changed for a fixed smaller panel with a sliding ventilator on top.

These carriages were most distinctive, and could be recognised immediately on any train, not only by the bulbous sides but more by the fact that the livery was particularly austere, having large expanses of both cream and chocolate relieved only by two narrow waistband linings, one roundel, and two numbers, one each end. Inscriptions were kept to a minimum and consisted of 'FIRST, GUARD, LUGGAGE, RESTAURANT CAR and THIRD CLASS' only, on the diners. This well known study, by Maurice Earley, *figure 349*, shows this magnificent stock to advantage. It was taken at Aldermaston in 1939 when these coaches were four years old. Surely Great Western at its greatest! The upper plate is the official picture of the Riviera at Teignmouth.

FIG 346

203

FIG 348

FIG 349

FIG 350

CARRYING CAPACITY

THIRD		
COMP		PASS
2		16
TOTAL. PASSENGERS		16

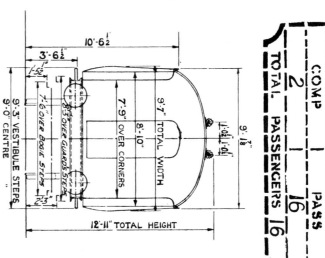

TARE 31ᵀ·16ᶜ

10'-6½"
3'-6½"
1'-5¾"
9'-3" VESTIBULE STEPS
9'-0" CENTRE
7'-6" OVER BOGIE STEPS
8'-3" OVER GUARDS STEPS
1'-3"
9'-7" TOTAL WIDTH
8'-10"
7'-9" OVER CORNERS
9'-1⅛"
1'-10½"·1'-10½"
12'-11" TOTAL HEIGHT

- G.W.R -
- BRAKE THIRD CLASS CARRIAGE -
— MAIN LINE SERVICE —
- SWINDON -
—APRIL 1938—
LOT 1536 (4R.&2L. HAND)

Veh Nos. 4575 - 4580.

DIA.D.120

The Centenarys

I am fortunate in being able to present the whole range in photograph and drawing, the latter being kindly loaned to me by Pendon Museum. The ordinary modeller like myself can produce a very satisfactory series of 'Centenarys' by virtue of the splendid kits issued by B.S.L. models. To describe the various vehicles in the prototype range we start off with *lot 1536*, under which order six brake 3rds were made. The diagram was *D.120*, and there were four right-hand vans and two left-handers. Notice in the photographs the unusual pattern of luggage doors and ends; only the door with the handle had the droplight, the other being blank. The van ends, although tapered to match the compartment end had no doors or lights therein. This was a real break with tradition. In *figure 350*, one can see the little red triangle on the end of No. 4575, which indicated to the traffic dept. the restricted use of the vehicles. The drawing also shows that there were only two compartments in these brake 3rds, one being for smokers. They were quite large compartments, being 6'3" x 6'10" wide. One other point to look for in the picture is the difference in the window configuration. The top picture is No. 4576 and the lower is No. 4547, both carriages being of the right hand van type. Complete details are:-

Lot 1536 of 1935; diagram D.120; Nos. 4575 to 4580.

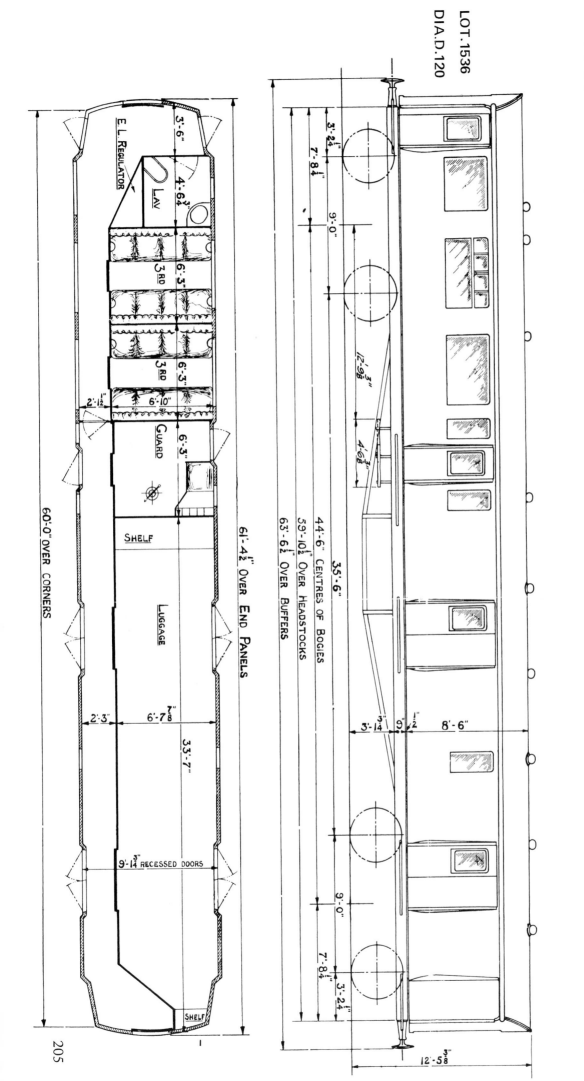

LOT.1536
DIA.D.120

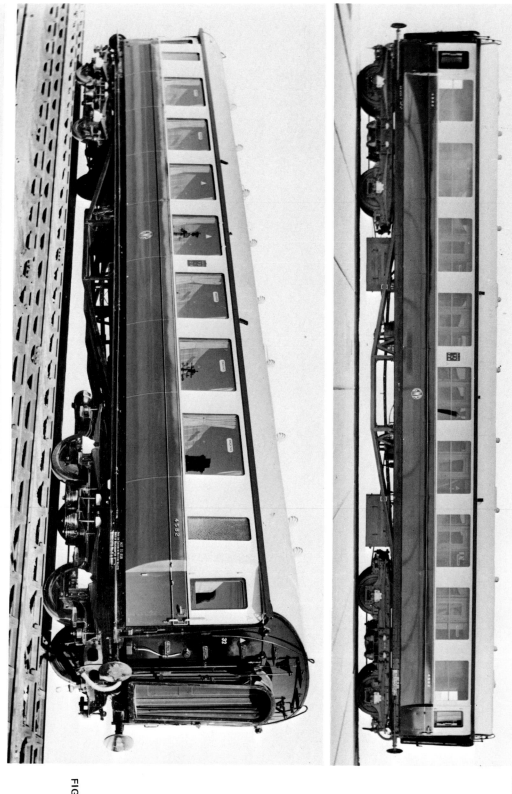

FIG 351

FIG 351A

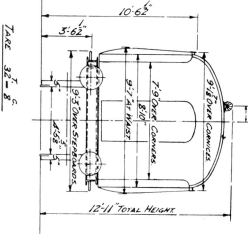

TARE 32-8 T. C.

10'-6⅜"
3'-6⅜"
9'-8¾" OVER CORNICES
7'-9" OVER CORNICES
8'-10"
9'-7" AT WAIST
9'-3" OVER STEPBOARDS
4'-5⅜"
1'-0⅝"
12'-11" TOTAL HEIGHT.

— G. W. R. —

THIRD CLASS CARRIAGE.

— MAIN LINE SERVICE. —

— SWINDON —   — APRIL 1938. —

— LOT 1537 —

VAN Nos 4581~4586
DIA.C.69

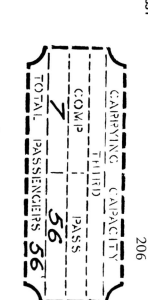

CARRYING CAPACITY
COMP   THIRD   PASS
7   56
TOTAL PASSENGERS 56

206

Built at the same time, under the consecutive *lot no. 1537*, were six full 3rds to *diagram C.69* with painted numbers 4581 to 4586. The outline followed that of the brake 3rds, but in this vehicle doors with drop lights were provided at each end and at both sides. Note that the panel for seat reservation numbers is situated in the centre of the coach, and not at the two ends as before. The inscription on the solebar reads "NOT TO RUN OVER THE EASTERN AND WESTERN VALLEYS NORTH OF WOLVERHAMPTON NORTH OF SALTNEY JCT. BETWEEN LITTLE MILL JCT. AND

MAINDEE JCT." This restriction was on every vehicle of the series and also included in the prohibited routes were Churchdown to Gloucester and between Andoversford Jct. and Red Posts Junction. Another point perhaps not known, is that this 'Centenary' stock was not allowed to run on any other Company's lines, owing to the extreme width. The photographs show No. 4582 at the top and centre, both sides of the vehicle, and with the original 'Beclawet' windows in place. No. 4581 in the lower picture has been given two sliding ventilators, (*figure 352*). Notice in the drawings the large vestibules at each end and — plenty of room to swing a cat here!

LOT.1537

DIA.C.69

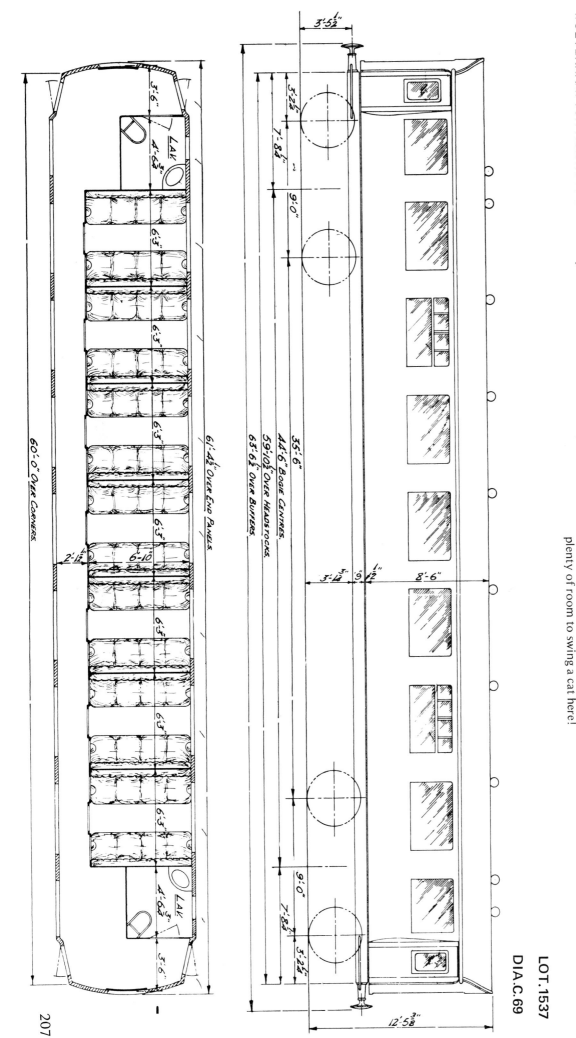

FIG 353

FIG 354

TARE WEIGHT 32T 12C

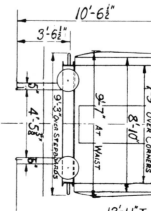

10'-6½"

3'-6½"

5'
4'-5½"
5'

9'-3" OVER STEPBOARDS

9'-1⅞" OVER CORNERS

7'-9" OVER CORNERS

9'-7" AT WAIST

8'-10"

12'-11" TOTAL HEIGHT

CARRYING CAPACITY				
FIRST		THIRD		
COMP	PASS	COMP	PASS	
4	24	3	24	
TOTAL		PASSENGERS		48

— G.W.R —

— COMPOSITE CARRIAGE —

— MAIN LINE SERVICE —

— SWINDON — APRIL 1938 —

— LOT 1538 —

Veh. Nos. 6658 - 6661
1 OFF

LOT.1538

The composite carriage in the 'Centenary' had one very unusual feature, which to my knowledge was not perpetuated. This was in the arrangement of the lavatories; instead of there being one at each end, the toilet cabins were side by side at the 1st class end, but accessible to both classes by means of a swing door in the corridor. (Note that this door was hung on the compartment side). There were four 1st class compartments, and three

3rds, and the vestibules at each end were of different sizes. In the photographs it will be seen that two have the original windows, and at the top, (figure 353), No. 6661, No. 6659 has been refitted. The central picture (figure 354), is of No. 6661, and the range was:-

Lot 1538 to diagram E.149, Nos. 6658 to 6661, only four being built.

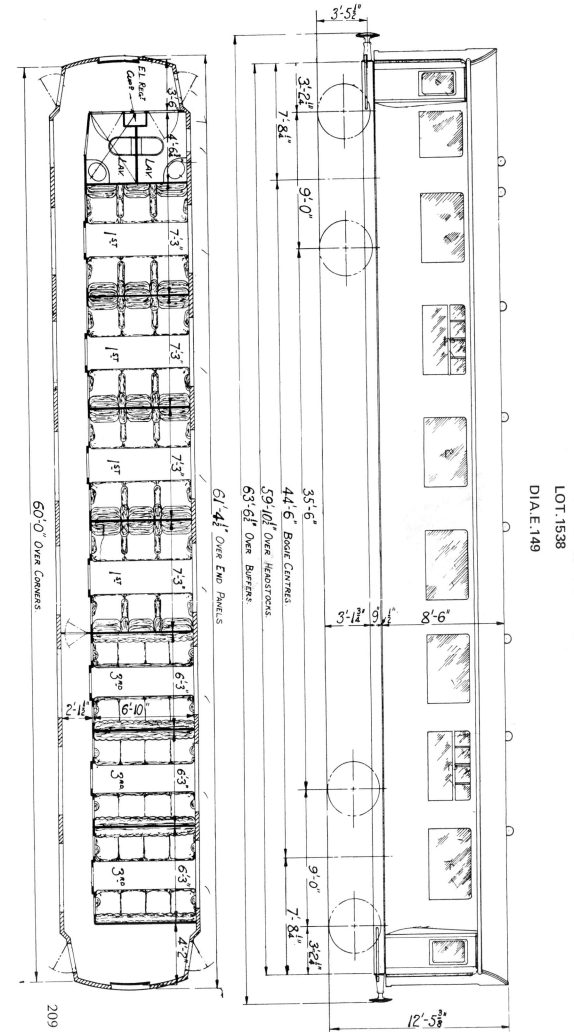

LOT.1538
DIA.E.149

FIG 356

Six other composites were included in the range, but this time with a brake and luggage compartment, making the *design E.150*. The picture on this page, *figure 356*, shows No. 6653 of this compilation in the crimson lake livery of British Rail. Still carrying the little red triangle, note that the restriction admonition has now been moved up on to the end over the buffer, where it was much easier to see than before. There were six vehicles in the brake composites design ranging from No. 6650 to No. 6655.

210

CARRYING CAPACITY		
FIRST	THIRD	
COMP¹ PASS	COMP⁰ PASS	COMP⁰ PASS
2	12	3	24
TOTAL PASSENGERS 36		

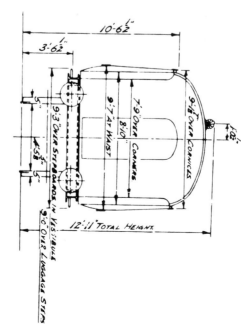

TARE 33ᵀ-7ᶜ

10'-6½"
3'-6½"

9'-3" OVER STEPBOARDS IN VESTIBULE
9'-7" AT WAIST
8'-10"
7'-9" OVER CORNICES
9'-8" OVER CORNICES
9'-0" OVER LUGGAGE STEPS
12'-1½" TOTAL HEIGHT

— G. W. R. —

— BRAKE COMPOSITE CARRIAGE —

— MAIN LINE SERVICE —

— SWINDON —   — APRIL 1938 —

— LOT 1539 —

VEH. Nos. 6650 – 6655

DIA. E.150

The drawing on this page shows the internal layout of the brake Composite which has three 3rd class and two 1st class compartments, plus a guard/luggage space. Note that the lavatories are back in their usual place, one at each end. Also, compared with the brake 3rds of the series, they differ in having entrance doors at both ends of the carriage, and the 1st class passengers were expected to enter through the van end door, and sidle along to their seats past the luggage van!

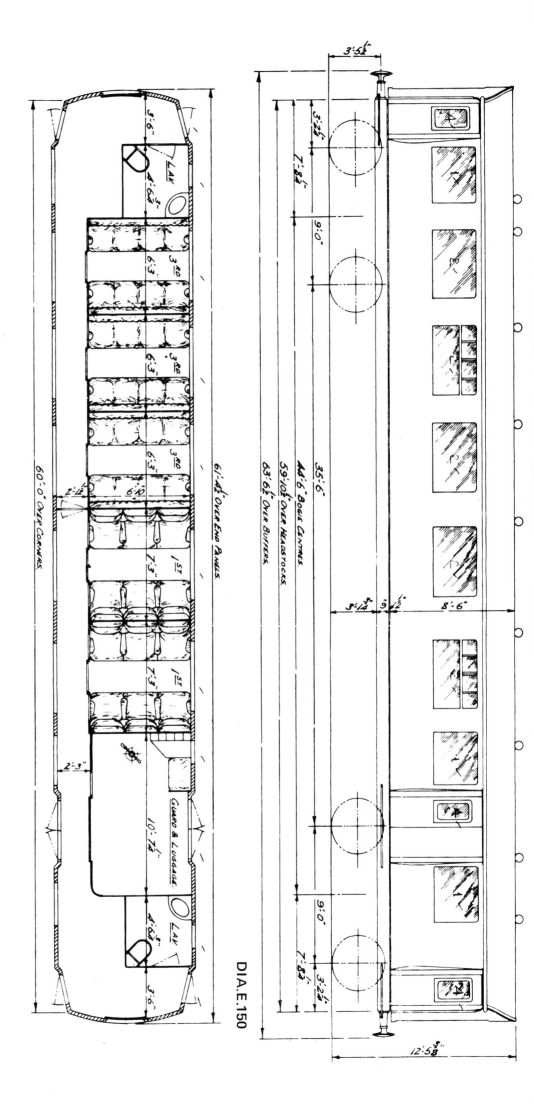

DIA. E.150

FIG 357

Three more offical photographs showing No. 6652, both sides as built, in the top and centre pictures, whilst No. 6651 in the lower view has the sliding ventilators, (*figure 359*). Note in the centre picture, (*figure 358*), how the smokers were divided up in the five compartments.

FIG 358

DIA.E.150

The two interior views, on *page 213*, illustrate mainly the operation of the 'Beclawet' windows. The action was by means of the small lever in the centre of the sill. When this lever was to the right, the window was fastened; when the lever was moved to the left, the window could be lowered by pulling it down from the top. Other details can be seen, such as the new tartan pattern upholstery. This was dark brown and gold with gold curtains, in this carriage, being a 3rd class vehicle No. 6650. The 1st class interior was green and blue, with blue curtains, and white head cloths for each seat. The small fittings below the window handle were to accommodate a collapsible table which was stowed in the corridor. Note also the neat housing for the communication cord.

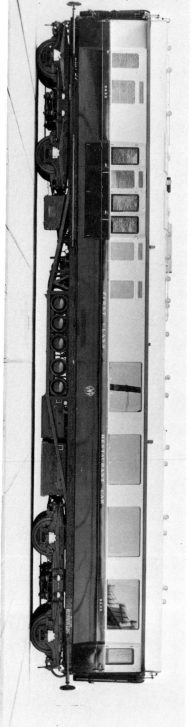

FIG 364

FIG 363

FIG 362

B.R-W.R

FIRST CLASS RESTAURANT CAR

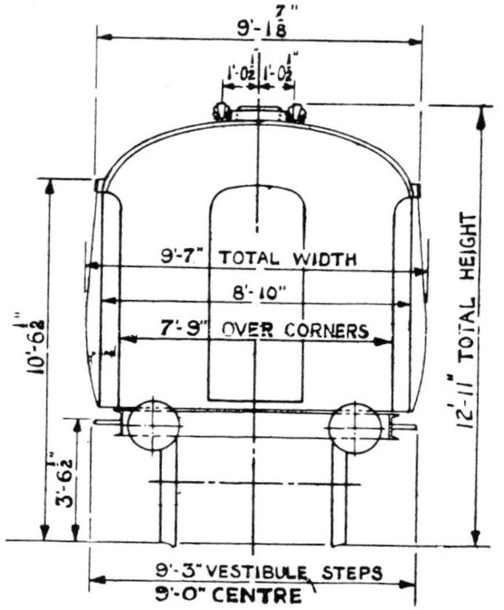

MAIN LINE SERVICE

SWINDON JANUARY 1928

Nᵒˢ 9635 & 9636

LOT 1540

LOT.1540

DIA.H.43

TARE 42ᵀ· 8ᶜ·

10'-6½"

3'-6½"

9'-3"-VESTIBULE STEPS

9'-0" CENTRE

9'-7" TOTAL WIDTH

8'-10"

7'-9" OVER CORNERS

1'-0⅛"

1'-0½"

9'-1⅛"

7"

12'-11" TOTAL HEIGHT

214

The system of dining used on the 'Centenary' make was again different to the standard practice of a separate kitchen car and two saloons, one 1st and one 3rd class. A kitchen car with 1st class saloon combined was used, the latter having seating for 24 passengers, the 3rd class voyageurs (having seating for 64 was in a separate saloon. *Figure 367*) The photographs *figures 362 and 364*, show No. 9635 from both sides, and a three-quarter view, *figure 363*, gives most of the salient points. Notice the vehicle has only three battery boxes under the chassis, but also five large gas tanks set transversely for storing gas used in the kitchen cookers, etc. Only two vehicles like this were made, Nos. 9635 and 9636, to diagram H.43.

The offical drawing of the *H.43*, shows the layout of both the kitchen, pantry and the 1st class saloon. In the latter, each diner had individual seats, those on one side of the gangway in pairs, and on the other, in foursomes. There was no lavatory. Those in need, had to pass through the gangways into the next adjoining vehicle. Also note that one end by the pantry had the same blank panel as had the brake 3rds. Stainless steel was used on the walls of the kitchen. The serving hatch has gone back to the corridor, even though there is a vestibule between pantry and kitchen.

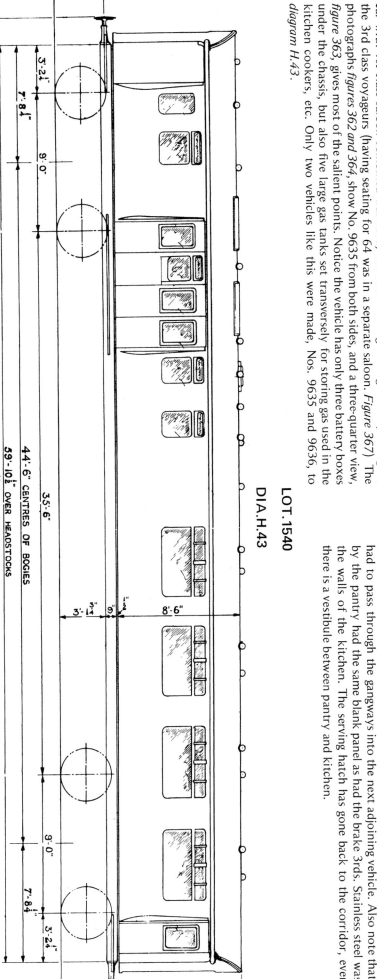

LOT.1540

DIA.H.43

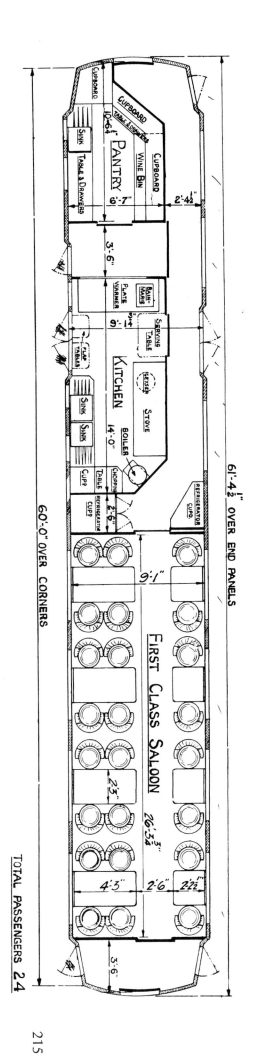

61'-4½" OVER END PANELS

63'-6½" OVER BUFFERS

59'-10½" OVER HEADSTOCKS

44'-6" CENTRES OF BOGIES

60'-0" OVER CORNERS

TOTAL PASSENGERS 24

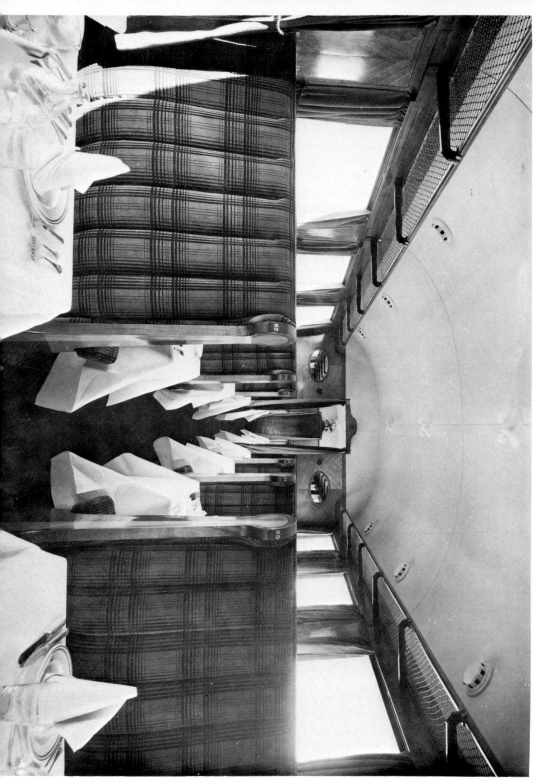

FIG 366

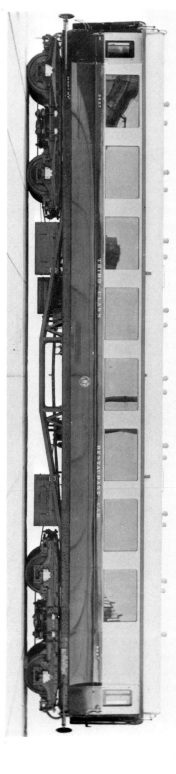

FIG 365

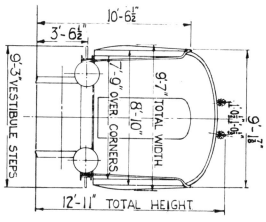

- G.W.R -
- THIRD CLASS DINING SALOON -
- MAIN LINE SERVICE -
- SWINDON - OCTOBER 1947

LOT 1541

Nᵒˢ 9637 & 9638

1 OFF

LOT. 1541

DIA. H. 44

TARE 33ᵀ-5ᶜ

10'-6½"

3'-6½"

9'-3" VESTIBULE STEPS

9'-7" TOTAL WIDTH

8'-10"

7'-9" OVER CORNERS

1'-0½"-1'-0½"

9'-1⅞"

12'-11" TOTAL HEIGHT

CARRYING CAPACITY		
SALOON	COMP	PASS
SALOON		
TOTAL		
TOTAL PASSENGERS	64	

216

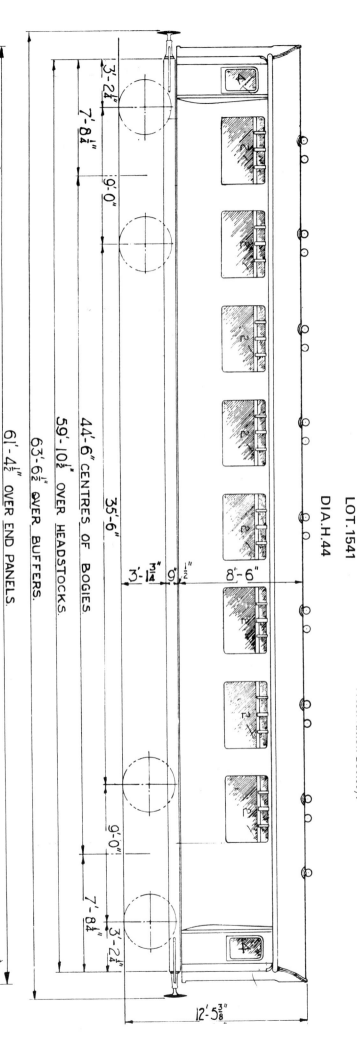

FIG 367

LOT.1541

DIA.H.44

Finally, to complete this magnificent range, the 3rd class diner is shown here in photograph and drawing. The interior view, *figure 366*, illustrates the centre gangway with double seating on both sides, which incidentally made use of tip-up seats. There were two saloons, with large linen cupboards at one end. All tables had small lamps thereon, in the style of the 1st class diners. There was no toilet facility. Note the sensible design of the luggage rack and oval mirrors. The *lot no.* was *1541* and two vehicles were made to *diagram H.44*, Nos 9637 and 9638. The two exterior photographs show No. 9637 from both sides, as built with the original windows, and later with the narrow sliding toplights (*figures 365 and 367*). No. 9635 is preserved at Ashchurch by the Dowty Railway Preservation Society.

217

Two types of rail cars are shown here, the trailer car at the top of the page, and two more examples of the diesel streamlined coach, centre and bottom left respectively. No. 216 which was originally No. 64 steam rail car, built by Kerr-Stuarts is here shown as converted in 1936 to *diagram A.29*. Notice the double doors in the centre which betray its non-Swindon building. (*figure 368*) The two diesels shown are part of a batch in which the bodies were made by the Gloucester Railway Carriage and Wagon Company. The layout was similar to that of No. 1, but two engines were installed instead of one, and there was only one lavatory. Sliding doors were fitted in place of the outward-opening type of the earlier cars. No. 8 was to *lot 1547*, *diagram W* (*figure 369*). No. 12 was to the same lot but *diagram 'X'* (*figure 370*).

DIA.X

FIG 368

LOT.1545

DIA.A.29

FIG 369

FIG 370

LOT.1547

DIA.W

Maurice Earley, very fascinating to me, as the three trains are made up with many of the vehicles described in these books. The trains are, centre, Down Milk Empties at Sonning in 1925, top, Milk Train at Twyford, Engine No. 509, in 1928, bottom, Penzance sleeper near Reading in 1930.

219

FIG 371

In 1933 Messrs. Fry the chocolate people, commissioned a show train to tour the Great Western system, exhibiting their products. The end doors of two Monsters, Nos. 590 and 593 of *lot 1265*, were removed and gangways fitted in their place, one end only. A similar tour was organised by His Master's Voice Ltd. in 1934 and afterwards the vehicles were restored to their original condition. At a later date, two other Monsters, Nos. 587 and 591, were fitted permanently with gangways and the ends boarded up and so became again the official 'Giants'. No diagram has been found, however, to show this change, so it is possible that the alterations still came under the *diagram P.18* classification. The two photographs show No. 591 in Old Oak Common carriage shed in 1948 and below, No. 587 at Bristol in 1947. *Lot No. was 1223*, (*figures 371 and 372*).

FIG 373

LOT.1555

DIA.D.121

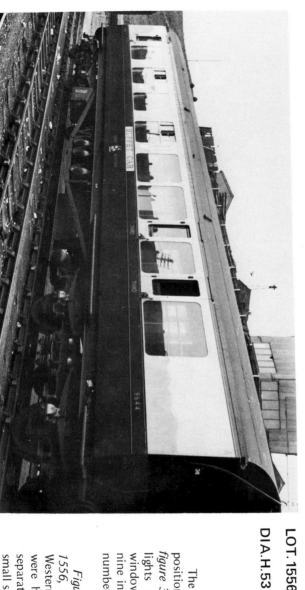

FIG 374

LOT.1556

DIA.H.53

The main line stock built in 1936 was unusual only in the positioning of some of the droplights in the sides. It will be seen in *figure 373* that No. 4083, the brake 3rd, has corridor lights and door lights of an extra height, but that the van, guard, and vestibule windows come down to the waistline, but are all on a line, a good nine inches above. *Lot 1555* was for 36 vehicles to *diagram D.121* and numbers were from 4066 to 4069, 4073 to 4102, and 4104 and 4125.

Figure 374 on the left is one of the two buffet cars, made to *lot 1556*, *diagram H.53*. Nos. 9643 and 9644 are shown in the last Great Western livery, again with the standard droplights. These two carriages were half compartments and half buffet counter, there being four separate 3rd class compartments and a short side buffet counter in the small saloon. Note the 'BUFFET CAR' panel.

FIG 375   222

There seemed to be no rhyme or reason to the design of these carriages at this time, regarding both side window sizes and coach lengths. For instance, the vehicles described on the previous page, (lot 1555) were 60'11¼" long. The vehicle in figure 375 is lot 1557, No. 6932, and has all the windows in a line, again with a length of 60'11"; yet lots 1556 and 1560 are 60' and 58'7" respectively and the windows are staggered! Figure 376, lot 1557 was for diagram E.152 and numbers 6859-62, 6925, 6932, 6940, 6965, 6967, 6971, 6973.

Lot 1560 for 10 composites was to diagram E.151, and the numbers were 6606, 6607, 6611, 6612, 6614, 6617, 6618, 6620, 6622, 6623. The example shown in B.R. ownership is No. 6617.

FIG 375

LOT.1557
DIA.E.152

FIG 376

LOT.1560
DIA.E.151

DIA.A.21
LOT.1566

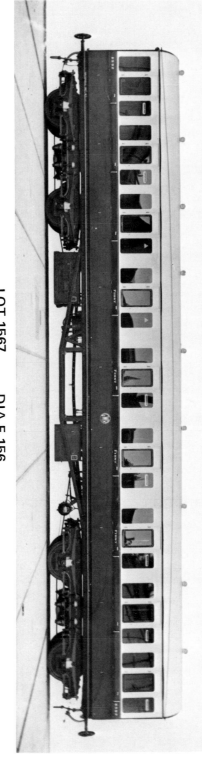

FIG 378

LOT.1567   DIA.E.156

FIG 378A

DIA.C.75

During the second half of 1937, eighty-four vehicles were constructed of the non-corridor suburban stock, measuring from 55'3½'' of the full 3rds to the 59'3½'' of the composites. Built under *lots 1566 to 1570* they consisted of 10 firsts to *diagram A.21*, numbers 8033-42; four composites of *E.156 diagram*, Nos. 6591-4; twenty brake composites of *diagram E.157 numbering 6218/23/6/7/30 /43/4/5/65/96/6300/3/5/7/9/12/13/14/17/18*; thirty-five full 3rds, to *diagram C.75* Nos. 1384 to 1418; and twenty brake 3rds to *diagram D.125* numbering 1419-35, 1437-9. Except for the length they were very similar in outline, varying only in the number of compartments. Three examples are illustrated here. At the top of the page is No. 8034, one of the full 1st class carriages of *lot 1566*. In the centre is No. 6592, a composite of *lot 1567*, and at the bottom of the page is No. 1392, a full 3rd having nine compartments, seven for smokers and two only for non-smokers. These were some of the last stock to be built with rain strips on the roof.

FIG 379

FIG 380

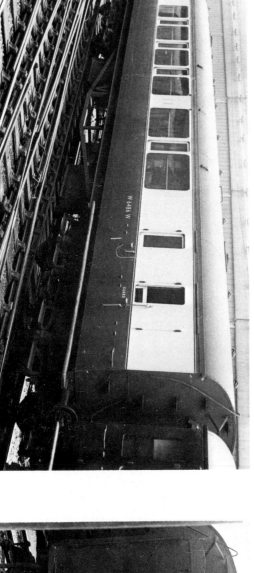

FIG 381

FIG 382

Four coaches of the 1936-7 period are illustrated on this page.

DIA.D.125 LOT.1570

DIA.E.153 LOT.1572

Figure 379, shows one of the brake 3rd non-corridor suburban stock, No. 1433, it was built to *diagram D.125* under *lot 1570* with nineteen others of the same pattern, numbered 1419-1435, 1437/8/1439. The length was 57' x width 8'11''. The other three pictures show examples of the brake composites *diagram E.153* built under *lot 1572. Figure 380* shows No. 6490 at Henley. Bottom left, *figure 381*, is No. 6486 at Paddington and bottom right, *figure 382*, is No. 6385 at Didcot. Note that with this design all the corridor side windows come to the waistline and the compartment sides have the sliding ventilators at the top of the large windows. Nos. in this lot were 6378/79/84/5/97, 6400/06/07/66/67, 72/73/84/86/89/90/96/99, 6529.

FIG 383

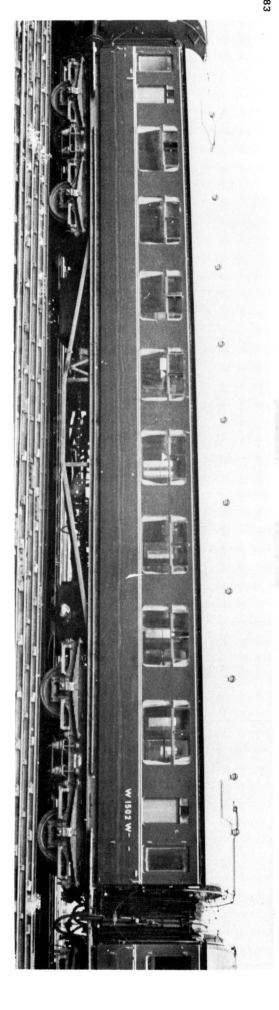

LOT.1573
DIA.C.73

Of the same outline as the previous stock were the seventy-four corridor 3rds built to *lot 1573* of 1937. The photograph in (*figure 383*) shows the compartment side of No. 1502 in the maroon of B.R., and in the lower picture, *figure 384*, the corridor side of No. 1456 is shown as built and in the livery of 1937 (note the white roof as outshopped). Diagram was C.73 and numbers 1442 to 1516 inclusive.

FIG 384

FIG 385

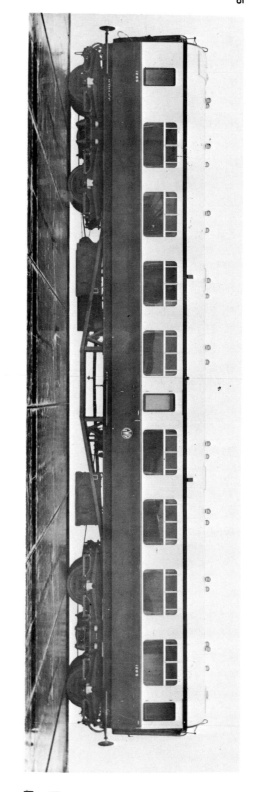

Two more later patterns of the open excursion stock already mentioned are shown here. Following the general outline of the contemporary stock, the interior was to the same plan as the orginal 'Excursion' stock, having open plan saloons. The only difference was to be found in the window design. These two lots have the fixed windows on both sides with the large sliding ventilators set at the top. *Diagram was C.74 for the 3rds*, numbering 1271 to 1297, *(figure 385)*, and *diagram D.123* for the brake 3rds the numbers 1298 to 1301 *(figure 386)*.

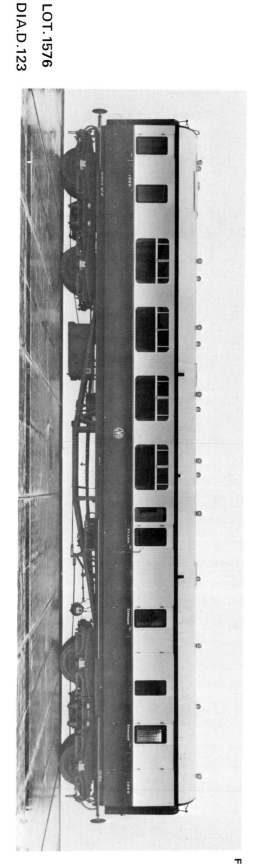

LOT.1576
DIA.D.123

FIG 386

226

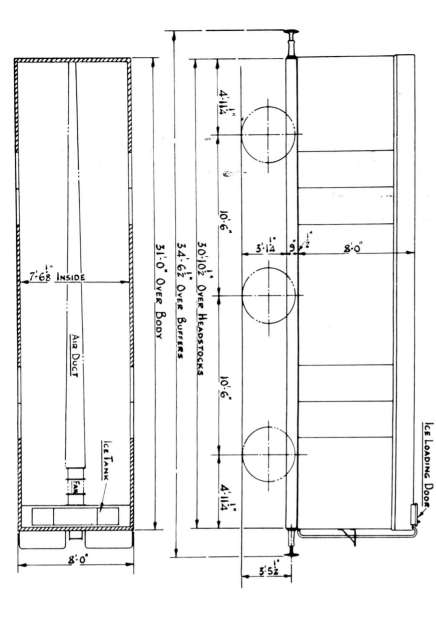

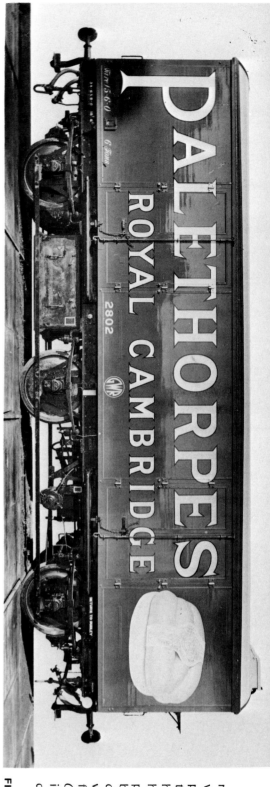

FIG 387

A six-wheeled vehicle which is rarely seen modelled is the sausage van, depicted on this page. It was very colourful in its milk-chocolate livery, with pale blue lettering, and the bunch of pink sausages on the right. The length was 31' and width 8', the roof had an ice box set in one end and there was a special hand rail and steps to this particular end for the purpose of loading ice into the chamber. Lighting was by electricity and the van was fitted with insulated doors similar to those used on the 'Siphon J's'. These vehicles were some of the very few six-wheelers to be fitted with a dynamo and control gear. *Diagram was O.46 and numbers 2801 and 2802. Date 1936.* An internal electric fan was also fitted to circulate the cool air. (Note—the drawing is not to 4mm scale.)

7'·6⅝" INSIDE

AIR DUCT

ICE TANK

FAN

8'-0"

31'-0" OVER BODY

34'-6½" OVER BUFFERS

30'-10½" OVER HEADSTOCKS

4'-11½" 10'-6" 10'-6" 4'-11½"

3'·1¼" 9" 1½"

8'-0"

ICE LOADING DOOR

3'·5½"

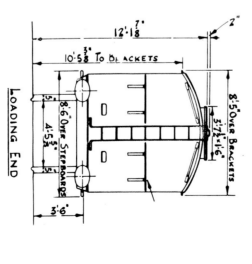

LOADING END

12'·1⅞"

10'·5⅞" TO BRACKETS

8'·6" OVER STEPBOARDS

4'·5⅝"

3'·7½"×1'-6"

8'·5" OVER BRACKETS

3'-6"

2"

LOAD · 6 TONS
TARE · 15'·6'

DIA.O.46

G.W.R
—
INSULATED VAN
—
FOR SAUSAGE TRAFFIC
—
SWINDON — DECEMBER 1936
—

FIG 388

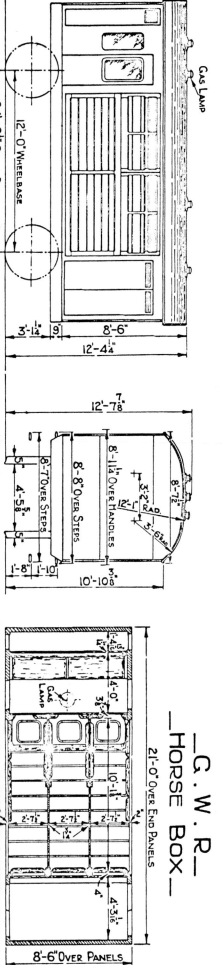

LOT.1577
DIA.N.16

GAS LAMP

12'-0"WHEELBASE

3'-1¼" 9" 8'-6"

12'-4¼"

12'-7⅞"

8'-11¼"OVER HANDLES

8'-8"OVER STEPS

8'-7"OVER STEPS

8'-7½"

3'-2"RAD.

12'-1"

3'-6"RAD.

5"

4'-5⅝"

5"

1'-8" 1'-10" 3'-5⅛"

10'-10"

GAS LAMP

1'-4"

4'-0"

3'-6"

10'-1⅛"

2'-7½" 2'-7½" 2'-7½" 2"

1'-4"

4"

4'-3 3/16"

_G.W.R._
HORSE BOX

21'-0"OVER END PANELS

8'-6"OVER PANELS

546

With the exception of the roof contour, there were few curves on the 1937 series of horse boxes, the sides and ends being perfectly straight. Although this made the prototype look very austere, it does mean that modelling such a vehicle is that much easier! In general lines the design is identical to the previous order, *diagram N.15* except for the total lack of tumble-home. Painting followed the usual horse box and brown vehicle pattern, being milk chocolate body sides, with black underframes, straps handles and ends, light grey roof, with the roundel and number in yellow. They were equipped with gas lighting and its attendant reservoir. Note the use of the old 'Mansell' wheels. Some numbers under *lot 1577* were 601 to 613, 620, 621, 626-719; also, the numbers 515 to 599 were mixed between *lot 1461* of *diagram N.15* and of this *N.16* series.

FIG 389

LOT.1579

DIA.H.54

One of the last lots of 'Siphon G' built to *diagram O.33* for the Great Western was *lot 1578* of 1937. An example of this inside-framed Siphon G is shown at the foot of this page. (*figure 390*) No. 2792 was one of fifty such vehicles numbering from 2751 to 2800. It can be seen that these vans, ventilated by louvres in doors and sides, were still called officially 'Milk vans'. But apart from this they were generally used on all types of passenger trains for parcels traffic. Being mounted on standard heavy 9' bogies their carrying capacity was 14 tons.

The photograph of the run-down kitchen car, *figure 389* was taken at Henley in 1947 and shows No. 9665, one of the six cars specially built in 1937 to run with the open 'Excursion' stock mentioned. The idea was to provide a compact car like this, self contained with full facilities and staff. They were fitted with two lavatories and even a compartment reserved specially for the car's crew, from which 'excursionists' could be fed at their own tables in their carriages. However, the difficulties of serving a hot meal to a coach of day-trippers, some five vehicles away from the kitchen car, soon became apparent and H & R Dept. staff would have none of it. These kitchen cars thus eventually found their way into standard main line express service. *Diagram no.* was *H.54* and numbers 9663 to 9668.

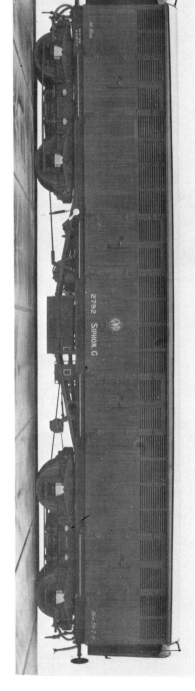

LOT.1578

DIA.O.33

FIG 390

LOT. 1581
DIA. A.20

LOT. 1582
DIA. E.155

FIG 391

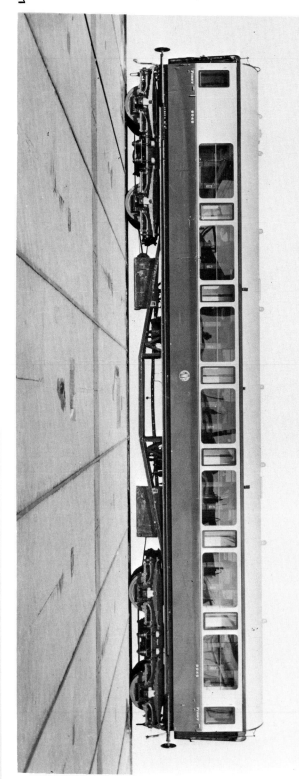

230

Two consecutive lots of mid-1937 are shown on this page. *Figure 392* is one of the main line corridor composites built to lot 1582 to *diagram E.155*. This coach is shown in the 'Cheltenham Flyer' rake standing at Worcester in 1947. The design had three 3rd class compartments and four 1sts with two toilets, one at each end. Running numbers were 6049/53/56/57/59/62/84/6106 6109-12/6114/6/6128/32/6/6140.

In the upper official photograph is seen No. 8045, a 60'1" corridor 1st of the period built to *lot 1581, diagram A.20 (figure 391)*. There were ten in this batch, numbering 8043 to 8052. Note the deep droplights on this, the corridor, side; opening doors are only at each end, as with *lot 1582*. Another point of interest is that, whereas the composite carriage had two lavatories, this 1st vehicle of seven compartments had only one — at the left hand end.

Here are two pictures of the 60'1" main line corridor 1sts of 1938, containing seven compartments. Again there was a lavatory at one end only. In the top picture of No. 8092, *figure 393*, notice the compartment side with doors only at the two ends and the large windows with equally large sliding ventilators to each compartment. On the corridor side, however, (*figure 394*), there are four doors divided neatly between the seven compartments and only two of the windows have the ventilator. *Diagram No. A.22* under *lot 1586* and numbers were from 8092 to 8111.

FIG 393

FIG 394

LOT.1586

DIA.A.22

FIG 395

LOT.1588
DIA.E.160

LOT.1589
DIA.E.159

FIG 396

These two composites are of the same series as the previous page and with windows set out in similar fashion. Built consecutively, the composite at the top, (figure 395) No. 6142, is from lot 1588 of diagram E.160. Other numbers were 6144 6162 6169-74 6196 6266/74/5/91/6302/6/11/51/2. The length of this stock was only 58'7" as compared with the standard 60'11¼" of composite shown below, figure 396, No. 6487. This brake composite had two 1st and three 3rds as well as the brake/luggage compartment. This lot was 1589, diagram E.159 and numbers were 6355/6/6408/21/6485/87/6533/9/40/6543/4/6/6550/2/9/6562/4/95/9/6600/3/5/8/9/10/9.

232

Lot 1591 was an order for ten open-type corridor 3rds of the 'Excursion' pattern and were with *diagram C.74*, the last of this style to be built for the Great Western. They were longer than the previous batch, being 60'11¼", as against the *diagram C.74* which was 60'. Only two doors were provided on the side with the single lavatory, one at the end opposite the toilet, and the other carving into the centre semi-vestibule. Their diagram was C.76 and running numbers were 1530 to 1539. *Figure 397* shows No. 1538 at Worcester in 1947 and *figure 398*, depicts No. 1530 as outshopped in 1938. It is interesting to note how the design has come full circle. The Dean clerestory (*diagram C.17*) of 1899 had this open saloon plan and here it has been revived after nearly forty years; in 1972 70% of main line stock was built to this 'Excursion' pattern!

LOT.1591

DIA.C.76

FIG 397

FIG 398

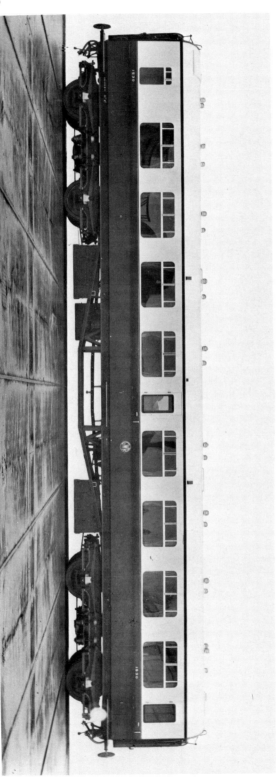

FIG 399

The brake 3rd of the 'Excursion' style of 1938 is shown at the top of this page, *figure 399*, in the official works photograph of No. 1541. It will be noted that it follows closely the full 3rd design of *lot 1591*, except that the guard/luggage section can be locked off from the saloon. Painted numbers were 1541 and 1542 to *diagram D.126*. The lower illustration shows No. 1080 of *lot 1593*, one of a large batch of main-line corridor 3rds built at the end of 1938 to the *diagram C.77*. This style reverted to the separate compartment design, having eight 3rd class compartments served by four doors on the corridor side and two on the reverse. Note that some windows have sliding vents, and that all drop lights are shorter than the fixed windows. Numbers were 1080-9/91/3-8/1100-16/8-28/30-4/1136-55. (*figure 400*).

LOT.1592
DIA.D.126

FIG 400

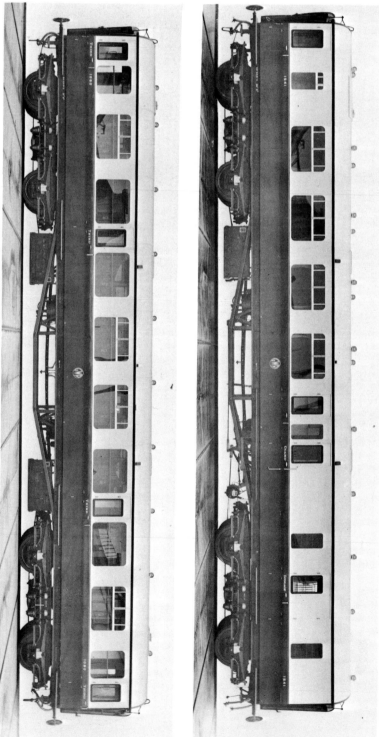

LOT.1593
DIA.C.77

I consider myself very fortunate in being acquainted with that superb railway enthusiast and photographer Maurice Earley. Although this book is primarily a work on coaches, I could not resist including this lovely shot of No. 5070 picking up water on Goring troughs in 1938. My excuse is that the train consists mainly of vehicles which I have just been describing and why not a shot of them in action? The fourth vehicle looks like the 'Buffet' car, but this is only a guess! On *page 236* are two interior shots of Corridor 3rds. No. 1080, *figures 402 and 403*, give a good idea of the styling of the *C.77 diagram*. These two pictures are of the same compartment, the last on the right hand of the vehicle shown in the exterior view. How do I know this? Well, the small letter 'H' on the compartment side tells that this is the eighth cabin and the smoking sign on the window can just be seen on the exterior shot, *figure 400*, on the right hand side of the carriage. Note the new patterned upholstery; this was in a brown-ochre colour, the curtains being mid-brown, ceiling white and woodwork varnished. The modernity of the 1936 decor has given way to the more traditional style in the luggage rack supports and lighting. *Figure 402* is looking at the compartment window, and *figure 403* is looking at the corridor door.

FIG 401

235

FIG 404

At the end of 1938 eight non-corridor composites were built which had an unusually non-standard length of 59'3½". Having three 3rd class compartments one end, and two at the other, with four 1st class compartments in the centre, the width nevertheless was the standard 8'11". Note that by this period rain strips were not fitted, and also that the Great Western roundel was seldom situated in the dead centre of the carriage side, nearly always being off-set to the right, away from the door panel. The vehicle shown at the top of the page is No. 7097 of *lot 1596* to *diagram E.156*. Other numbers were 7091-6 and 7098 (*figure 404*).

The two other photographs on this page illustrate an interesting departure in coach construction, being a suburban brake 3rd which had the van end built with a driver's compartment for use as an Auto train. Unlike previous clerestories which had been rebuilt with this feature, these four vehicles were designed with this purpose in mind and so were 'Trailer cars' which were built with compartments. The small picture shows the single end-window and auto gear fitted to this stock, and the official photograph illustrates the side elevation of the same type, (*figure 406*). As they were officially 'Trailer cars' their *diagram was A.34* in that series, not the be confused with the 1st class 'A' series in the coach programme.

Lot no. was 1600, painted numbers 1668 to 1671, the inscription on the solebar reads *'To work between Lydney and Berkeley Road'*.

FIG 405

FIG 406

FIG 407

At the same time as the brake 3rds were made as Auto trailers (just described), two brake composites were also converted and *figure 407* shows No. 6820 of *lot 1550* refitted with driver's compartment. It will be seen that this compartment had no doors, being entered from the luggage van.

On *page 239* two driving ends are shown, that in *figure 408* being of No. 6820. Note that there are no grab handles on the coach side, and the sliding door can just be seen through the window. *Figure 409* illustrates the end of one of the brake 3rd type; this has a larger window and side grabs. The small white hose was for linking the electric bell code to other vehicles or engines.

LOT.1603
DIA.H.56

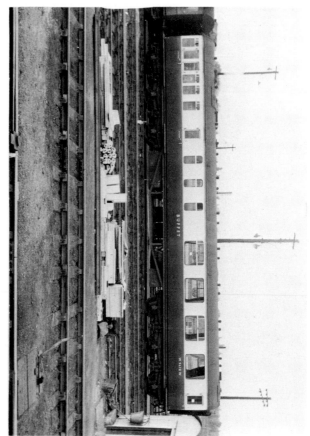

FIG 411

LOT.1602
DIA.H.55

FIG 410

The buffet cars in the late thirties were becoming popular, both with the travelling public who only required a light snack and not a sit-down meal, and also with the Hotel and Refreshment Dept. as these vehicles only required half the crew of a full diner. Built for cross country services and capable of running over other Companies' lines, the five cars to *lot 1602* were 60'11" long 8'11" wide and mounted on six-wheeled bogies. Diagram was *H.55* and numbers 9676 to 9680. *Figure 410* shows No. 9678 in B.R. days from the kitchen side (*far left*), the three central windows being those behind the counter and the four large saloon windows on the right. An official photograph of No. 9676 from the other side appears on *page 108 of Great Western Coaches by M. Harris*.

The subsequent lot of these buffet cars was no 1603, which ordered two kitchen cars to the same length and width as the previous stock. Numbered 9669 to 9670, again on six wheel bogies, they were intended for the 'Vestibule Train' set No. 5 alias the final 'Excursion' set built already described but under *diagrams C.76 and D.126*. My photograph *figure 411*, shows No. 9670 at the end of the war in the carriage sidings at Henley-on-Thames awaiting the journey to Swindon for a major refit. On being outshopped they worked on many main line services, including the Newbury Race specials, and lasted well in the 1960's.

LOT.1605
DIA.W.14

Two further batches of existing 'Brown' vehicle types were also constructed in 1938. Several Beetle C's were made on *lot 1605* to *diagram W.14*, numbering from 720 to 730. Note the position of the angle irons on the vehicle's end panels and the re-use of the old 'Mansell' coaching wheels. (*figure 412*).

FIG 412

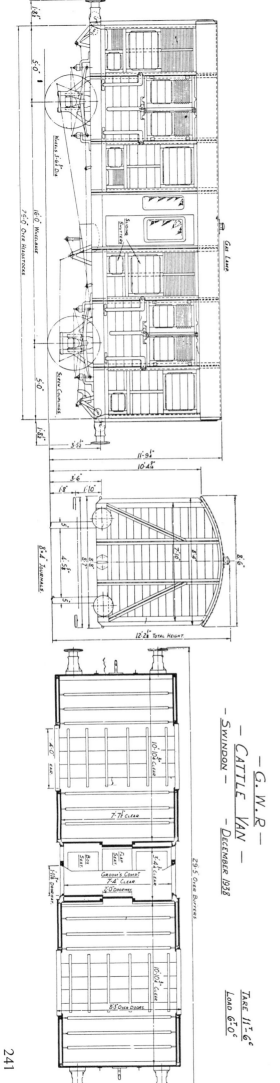

- G.W.R -
- CATTLE VAN -
- SWINDON - DECEMBER 1938 -

TARE 11⊺ 6ᶜ
LOAD 6⊺ 0ᶜ

241

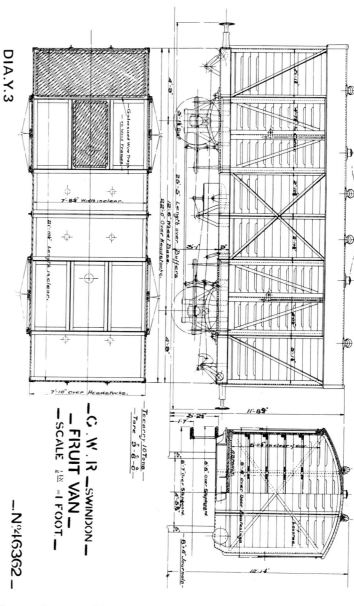

DIA.Y.3

LOT.1606
DIA.Y.9

N.º 46362

— C.W.R —SWINDON—
— FRUIT VAN —
— SCALE $\frac{1}{2}$ IN = 1 FOOT —

The two photographs, *figures 413 and 414*, on this page illustrate the 'Fruit C' van of which 50 were built between 1938-39 to the *diagram Y.9*. In *lot 1606*, the numbers were 2803 to 2832 and in *lot 1634*, the numbers were 2847 to 2866. These vehicles were gas lit by two internal lamps, which were turned on when the traffic via a lever on the solebar, having bypass jets on the mantels. Note the projecting flush doors now fitted and end vents in place of louvres. No. 2821 on the left has disc wheels and No. 2803 on the right has spoked wheels. Both are branded 'return to Worcester'. The drawing of the earlier type gives the dimensions, but not the different doors fitted, and is *dia. Y.3*.

FIG 413

FIG 414

242

FIG 415

Two different types of surburban stock built for special services are illustrated on this page. At the top, *figure 415*, is one of the two brake 3rds which were designed expressly for the Highworth branch. This little line, which left the main line east of Swindon and meandered through the meadows for about six miles through the villages of Stratton and Hannington, had two very low bridges and so this stock had their roof ventilators mounted on the sides of the roof rather than on top. These ventilators are known to modellers and such as 'shell' vents. Swindon knew them as 'Ash' ventilators! Coach Nos. were 1239-40, to *diagram D.125*. In the same 'Highworth' series were two 3rds, Nos. 1237-8, C.75, and two brake composites Nos. 6830-1 to *diagram E.161*. But for a really low roof profile and narrow width the stock constructed specially for the Burry Port and Gwendraeth Valley were the ultimate! They were only 8'8" wide, and the height had to be no more than 11'3". These seven carriages were built and mounted on old 9' bogies of the 1910 era. There was only one full 3rd, No. 1329 shown here in the lower photograph, *figure 417*, it contained nine compartments and was only 55'3½" long. The other six were brake 3rds, each having seven compartments and the central photograph shows No. 1323, other numbers being 1324-1328. (*figure 416*)

FIG 416

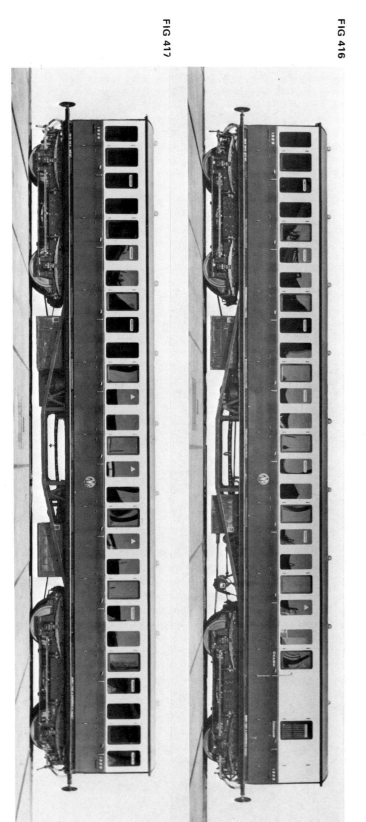

FIG 417

FIG 418

DIA.Y.11

This interior illustrates one of the 3rd class compartments of the low-roofed Burry Port stock, and shows the contemporary upholstery in the trim, the internal part of the snap-lock and the cluster of three bulbs in the light fitting. The low arc of the roof contour can be seen just above the luggage racks and notice also the comparative narrowness of the compartment for this period. This photo is one of the brake 3rds, No. 1323.

The last type of 'Fruit' vehicle to be built by the Great Western was the Fruit D alias *diagram Y.11. Figure 418* illustrates this van which has the long 18" wheelbase and three double doors on each side. They were fitted with gas lighting, and had many uses apart from the carriage of fruit, being also used for express parcels traffic. The example shown is branded 'Return to Old Oak Common'. Although seen later on freight trains, these vans were were proper 'brown' vehicles, and registered on the carriage list. No. 2881 was one of a batch built under *lot 1649* and other numbers were 2867 to 2916. Many more were built up to 1955.

FIG 419

Moving now into the war years, the 5'9110" composite illustrated in *figure 421* is the official photograph of No. 7309. This shows the corridor side of the vehicle. Containing three 3rd and four 1st class compartments, it follows the practice of four doors on one side and two only on the other. Forty were built under *lot 1621* to *diagram E.158* numbering from 7301 to 7340. Note the dark roof and the coat of arms replacing the roundel. The other photograph is of special saloon No. 9002. This is another of the 1st class special vehicles for V.I.P's, being self contained, with a kitchen, etc., and mounted on six wheeled bogies. It was one of two Nos. 9001-2 which were 60'11" long built under *lot 1626* to *diagram G.62*.

FIG 420

LOT.1621
DIA.E.158

FIG 421

LOT.1626
DIA.G.62

FIG 422

DIA.G.62

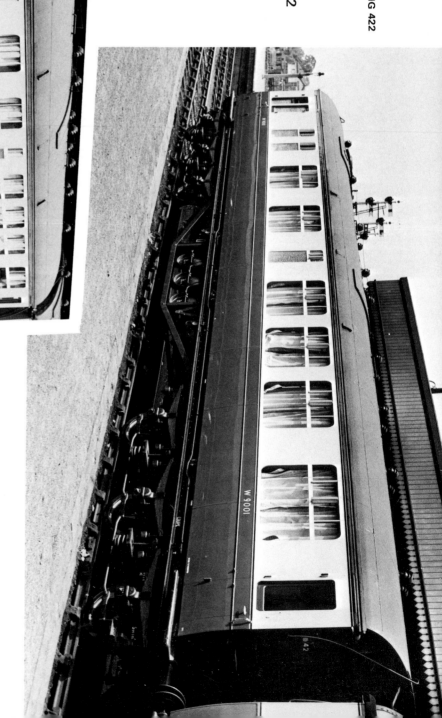

These two pictures, *figures 422 and 423*, were taken by my friend Dick Blenkinsop at Didcot in British Rail days, and show No. 9001 in excellent detail. This was the other vehicle of the pair constructed under *lot 1626* mentioned briefly on the previous page. Both ends are shown, and also of importance to modellers is the fact that these photographs illustrate the opposite side to that of 9002. The large round dome on the roof is the stove vent from the small kitchen, and one can also see the water tank filter cap. Note the weight — 42 tons.

FIG 425

FIG 426

FIG 424

Figure 424, a rather nice photograph by R. Blenkinsop shows the large six-wheeled bogie which was used on the heaviest stock. Notice that there are two transverse beams of channel section with flanges down. The stabilizers are connected through these beams and sprung with coil springs of a similar pattern. Four-wheel instead of six is shown in *figure 426,* this is the heavy duty bogie used between articulated coaches. The standard pressed-steel 9' bogie seen in *figure 425* has the transverse beams with flanges upwards, and 4 volute springs instead of coil-springs on each side.

FIG 427

FIG 428

FIG 429

FIG 430

Figure 427 shows the 9' wheelbase, Churchward bogie, with wooden beam, and volute springs, with coils over the axle boxes. *Figure 428* shows a rare experimental type, 9' again, but with the transverse spring similar to the so-called 'American' type. *Figure 429* shows the similar 7' pattern but with coil springs instead of volute, used mostly on brown vehicles.

The missing example from this page is the 9' wheelbase 'plate frame' known as the 'fishbelly' due to its shape; an example can be seen on *page 96*.

Many references have been made to the 'American bogie', so I have shown this type in close-up in *figures 431, 432 and 433*. It was termed "American" as it was designed by Churchward after he had studied the heavy bogies then running in the United States. The design consists of a double equalizing beam bearing on the axle boxes each side and sprung with coil springs. A central transverse spring takes the shocks on the bolster. There were two sizes, the standard 9' wheelbase as shown, and a lighter form, with an 8' wheelbase and double transverse springs, instead of triple. There was one other form which had volute springs in place of the large semi-eliptic, but I have only seen one example, (see part 1 *page 226, figure 228*).

FIG 432

FIG 433

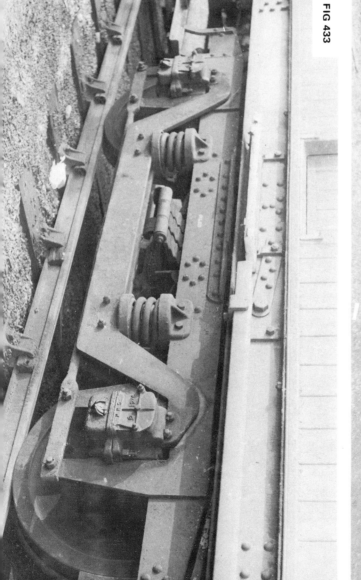

FIG 434   FIG 436

FIG 435

Here are a few more chassis details, which might prove useful to model-makers. *Figures 434* shows clearly the construction of the flat bar trussing. This was on vehicle No. 131, a breakdown van dating from 1911. It is possible to see the adjustable queen post and its seating. The small gauge is for indicating the quantity of gas in the cylinder seen on the right. An example of the Bars II is illustrated in *figure 435* which shows how this system of cantilevered underframe trussing was arranged, and in *figure 436* are details of the large round head buffer, in its rectangular shank, showing the fixing onto the head stock.

The Python built under *lot 1197* has been described previously but, I assumed readers would be interested in knowing about this adaption of No. 560. At the outbreak of the 1939-45 war, the Great Western authorities were very concerned about damage to property by incendiary bombs and so a mobile 'FIRE TRAIN' was brought into being.

The coach No. 7995 was utilized as accommodation for the fire-fighting crew and for other impedimentia, whilst the Python shown in *figure 437* contained a Coventry Climax Fire pump which could be swung out of the specially enlarged side doors on a derrick and lowered on to the ground. The vehicle was painted in the standard brown with black ends, and the words "FIRE TRAIN" were in post office red. The location is Reading.

250

FIG 437

251

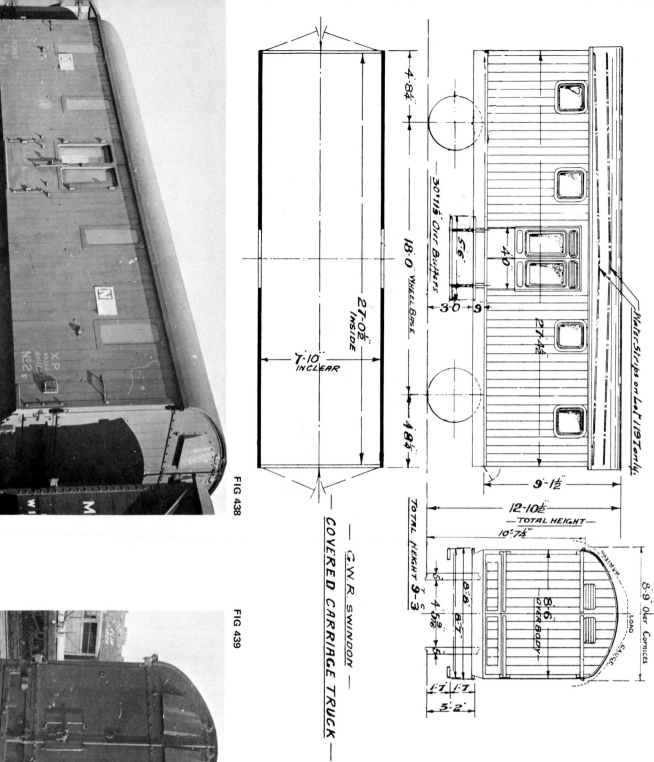

FIG 438

FIG 439

WaterStrips on Lot 1197 only.

30'11½" Over Buffers

18-0" WHEEL BASE

4-8¼"   4-8¼"

5'6"

40

3'0"   9"

27-1¼

9-1½"

27-0½" INSIDE

7-10 IN CLEAR

— G.W.R. SWINDON —

— COVERED CARRIAGE TRUCK —

TOTAL HEIGHT 9-3

12-10½"

— TOTAL HEIGHT —

10-7¼"

8-9" Over Cornices

LOAD GAUGE

MAXIMUM

8-6 OVER BODY

8-2

8-7

4-5½

3-5

1-7 1-7

3-2"

The Python B was the last four-wheeled covered carriage truck type to be built for the Great Western of *lot no. 1650*, to *diagram P.22*. There were only six, numbering from 1 to 6, these two pictures show No. 2 at Banbury in the hump yard on the left, and in the up platform on the right. Note the flush windows, and the strengthening webs under the sides. The length of the vehicle was 32' and the wheelbase 20'. The drawing is of the *P.14* Python and is only put here to show the comparison.

LOT.1650

DIA.P.22

Although slightly out of sequence, I have shown the 'Express Parcels' diesel rail cars here, so that comparison can be made with the first type No. 17, and the second type No. 34. The idea behind the building of these vehicles was to provide a fast service between Paddington and Reading for small parcels, and No. 17 was designed for this purpose. Used mostly at night or 'off peak' times it was an elusive vehicle to photograph. The drawing is the official diagram and it can be seen that the vehicle retained the streamlined outline, with the headless buffing gear, and recessed sliding doors. When first turned out, the roof was painted white, the style was the Great Western chocolate and cream, with 'EXPRESS PARCELS' in yellow ochre shaded black. The diagram was Y and *lot No. 1547.*

FIG 440

LOT.NO.1547

DIA. Y

(Drawing not to 4mm scale.)

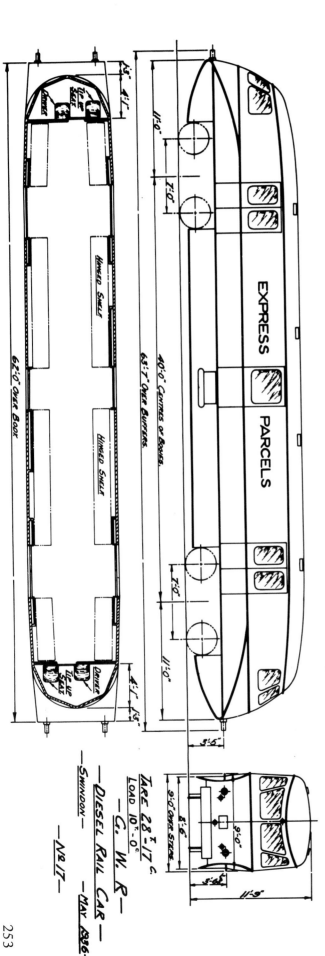

253

The diesel parcels car proved quite successful, so much so that another similar vehicle was built at Swindon in 1941. It will be seen from both drawing and photograph that although following the general lines of the previous vehicle, No. 34 was different in many small ways. For instance, the outline was more angular, and the doors were flush with the sides, and hinged opening outwards. No front skirt was fitted, and full standard drawgear buffers and hoses were built in. It was one foot shorter than No. 17 but slightly wider than its sister. Note also the roof colour is now dark grey. *(figure 441)*

(Drawing not to 4 mm scale)

FIG 441

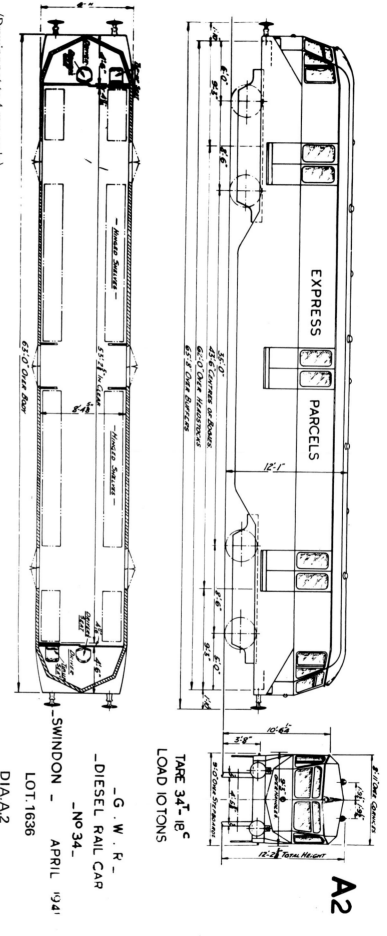

- HINGED SHELVES -

- DIESEL -

53'-2½" IN CLEAR

8'-4½"

- HINGED SHELVES -

63'-0" OVER BODY

65'-8" OVER BUFFERS

EXPRESS

PARCELS

35'-0"

43'-6" CENTRES OF BOGIES

62'-0" OVER HEADSTOCKS

6'-0"

9'-3"

8'-6"

12'-1"

8'-6"

9'-3"

6'-0"

TARE 34T-18°

LOAD 10 TONS

- G . W . R -
- DIESEL RAIL CAR
- No 34 -
- SWINDON -   APRIL 1941

LOT. 1636

DIA. A.2

10'-6¼"

3'-8"

9'-0" OVER STEPBOARDS

4'-5¾"

9'-3" OVERHANGERS

8'-11" OVER CORNERS

8'-11" OVER STEPBOARDS

12'-2" TOTAL HEIGHT

A2

No. 34

EXPRESS

PARCELS

FIG 443

FIG 444

LOT.1637

DIA.A.

the first two years of the war, being developments of the original design. These cars had AEC engine units but the chassis and bodies were built at Swindon. It will be seen from *figures 442-444* of Nos. 19 and 20 that all pretentions of streamlining have given way to a more austere outline to give more room inside, and the coach sides have been terminated above the bogies to allow easier accessibility for maintenance. Also, brake gear is now of the railway type, being applied through brake blocks on the wheels rather than the original drums. Standard buffing and draw-gear was fitted to allow a tail load to be added. It is interesting to note that Nos. 19 and 20 were fitted with a special gear-box to allow high speed for single cars, and low speed for cars with a tail load. Built under *lot 1635* fifteen were built to *diagram A*, Nos. 19 to 33.

The official photograph, *figure 444*, shows the further development of the railcar idea and surely the seeds of the multiple unit of today. Two cars as a twin set were coupled together, each having a driving compartment at one end only. The other ends were fitted with standard draw-gear and gangways. The unit could be used simply as a two coach set, or could be strengthened by the insertion of a standard coach between the two. Their use was on the express run

between Birmingham and Cardiff, where they were so successful that they eventually had to be replaced by a steam train! They then found service on the Bristol-Weymouth route and Reading-Newbury line. Of the two shown, No.36 had a buffet counter and its twin, No. 35, had lavatory facilities, thus making a compact cross country unit.

255

FIG 445

Two final examples of the *A.1 diagram* type of diesel rail car are shown here in British Railways 'strawberry and cream' livery. Very little difference can be noted except that, during a major refit, the side windows in the driving compartment have been sub-divided to allow part opening.

I have travelled in these cars on the South Wales run and can vouch for their speed and comfort, far superior to the up and down ride on the M.U's of today. Diagram for the twins was A.3 for the buffet cars, Nos. 36 and 38, and A.4 for the toilet cars Nos. 35-37.

LOT.1635

FIG 448

LOT.1652

DIA.K.42

Thirty 57' passenger brake vans were built to *diagram K.42* under two separate lots during the war years 1940-45. The first batch, *lot 1652*, numbered from 121 to 130 and the interior of one of these, No. 124, is shown in the large official picture, *figure 448. Figure 447* shows the van side of No. 98, one of the second series completed in 1945 under *lot 1655*. Other numbers were 91-97, 99, 100, 268-277.

FIG 447

257

FIG 449

258

lounge, and guard/luggage space. Three years later these two vehicles formed the nucleus of a new Royal Train for the Great Western Railway. They were refitted to a style worthy of royalty, and air conditioning was installed. The train was made up of 9006 and 9007, strengthened at each end by a brake composite of the E.164 diagram, their numbers being 7372 and 7377. In B.R. days the two specials were painted in Royal maroon, and were adapted for a portable stairway which allowed entry to the vehicles from ground level.

LOT.1673
DIA.G.64,65

Two special vehicles ordered during the war, but not put into service until 1945, were Nos. 9006 and 9007, shown here. They were unusual in several ways, one being that their underframes were from earlier stock which had been damaged. No. 9006, *figures 450 and 450a*, was built on to the chassis of No. 1133, a 1938 corridor 3rd of *diagram C.77* No. 9007, *figure 449*, received the underframe from a brake 3rd, No. 1598 of *diagram D.125*. These two specials had different diagram numbers as they differed slightly in interior layout. No. 9006 had a kitchen and a sleeping compartment for staff, a dining room with accommodation for eight, a bathroom, two bedrooms and a saloon at one end with windows each side of the gangway. In contrast, No. 9007 had two larger bedrooms, no kitchen, a large

FIG 450

FIG 450A

FIG 451

W 768

FIG 452

W 8003

No. 768 illustrated at the top of the page (*figure 451*), is one of the full 3rd main line carriages built during the war and is placed here to compare with the new 'Hawkesworth' stock shown in the lower photograph, *figure 452*. The full 3rd has the side window layout with eight fixed large lights, four more windows fitted with sliding vents, and four shorter droplights. The 'Hawkesworth' has a similar design of windows but only six large fixed lights. The length has increased from the standard 60'11" to 64' and the most notable change is in the roof. The ends are now sloped down after the Gresley fashion on the LNER and the train boards were altered from a roof position on to a new place along the cantrail. Today, the nameboards are once again going up on the roof sides and are being painted in the old Great Western style. The full 3rd was of *diagram C.81* in which numbers ran from 751 to 780, and the 1st class vehicle was from *lot 1688, diagram A.23* and numbered from 8001 to 8003.

LOT. 1688
DIA. A.23

LOT.1691
DIA.C.82

FIG 453

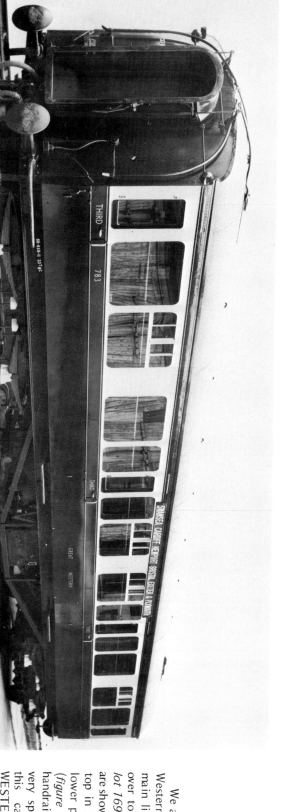

FIG 454

We are now getting close to the end of the Great Western as an individual company. Large quantities of main line stock were ordered before the final hand over to the government. Amongst these vehicles was *lot 1691* which ordered fifty-two corridor 3rds. Two are shown here in official photographs. No. 796 at the top in *figure 453* is shown broadside on and in the lower picture is No. 783 giving a three quarter view, (*figure 454*). Notice in the latter that although handrails are fitted for access to the roof, steps are very sparse. Also, the coat of arms is missing from this carriage, having only the words 'GREAT WESTERN' on the middle waist. The diagram was C.82 and numbers ran from 781 to 832.

LOT.1693

DIA.C.83

The non-corridor 3rds built at this late time in Great Western history were ¼″ shorter than the corridor stock, although to the same width. They were fitted with ten compartments, with all window and droplights to the same height. The roof contour did not follow the curved end shape of the main line stock but was the standard straight profile. The lot number of the example illustrated in *figure 455* at the top of the page was *lot 1693* to *diagram C.83*, and numbers ran from 374 to 413. No. 387 is seen at Banbury Loco sidings in 1950.

The lower photograph is of a later corridor 3rd built to *lot 1706, diagram C.84*. There was very little difference between this series and those of C.82. Nos. were from 1713 to 1737, this example being No. 1732, *(figure 456)*.

LOT.1706

DIA.C.84

FIG 456

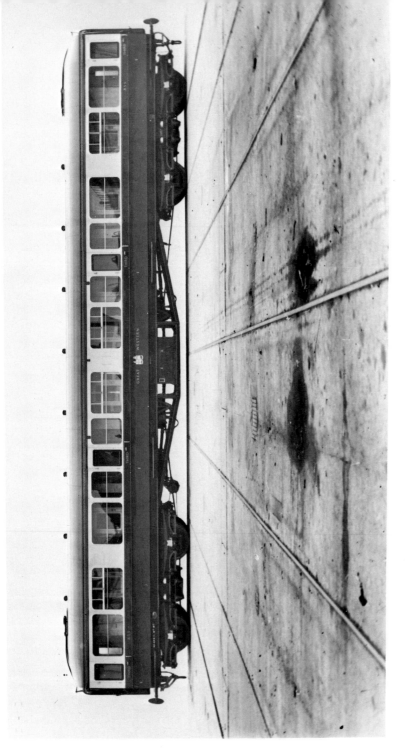

Another batch of seventy was built in 1948 to the same size and *diagram, C.82* as the previous 3rds built under *lot 1691*. These numbered from 855 to 924, built to *lot 1714*. The photograph shows the first of the batch, No. 855 and the only thing of note is that the coat of arms now has the words 'Great Western' each side of the transfer in the middle of the waist, (*figure 457*).

At the lower left *figure 458* is an example of one of the last Siphons built for the Great Western. This was the Siphon G, which had louvres at the bottom of the sides which could be covered up with sliding panels. The vehicle shown, No. 1317, was being used as a demonstration exhibit for the 'Tote System'. Lot number was *1721, diagram O.62* and numbers 1310 – 1339. Other later Siphons were:-

Diagram O.62 lot 1751 1001-1030 of 1951 (British Railways)
Diagram O.62 lot 1768 1031-1050 of 1955 (British Railways)

LOT.1714
DIA.C.82

FIG 457

LOT.1721
DIA.O.62

Just to show how the designs lingered on after national-ization, two Monsters are shown here built in the 1950's, (*figure 459*). On the left is end-door Monster of *diagram P.23* at Bristol, painted number 493, fitted with modern bogies under *lot No. 1753*. Others were 494-8. On the right is 'Giant' at Old Oak Common, which was fitted with gangways instead of end doors like the old 'Monster', (*figure 460*). These vehicles were built under *diagram P.24* and numbers were 596 to 600. The one shown is No. 597.

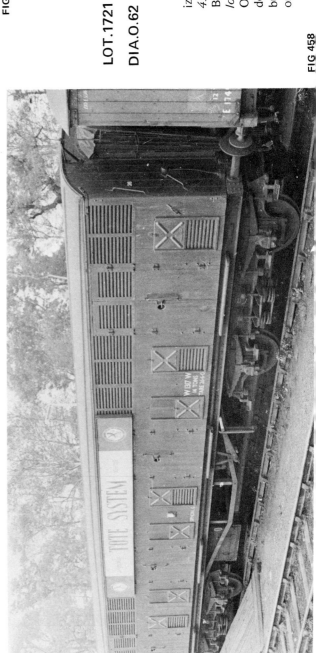

FIG 458

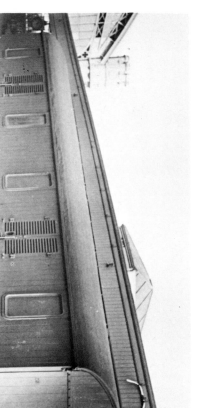

FIG 459

FIG 460

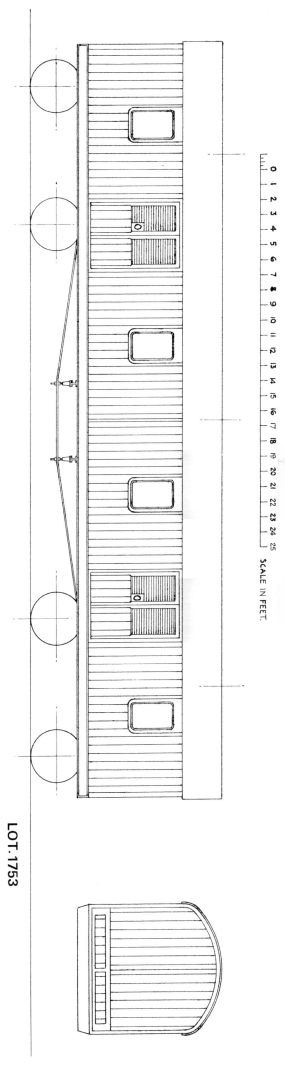

DIA.P.23

LOT.1753
DIA.P.24

SCALE IN FEET.

0 1 2 3 4 5 6 7 8 9 10 11 12 13 14 15 16 17 18 19 20 21 22 23 24 25

263

The last 'Slip' to be dropped off a British train was this vehicle shown off the 5.10p.m. Paddington to Birmingham. 1960 saw the end of this practice which the Great Western had perfected to a fine art over three-quarters of a century. However, economies finally put an end to it, due to the cost of supplying an experienced top link guard for each slip worked. It was found cheaper to stop the whole train, which meant adding another 10 minutes on the schedule, but also had the advantage of being able to pick up passengers as well as set down. No. 7374 was built with thirteen other similar vehicles to *lots 1690* at the very end of the Great Western's reign. The diagram was *E.164* as they were constructed to the brake composite design, and only three of them were converted to slip use in 1958. Other numbers were 7372 to 7385. The two photographs which I took of this final service at Bicester show No. 7374 actually being slipped. The point of release was about 100 yards south of the up advanced starter, fairly close to the station as the gradient here is uphill going towards Birmingham. The slipped carriage ran on after being dropped and was brought to a halt outside the Down home signal, and was finally drawn into the platform at Bicester by the engine of the 4.40p.m. Paddington — Banbury which always waited in the platform road for

FIG 462

FIG 461

264

that very duty. At the bottom left, *figure 462*, the guard has just "slipped" and one can see the open hook and the lowered droplight in the end of the vehicle. The upper picture is of the coach as it passed by and the special tail lamps can be seen, indicating that one slip portion only has been released. (*figure 461*)

To me these pictures are very nostalgic, as they were the last coach pictures I took of Great Western stock, and they signified the ending of a phase of not only steam transport but a way of life. The only way I can recapture any of the tradition — timekeeping, service and dare I say it, romance, of the railway I knew and grew up with — is in model form and it is with great pleasure that I see interest, not only rekindled but growing apace, in things Great Western, all of which has made these books worthwhile. So to modellers and enthusiasts alike, here's hoping my humble efforts will prove interesting.

Following on from the elaborate livery of the 1900's, shown and described briefly in *Part I* of this work, we come now to the change which took place when an all-over brown superseded the chocolate and cream.

In July of 1903 a trial train of six coaches was painted 'dark lake', as an experiment "to test the advisability of changing the standard painting" (quote from the Locomotive Magazine, Vol. 9). It ran down to Penzance on the 11.45a.m., and returned on the 8.00a.m. ex-Penzance the next day. However, little was proved, but on September 1st 1908 all coaching stock was outshopped in all-over brown, lined out with gold leaf and black, with white roofs. The gold leaf soon gave way to yellow ochre for lining, but in the Great Western magazine for October 1912, it was stated that gold leaf was again to be used. Also in that month and year the coach roof boards were changed from cream and brown to red lettering shaded black, on a white ground, so that they would be conspicuous on a brown coach!

The crimson lake period commenced in 1912, and continued through to 1922, although standards of paintwork suffered during the war years of 1914-1918. An exception to this style was provided by the home ambulance trains, which were fitted out and marshalled for Government use. These rakes of vehicles were painted on olive green shade, with large white circles on the coach sides, which contained the red cross of the ambulance service.

In July 1922, two trains for the 'Cornish Riviera' were turned out in the chocolate and cream livery once more, but yellow ochre took the place of the gold leaf, and the chocolate line which used to be on the cream panels was not restored. Also, coach ends were now black and name boards were lettered black on a painted brown. Roofs were still white, and name boards were lettered black on a white ground.

From here on, stock was turned out in the two-colour livery, and steel panelled carriages still had their 'panels' painted in, indian red paint taking the place of the erstwhile mahogany bolections! However, in 1927 all this pseudo panel lining was dispensed with, and the chocolate lower half was separated from the upper cream by a yellow ochre line. (Except for the principal expresses which had the double waist lining.)

In the 1928 period the garter crest was replaced by the heraldic arms of London and Bristol, side by side, above the Company's device, and surmounted by the letters G.W.R.

From 1934 until 1943 the coat of arms was replaced by the circular totem, which appeared on everything, from locomotives and platform trollies, to staff uniform buttons! I suppose it was in the spirit of the times but I did not know a single 'Western' man who preferred this modern motif to the character and tradition of the old arms transfer. During this period some of the lesser carriage stock was painted all-over brown again. When the second World War broke out in 1939, and shopping recommenced at Swindon a couple of years later, main line and all passenger stock was also turned out in this milk chocolate shade with a single orange line at the waist.

Chocolate and cream came back into being in late 1943, and coaches were lined with a single gold line, shaded black at the division of the cream from the chocolate, although the very best stock was still given the much more dignified coat of treatment. The awful totem at last gave way to the much more dignified coat of arms of the 1928-34 period, with G.W.R. above as before. Finally, just a few years before nationalization, these letters were replaced by the words GREAT and WESTERN, placed one on each side of the arms transfer.

BROWN VEHICLES

The 1903 style of lettering for the brown vehicles was of the large 25" size, and the yellow letters G.W. appeared wherever there was large enough space on the vehicle side. On several Siphons these letters were even spread over the louvres. Numbers were also in large format, being 1'6" high and often placed between the letters G & W. By 1920, however, the numbers were reduced in size to the ordinary freight stock style, but still in the yellow paint, and the letters meantime dropped to a mere 16" high. This style lasted until 1934 when the circular totem was adopted, and this device in yellow ochre took the place of the letters G.W. Many readers have asked about the position of the 16" letters on the Siphon F and C. On *page 43* it can be seen that the 'G' was in the upper triangle of flat boards, directly below the left-hand bracket of the roof board in *figure 54*, whilst the 'W' was in the upper triangle below the right-hand roof bracket. This is for the Siphon F. The Siphon C lettering was in similar panels, one on each side of the central double doors (not like No. 1777 on *page 50*, which is in the lower panels). In *figure 71*, one can see the roundel in the position where the 'W' used to be, (the 'G' was in the left-hand panel on the other side of the doors!)

Several of the 'browns' had their code names painted on the body side, but not all types. Vehicles so treated were Monsters, Fruits, Bloaters, Goliath, Fish and Siphons F, C, G, H, & J. Roofs were white when turned out of the factory, and although originally some of the ends were brown, in my time on the Great Western (1928-45) the ends were painted black, as was everything below the solebar. However, models look much more realistic with the roofs painted grey, as this was the colour they quickly became.

TELEGRAPHIC CODE NAMES FOR CARRIAGE STOCK & VAN

Beetle	18' 6" Cattle Box
Beetle A	18' 6" Cattle Box Dual Braked
Beetle B	23' and 26' Cattle Box, with compartment. Dual Braked
Beetle C	23' and 26' Cattle Box, with compartment. Vacuum brake only
Bloater	28' 6" Fish van
Chafer	Invalid Carriage
Chintz	Family Carriage
Chub A	Bogie saloon
Chub B	Bogie saloon with brake
Cricket	Bogie composite
Cricket A	Bogie composite
Cricket B	Bogie composite with brake
Cricket C	Bogie composite with luggage compartment
Cricket D	Bogie composite corridor fitted
	Bogie composite corridor and brake compartment
Emmett A	Bogie Third with brake
First A	Bogie First
Fish	21' 0" Fish van
Fruit	16' Fruit van
Fruit	22' Fruit van
Fruit C	22' Fruit van
Fruit D	50' bogie covered van with corridor
Giant	50' bogie open carriage truck with corridor
Goliath	19', 21', & 25' 6" well wagon. Capacity 8 tons
Hydra	20' 10" well wagon
Hydra	30' 6" well wagon. Capacity 5 tons
Hydra A	28' 6" well wagon. Capacity 15 tons
Hydra C	Bogie 70' Slip, double ended
Hydra D	Bogie 70' Slip, single ended
Gnat	Bogie 63' Slip, double ended
Gnat A	Bogie, van end, Third
Gnat B	Bogie brake third, not wider than 9' 3" with corridor
Melon	Bogie brake third, not wider than 9' 6" with corridor
Melon	Bogie brake third, not wider than 8' 6" with corridor
Melon B	Bogie brake third, not wider than 8' 6" with corridor and clerestory roof
Melon C	Bogie brake third, 9' 7" wide with corridor
Melon D	50' bogie covered scenery van
Melon E	16' Horse box
Monster	
Paco	

(Beetle – Beetle C grouped as "Van List"; Hydra A – Hydra D grouped as "Wagon List".)

Paco A	16' Horse box dual braked
Paco B	21' Horse box with fodder compartment
Paco C	21' Horse box with fodder compartment dual braked
Python	Covered carriage truck
Python A	Long covered carriage truck strengthened for elephants
Python B	Long covered carriage truck
Scorpion	Open carriage truck
Scorpion A	Open carriage truck dual braked
Scorpion B	Open carriage truck 21'
Scorpion C	Open carriage 21'
Scorpion D	Open carriage truck 45' dual braked
	Open carriage truck 21' dual braked
Siphon	27' 6" Milk Van
Siphon A	27' 6" Fish Van (six wheel)
Siphon B	18' 0" Milk Van (four wheel)
Siphon C	28' 6" Milk Van, with end doors (four wheel)
Siphon D	27' 6" Milk Van (six wheel)
Siphon F	40' 0" Bogie Milk Van with end doors
Siphon G	50' 0" Bogie Milk Van corridor ends
Siphon H	50' 0" Bogie Milk Van with end doors
Siphon J	50' 0" Insulated Milk Van with corridor
Tadpole	Open Fish Wagon
Tadpole A	Open Fish Wagon with guards compartment
Snake	Four wheel Brake Van
Snake	Six wheel Brake Van
Snake A	Eight wheel Brake Van
Snake B	Eight wheel Brake Van with side corridor
Snake C	Eight wheel Brake Van with gangways
Snake D	Four wheel Third
Termite	Eight wheel Third
Termite	Eight wheel 8' 6" clerestory
Termite A	Eight wheel 9' 0" 10 compartments
Termite C	Eight wheel 9' 0" 8 compartments
Termite D	Eight wheel 9' 6" corridor
Termite E	Eight wheel 9' 6" corridor
Termite F	Eight wheel 10 compartments non-corridor
Termite G	Eight wheel 9' 7" wide corridor
Termite H	Eight wheel Open excursion stock
Termite J	

(Tadpole – Tadpole A grouped as "Wagon List".)

Through the efforts of many Great Western enthusiasts, it is still possible to see a wide representation of early carriage stock. Not only is there a fine collection of superb models at Pendon Museum, near Didcot, but also many full sized examples of G.W.R. stock have been preserved by various societies, and a list of both model and restored carriages appears hereunder.

Models at Long Wittenham, near Didcot.

Dia. No.	Painted No.	Type
F.16	7109	Toplight Double ended Slip
E.88	7745	Toplight Composite (Bars 11)
C.30	2430	Toplight Third
H.38	9601	Toplight Third
G.65	9116	Bow-ended Dining Car
D.45	3542	Super Saloon
E.109	7604	Toplight Brake 3rd (Bars 11)
C.54	4796	Steel panelled Composite 70'
C.54	4800	Bow-ended 57' Third
E.83	7540	Bow-ended 57' Third
E.128	6515	Tri-Composite Brake
D.29	2341	Steel Panelled 57' Brake Composite
E.73	7474	Clerestory, Brake 3rd
D.30	2085	Clerestory, Composite
E.40	7250	Clerestory, Brake 3rd
E.40	7249	Brake Composite, Low roof
E.147	6762	Brake Composite, Low roof
E.147	6763	Bow-ended, 'B' set
A.28	171	Bow-ended, 'B' set
A.28	174	Auto Trailer
K.38	1174	Steel panelled Passr. Brake
K.40	77	Steel panelled Parcels Brake
K.22	1147	Steel panelled Full Brake
M.15	1204	708 Newspaper Van
O.4	964	Low Siphon
O.4	981	Low Siphon
O.4	960	Low Siphon
O.11	1448	Siphon G
O.31	1221	Siphon J
O.31	1219	Siphon J
S.11	2700	Bloater
S.11	2401	Fruit C
Y.3	105	Cordon

All the above are built to 4mm scale, and are perfect reproductions in miniature, and can be seen running at the Pendon Museum, Long-Wittenham, on any Sunday.

Full sized preserved coaches at Bewdley, owned by the Severn Valley Line.

Dia. No.	Lot No.	Painted No.	Type
D.62	1275	3755	Brake 3rd, Main Line & City
D.62	1275	3756	Brake 3rd, Main Line & City
E.159	1590	6562	Composite
E.162	1639	7284	Composite
E.162	1639	7285	Composite
D.116	1490	5787	Brake 3rd
D.104	1399	5136	Brake 3rd
G.65	1471	9113	Super Saloon
D.101	1392	5539	Brake 3rd
C.32	1246	3930	Third
C.82	1691	829	Third
C.82	1720	2119	Third
G.62	1626	9001	Special Saloon
A.28	1410	178	Auto Trailer
D.133	1732	2202	Brake 3rd
C.77	1593	1086	Third
C.77	1593	1087	Third
C.77	1593	1116	Third
C.77	1593	1146	Third
J.18	1702	9082	Sleeping Car
J.18	1702	9084	Sleeping Car
J.18	1702	9085	Sleeping Car
U.14	990	6290	4 wheeled Composite
G.58	1400	9103	Saloon
G.56	1250	9369	Saloon
C.30	1167	9918	Third
G.43	1209	9055	Saloon
H.39	1468	9615	Dining Car
H.40	1469	9627	Dining Car
O.13	1299	1399	4 wheeled Milk Van
K.14	883	933	40' Brake Van
A.1	1635	22	Diesel Rail Car
C.54	1374	4887	Third

Full sized carriages owned by Great Western Society, at Didcot, Berks.

Dia No.	Lot No.	Year	Painted No.	Type
K.41	1512	1934	111	Brake
A.30	1480	1933	190	Trailer
A.26	1542	1936	212	Trailer
A.38	1736	1951	231	Trailer
Ex Cambrian Rly.			238	Composite
C.77	1623	1940	416	Brake 3rd (4 wheel)
	992	1902	536	Third Corridor
K.40	1413	1930	975	Third (4 wheel)
C.74	1575	1937	1111	Third Corridor
C.22	1038	1903	1184	Brake Van
			1289	Excursion 3rd
			1357	Third Clerestory
			1941	Third Clerestory
C.30	1167	1910	2434	Third Toplight
G.20	740	1894	2511	Saloon
C.24	1098	1905	3299	Third 'Dreadnought'
C.67	1527	1935	5952	Third Corridor
E.158	1621	1940	7313	Composite Corridor
E.159	1640	1941	7362	Brake Composite Corridor
E.159	1690	1948	7371	Brake Compo. Corridor
G.4	840	1897	9002	Special Saloon
G.60	147	1932	9112	Super Saloon
G.61	147	1932	9113	Super Saloon
G.61	147	1932	9118	Super Saloon
J.6	1123	1907	9083	Sleeper
Camping Coach			9891	Ex Toplight
V.	1522	1934	4	Diesel Rail Car
A.1	1635	1940	22	Diesel Rail Car

Full sized carriages owned by the Dart Valley Railway, Buckfastleigh.

Dia No.	Lot No.	Painted No.	Type
G.3	745	249	Directors Saloon
Q.1	1170	6479	Inspection Saloon
G.31	804	8231	Family Saloon
U.4	944	6008	4 wheeled Composite
—		790	Dynamometer Car
G.60	1471	9111	Super Saloon 'King George'
G.61	1471	9116	Super Saloon 'Duchess of York'
E.164	1690	7377	Composite
C.74	1575	1285	Open Excursion 3rd
C.74	1575	1295	Open Excursion 3rd

Full sized carriages owned by the Dowty Preservation Society, Ashchurch.

Dia No.	Lot No.	Painted No.	Type
H.43	'Centenary' (was 248)	9635	Kitchen-First Dining Car
		9044	Saloon Clerestory
N	1126	38	Trailer Car

PHOTOGRAPHIC CREDITS

To British Railways All on pages 3, 4, 5, 6, 7, 13, 17, 18, 22, 27, 28, 29, 31, 32, 40, 46, 52, 59, 60, 72, 84, 93, 120, 121, 122, 123, 124, 125, 131, 132, 145, 147, 154, 155, 156, 158, 159, 162, 167—8, 173—5, 177—9, 183, 185, 190, 193, 200—1, 205—6, 214—5, 217—8, 219—24, 227—8, 230, 232, 240, 242—3, 249—50, 252—3, 262—5, 266, 274—7, 279, 283, 285, 290, 290a, 292—302, 311—3, 317, 319—20, 323, 325, 328, 329, 333, 337—8, 343—4, 346, 348—55, 357—68, 370, 376—8, 384—88, 390, 392, 393—6, 398—404, 406, 407—9, 412, 415—7, 418, 420—1, 437, 438—41, 443—5, 447—9, 451—3, 456.

To Pendon Museum All on pages 14, 24, 25, 39, 41, 43—5, 47—8, 50—1, 56—7, 58, 61—4, 67—8, 83, 85, 86—9, 94, 98, 105—6, 107—8, 117, 117a, 119, 126—7, 133—9, 140—4, 149, 153, 160—1, 180, 186, 187, 194, 195, 197—9, 226, 235—8, 241, 244—6, 247—8, 254, 268—73, 280—1, 287—8, 303—6, 314—5, 321—2, 331, 334—6, 345, 345a, 410, 446.

To David Lee All on pages 16, 30, 38, 75—6, 77—8.
To Alan Wild All on pages 97, 331, 339, 342, 356, 372, 375, 383, 405, 455.

To Maurice Earley All on pages 162a, 291, 347, 219.
To Railway Modeller On pages 130, 233.
To the late Mike Longridge On pages 70, 369.
To Nick Campling On pages 259, 332.
To James Arnold Those on pages 257, 258, 260, 329.
To Dick Blenkinsop On pages 422, 424.

All other photographs are by the author.